LETHAL LOVERS' QUARREL

Michelle said that when she got home, she felt crummy and wasn't in the mood to talk to her husband, Brandon. She wanted Devon to come over, and so a call was made to ask her to come. When Devon showed up with her girlfriend, Keary, Michelle couldn't handle it. She grew furious and yelled at Brandon not to let her in the house.

Later, Devon returned alone. She and Michelle began arguing in the living room. The fight escalated into a battle of pushing and hair-pulling. Brandon jumped between them to intervene. He grabbed Devon, holding her back to protect his pregnant wife.

Devon struck back, clamping down hard with her teeth. Brandon was hurt, and mad. He wanted to know why the two women couldn't talk like human beings. He said he didn't want to continue to watch them fight. A suggestion was made to take the argument outside.

On the way out, Michelle grabbed a wooden-handled knife from the kitchen.

LIPSTICK
AND
BLOOD

JOHN KEARNEY

PINNACLE BOOKS
Kensington Publishing Corp.
http://www.kensingtonbooks.com

PINNACLE BOOKS are published by

Kensington Publishing Corp.
850 Third Avenue
New York, NY 10022

All Kensington Titles, Imprints, and Distributed Lines are available at special quantity discounts for bulk purchases for sales promotions, premiums, fund-raising, and educational or institutional use. Special book excerpts or customized printings can also be created to fit specific needs. For details, write or phone the office of the Kensington special sales manager: Kensington Publishing Corp., 850 Third Avenue, New York, NY 10022, attn: Special Sales Department, Phone: 1-800-221-2647.

Pinnacle and the P logo Reg. U.S. Pat. & TM Off.

First Printing: October 2006

10 9 8 7 6 5 4 3 2

Printed in the United States of America

*For daughters who
dare to be themselves*

1

Spring air slicing through her spiked hair, Devon Guzman strode into the June night toward her new silver Pontiac Sunfire. Michelle Hetzel, her blond hair bouncing, raced to her own car, a new red Honda Accord. The tension of an unresolved argument lingered in the wake of their departure.

The argument involved Keary, of course.

It always came back to the three of them: Devon Guzman, Michelle Hetzel, Keary Renner. The trio's history had begun three years ago. In the year or so since leaving high school, Michelle and Keary had both gotten married, but that hadn't changed much. Everything still came back to the three of them.

Devon wore a gray T-shirt and black Adidas pants, with a beeper clipped under her belly button. A black-and-gray friendship anklet with the words "Puerto Rico" woven into it flopped on her right ankle, perhaps a reminder of the blissful days in the Caribbean she'd shared with Michelle just a short couple weeks ago. She flicked out her ignition key and yanked open the car door. If she looked at the dashboard clock, it would have told her the time was about 10:00 P.M. The date was June 14, 2000.

Michelle, looking tall in her size-five jeans and red Esprit shirt, jerked open the door of her Accord and lunged in.

Devon started her car, clutched it into gear and pulled away. On her rear bumper could be seen a rainbow decal. Most young people like her didn't have her nerve to display it openly like that. Maybe downriver in an out-front arts community like New Hope they did, but not here, not in Easton, Pennsylvania. But Devon was who she was, and she didn't care who knew. Michelle's car had a sticker to match, but a smaller one. Once upon a time, the rainbow might have been a symbol of the sisterhood, of their solidarity. Now, perhaps, it was another reminder of happier moments, like the Puerto Rico anklet or the envelope of photos sitting in her glove compartment, photos from the spontaneous Memorial Day escape to the islands, where Devon and Michelle had exchanged secret rings and vows.

From his small house, Rick Guzman observed the abrupt departure of his nineteen-year-old daughter and her friend. He felt for them. When they'd called from the islands over Memorial Day weekend to tell him they'd gotten married, they both sounded so happy. They'd asked if they could come live with him when they got back. Of course he said yes. He wanted Devon to be happy. Maybe other fathers would have had trouble accepting her, her relationship choices, her alternative lifestyle. But she'd been very open about things from pretty early on, and by now he hardly gave it a second thought. He did his best to love her without judgment and to respect her choices.

Although, along with some of these choices, trouble sometimes came. Not too long ago, Devon had told him she'd been threatened by Michelle's husband. He was going to kick her ass, "dyke her out," whatever that meant. And once, even Keary and Michelle had teamed up against her, furiously chasing her all the way home in Michelle's Honda. Devon had come running into the house, huffing and puffing, exclaiming that they were after her. Rick Guzman resorted to throwing something at the car and punching a window to defuse the situation and drive them away.

Not that he really worried about her with Michelle. Devon could handle herself. She might be petite, but she was feisty and athletic, whereas Michelle, though taller, could barely walk on her own two feet. If Michelle ever got rough, Devon would slap her silly. And the two would be laughing about it a minute later. That's how they were. Nonstop drama. Giggling one minute, bitching each other out the next, then back to their normal giddy selves a moment after that. In their own little world, those two. Faces always inches apart, so that no one else could get a word in edgewise. No, Michelle was nothing to worry about. If anything, it was Keary who concerned him, with her occasional rough physical handling of his daughter.

Still, as his daughter's taillights zigzagged into the night, Rick could take comfort in knowing that Devon was a tough kid. A little tiger. She could hold her own against anybody.

Even after the two cars were out of sight, he could hear them chasing each other recklessly, driving like nuts through the one-way streets all the way out to Freemansburg Avenue.

He shook his head.

In his mind's eye, those red taillights still blazed.

That's what he'd remember later. Seeing those taillights fade into the June night.

That's what he'd remember always.

* * *

Tires squealing, Devon and Michelle tore through the series of one-way streets, lucky not to attract the attention of police. Because, first of all, both of them had been drinking vodka shots. Rick, with his girlfriend, Holly, and his sister, Candy, had all been drinking since eight o'clock or so. And second, Phillipsburg High School, located on the Jersey side of the Delaware River, where Devon was born, had just held its graduation. The evening was now teeming with cars crammed with Class of 2000 grads kicking off the summer with a night of partying.

Racing along, Devon headed home to face Keary, with whom she shared a room at the Mineral Springs Hotel, a few miles away, on the Delaware River. Keary—the friend she'd enticed away from Michelle—was like Michelle in that she was being torn apart by a heterosexual marriage doomed to fail.

Keary would be waiting for her right now, even though she was supposed to be at work. She would be furious when Devon confessed that she'd lied earlier that night when she said she was not going to see Michelle. Yes, Keary would certainly be angry, and when Keary and Devon fought, things could take a scary turn.

Case in point was the knife incident. It had happened after Devon and Michelle's Memorial Day trip. Devon had told Keary she was leaving her, and the next thing she knew, Keary had a knife and Devon's hand was spilling blood. The gash turned out to be bad enough to send her to the emergency room.

As Keary described the incident, she was going to kill herself with the knife, and Devon had gotten cut trying to stop her. Who could tell whose fault things were anymore? There was so much competition and jealousy among the three, it blurred all the lines.

* * *

After chasing each other all the way out to Freemansburg Avenue, Devon sped east toward the Delaware River and Michelle peeled away in the opposite direction, toward Easton's South Side and her home on West St. Joseph Street. The trip Michelle had funded for herself and Devon, the gifts she'd bought, the promises they'd made, the plans to leave Brandon and Keary and go live somewhere warm and sunny, like St. Croix—all of it had happened only two weeks ago, but it might as well have been another lifetime.

Brandon Bloss was on the phone complaining to his mother-in-law about his missing wife when he heard her car pull up.

"Michelle's home," he told Mary Hetzel, and hung up.

Phone records would indicate that he had called his mother-in-law's house thirty-four minutes before. Her home was just two blocks away on West Nesquehoning Street. The call had been placed at 9:36 P.M.

He'd made the call after arriving home from his night job as a bartender and finding an empty house and his wife nowhere to be located. He called his in-laws, with whom he had a close, affectionate relationship, to air a common gripe. Many months later, in a court of law, Mary Hetzel would remember the conversation as follows:

"Michelle is out with Devon again," Brandon complained bitterly. "I wonder what her excuse is going to be this time."

Mary was quite familiar with this complaint, and sympathized with Brandon, because she realized that her hardworking twenty-five-year-old son-in-law was truly trying to make his four-month-old marriage to her daughter work. The same could hardly be said of Michelle.

"I just can't take it anymore," Brandon continued. He

sounded upset, frustrated, mad. "As long as Devon is around, Michelle and I will never be happy."

It was a familiar refrain, the blaming of Devon for interfering in his marriage, according to Mary.

"I could just kill her," she would recall his saying of Devon, at least once.

On West St. Joseph Street, Joseph Welsh, a computer consultant for the city of Easton, had just put his two sons to bed and was downstairs with his wife, enjoying the warm spring breeze coming in through open windows.

Suddenly he heard screaming.

Welsh went to a front window and looked out. Michelle, the lanky blond girl across the street, to whom he said hello now and then, was lying on the sidewalk in front of her house. Her husband, Brandon, stood on the walk just outside the front door.

Here we go again. It had not been even a week since the laundry incident, when the neighbor overheard Brandon declare to Michelle that she was "nothing but a fucking bitch" and watched him throw her laundry out the window.

Tonight's squabble was shaping up to be another doozy.

Michelle was on her knees. Her forehead hovered inches from the concrete. She was yelling loudly enough that he could hear her clearly, all the way across the street.

"What the fuck do you want from me?" she wailed.

"What the fuck do you want from me?" she yelled again.

"What the fuck do you want from me?"

Three, four times, she screamed it. He distinctly would remember this later.

Brandon seemed to be answering her, but Welsh couldn't hear what he said.

At last, Michelle picked herself up off the ground and headed for the house. The two of them disappeared inside.

A minute later, Brandon reemerged, sauntering over to where Michelle had been prostrate. Welsh watched him through the window. He stooped over to pick up something from the sidewalk. Welsh wondered what it could be. It seemed to be something small, like change or something. What it was, he couldn't tell.

When Devon arrived at apartment 3 at the Mineral Springs Hotel, Keary was waiting. Keary hadn't gone to work, because Devon hadn't been there to drive her. She'd paged Devon numerous times, but all night Devon had ignored the pages. Now Keary had just one question for her: "Was Michelle there?"

It wouldn't be the first time Michelle had used Devon's father's house as a meeting place. Knowing she couldn't call Devon at the Mineral Springs without riling Keary, Michelle often went through Devon's dad, showing up at his house and asking him to summon Devon there.

"No," Devon said, denying at first that she'd seen Michelle.

It was a lie. Devon had sworn it was just going to be a little birthday party with her and her dad, but it wasn't. Keary always knew when Devon lied about seeing Michelle. She always found out sooner or later. Usually Devon just admitted it.

Keary smelled the vodka on her breath, and the smell of alcohol triggered her temper. Devon could be a handful when she drank. Keary lunged for the bottle of vodka that sat on top of the refrigerator. She wrenched the cap off and chased Devon down and shoved the bottle at her face, as if to show her how pathetic it was.

Devon managed to twist the bottle away. She cocked her arm. Keary turned and ducked. The bottle caught her low in the back of the head, sending a searing pain down her neck.

Keary spun around and swung, connecting with an open hand. Blood bloomed on Devon's lip. Devon slapped her back. Then the yelling started, back and forth.

The volume in the apartment escalated to the point where people in other rooms, and even in the bar downstairs, would report having heard the two women brawling.

Keary persisted in asking why Devon hadn't returned her pages all night; Devon finally admitted having been with Michelle. "But you have nothing to worry about," she quickly protested. "I'm not going back with her."

"What do you mean?" Keary wanted to know.

Devon said Michelle had asked to marry her, but she'd rejected the proposal and returned the rings Michelle had given her. She and Michelle were through. The plan to run away together, back to the Caribbean, far away from Keary and Brandon, was over.

Now Devon and Keary could go to sunny Arizona as they'd planned, get married as they said they would, even have that baby they'd talked about, leaving all the jealous competition behind them.

Keary didn't know what to believe. Was it truly over with Michelle?

Devon's pager went off. She retreated to see who was trying to contact her.

The call was coming from Michelle's house.

She headed toward the door.

"Where are you going?" Keary demanded, blocking her.

"Downstairs."

Keary knew why. To call Michelle from the outside pay phone, so Keary couldn't hear.

"If it's really over, why don't you call her from here?" she dared Devon, still blocking her exit.

Devon plopped on the couch, picked up the phone and dialed.

The call was answered. Keary, sitting next to Devon, heard the rumble of Brandon's voice and, over that, Michelle screaming and yelling in the background.

After a minute or two, Devon hung up.

"Michelle's sick," she announced. "She needs me. I have to go."

Keary didn't buy it. There was Michelle, crying wolf again. Like always, conniving to get Devon away from her. How many times had she done it before? What was it that she claimed to have last time? A broken leg?

"What's wrong this time?" Keary demanded.

"She thinks she's going into cardiac arrest," Devon said.

Right. A heart attack.

"I have to go over there," Devon insisted. "I'd do it for you."

Keary gave this some thought.

"Fine," she said. "But I'm going with you."

She wasn't about to trust Devon alone with Michelle again, not after tonight.

Devon drove the 5½ miles or so, with Keary riding shotgun, snaking back down North Delaware Drive at top speed. Skirting downtown Easton on Larry Holmes Drive, the young women sped past the cocktail drinkers out on the open-air deck of the boxing champ's Ringside bar, then hung a left and dipped under a railroad bridge, entering into South Side, where Michelle and Brandon shared a house with a fenced backyard and their various pets.

Devon parked at the curb and ran to the door.

Keary watched her through the passenger window.

In the dark behind the house, Brandon and Michelle's dog, Sadie, slept in her cage, and their cats prowled the spring grass for mice.

Brandon's six-foot silhouette appeared in the doorway, dwarfing the slight Devon. An argument broke out between the two.

The commotion carried across the street, waking Joseph Welsh.

He glanced at the digital clock next to his bed: 12:35.

He got out of bed, went to the window and looked out. That silver Pontiac was parked out in front of his neighbor's house, the car that belonged to the little dark-haired girl who came by a couple nights a week. He didn't know her name, but he saw her standing on the front step, arguing back and forth with Brandon. What they were saying, he couldn't tell. He couldn't make out the words over the rumbling of his bedroom air conditioner—only an argumentative tone between them.

Welsh left the bedroom and made his way barefoot to the bathroom. The bathroom, like the bedroom, faced the front of the house. From inside the bathroom, he could hear more clearly. He heard a gruff voice, which sounded like Brandon's, telling the girl on the step that she couldn't do something. That he wasn't going to let her.

Welsh returned to the bedroom. He stood at the window in his pajamas and looked out to see what was going on. A flicker of movement inside the Pontiac caught his eye. Someone was inside the car, on the passenger side.

Abruptly the argument at the doorstep concluded. The girl marched back to her Pontiac and pounded her fist on the hood.

"Fuck this!" Welsh heard her holler at the person in the passenger seat. "I'm taking you home."

* * *

At 1:45 A.M., Keary was back at the Mineral Springs, working on a letter to her husband. It was a rambling, disjointed missive she'd been composing on and off for weeks now, begging him to take her back, to give her another chance if things didn't work out with his new girlfriend.

The telephone rang. It was Michelle.

"Where's Devon?" she wanted to know.

"She went back to see you," Keary shot back.

"Well, she never showed up. You're lying," Michelle insisted. "I know you're keeping her there. You won't let her go."

It wasn't the first time Keary had been accused of keeping Devon against her will.

"She's not here," Keary insisted.

"If she's there, just tell me," Michelle pressed.

"She isn't here!"

"I don't believe you."

Keary invited her to come over and see for herself, and then hung up. She wasn't worried. Devon had disappeared before. She always came back. And she and Keary never went to bed angry.

Around 2:30 A.M., Michelle pounded on the door. Keary let her in. Michelle looked around the place. It looked as if a bomb had gone off.

"Devon did this," Keary explained.

Michelle said she was worried about Devon and couldn't sleep.

"You should call the police," she pressed Keary. "You should report her as a missing person."

Keary thought notifying the police would be an overreaction. Plus, she didn't want to send the cops after Devon, in case she was out drinking and driving. Devon had been in trouble for that once already.

"She's left before," Keary told Michelle. "She always comes back."

But Michelle wasn't satisfied. She grabbed the phone and dialed 911.

"Northampton County Operator fifty-one," came the answer.

"Hi," Michelle said. "I would like to report a missing person. She was drinking. She was, she—"

"What's your address, ma'am?"

Michelle explained where she was calling from.

"Who are you to the missing person, ma'am?" the operator asked.

"To the missing person, I'm a friend."

"You're a friend?"

"Yeah. I'm here with the missing person's girlfriend."

"Is it a male or a female that you're reporting missing?"

"A female."

The operator verified the address and asked for a phone number. "And what makes you think that she's missing?"

"Well, at around six o'clock tonight, she started drinking. She was drinking very heavily and—"

"How old is she?"

"She's only eighteen years old—she's nineteen years old."

"Nineteen?"

"She's nineteen years old. And she was—she was with me, and I went home. She went back home with her girlfriend. And her girlfriend and her, they got in a little argument and she left and she was supposed to come to my house. She never came to my house, so now I'm here. She left at quarter after twelve and never came back here."

"OK. And who does she live with?"

"She lives here at that address that I gave you with her girlfriend."

"OK. Is she—obviously, at nineteen, is she on her own?"

"Yes."

"Does her parents—"

"Her parents have no control over her; she doesn't live with her parents."

"All right. What's your name, ma'am?"

"My name is Michelle."

"What's your last name?"

"Hetzel." Michelle spelled it for the operator. She continued to express her concern. "We don't know if she got in an accident. We don't know what's wrong with her. We don't know where she's at. It's three o'clock in the morning, she's never done this before and her girlfriend's really worried about her and she would have came home."

She gave the operator Devon's name, age and race.

"And you said she seemed very intoxicated?" the operator asked.

Michelle asked Keary, "When she left here, was she intoxicated?" Then she answered the operator, "Yeah. She was really loaded."

"Really upset, meaning, what, she could be suicidal?"

"I don't know. I don't know."

The operator asked if Devon might be at a friend's. Michelle said they already called her friends, as well as the hospital. "She had her pager," Michelle said. "She would call back, especially if Keary put in nine-one-one, she'd call."

"OK. Hang on. What apartment are you in now?"

"Three. The cops aren't gonna come here, right?"

"Yeah, they are."

"They are?"

"Yeah. Is that her parents' house or—"

"No, that's her own apartment."

"OK."

"Yeah."

"So that's fine that they come there? I mean, do you want to make a report that she's missing? They have to come there."

"OK."

"Let me get some information on her. OK. You said that she's a white female?"

Michelle described Devon as five foot seven (an exaggeration of a couple inches), a hundred pounds or less, with spiked dark brown hair.

"What was she last seen wearing?"

"What was she wearing? A gray T-shirt and black Adidas pants with white lines on them."

"Like jogging-type pants?"

"Right."

"All right. We'll send an officer over to make a report about it."

"OK."

"OK?"

"OK. Thanks."

"Yep, bye-bye."

"Bye-bye."

Sometime later, Detective Greg Dorney and a patrolman with the Forks Township Police Department showed up at the apartment to take the girls' statements for an attempt-to-locate (ATL) report. The ATL differed from a missing-person report in that the latter could go right into the FBI's National Crime Information Center (NCIC) database and was generally issued for children under eighteen, while an ATL couldn't be entered into NCIC right away and was issued for adults missing for a short period of time and for whom no one had submitted a sworn affidavit indicating that the person was in danger. Because Devon was over eighteen and had been missing only a short time, an ATL was issued. After the cops left,

Michelle and Keary spent the rest of the night calling friends, family, hospitals and police stations to find out if anyone had seen their friend.

When daylight came, Michelle went home to change clothes. Then she swung by the Mineral Springs to pick up Keary, and the two went out driving in Michelle's Accord to look for their missing friend.

2

The Morning Call, one of the two daily newspapers that competed aggressively in the Easton market, carried an average weekday's typical mix of stories about community happenings, political bickering and criminal doings that Thursday morning, June 15, 2000.

Community happenings included a children's sing-along at Centre Square downtown that day and a free "Rhythms of the River" folk concert on Sunday evening at Riverside Park. Graduation ceremonies had been held in schools the day before, and Thursday's paper contained names of valedictorians, lists of proud winners of various scholarships and end-of-the-year awards, and comprehensive rosters of graduates. Along with photos depicting the cheers, embraces, tears and farewells of the last day of school was a photo of a carefree thirteen-year-old showing off on a pogo stick.

Local political issues covered in Thursday's paper included a plan to keep adult entertainment businesses out of downtown Easton. No such businesses currently existed in the city, but the potential for one arose a month ago when Easton's most famous resident, boxing great Larry Holmes, floated the notion of a strip club on Northampton Street, the main thoroughfare cutting through the city. Backlash had prompted Holmes to kill his proposal voluntarily, but now city fathers wanted to put a nail in the coffin.

The paper that day published an essay by Northampton's county executive Glenn Reibman urging support of a $110-million bond intended to create jobs, preserve landmarks, redevelop industrial areas and preserve open space in the Lehigh Valley, a geographical designation encompassing Northampton County, Lehigh County and their three cities: Easton, Bethlehem and Allentown. He invoked a rosy image of the Eisenhower era, when "America was entering into a period of unmatched prosperity, and Bethlehem Steel was operating at full capacity." The essay went on to point out that a decline in steel and heavy manufacturing, as well as a shrinking corporate tax base, had brought the Lehigh Valley to an economic crossroads. Reibman, a Democrat, wrote of his vision for the area "to rise above partisan politics and historical disputes" and a desire "to return this once-great center of commerce and industry to the powerhouse that it was." A vote on the bond would take place that very night.

Criminal doings reported in the paper included coverage of the verdict reached after just three hours of jury deliberation in the trial of Lawrence Peterson Jr., a thirty-year-old Easton man convicted the day before of rape, attempted murder and other offenses. Peterson had smoked thirty-six bags of crack, over a three-day stretch, before setting out on a rampage of terror and violence. He beat a woman with a wooden paddle until it broke over her head, and then he stole money and her car. He stuffed a rag soaked in pine cleaner into the mouth of a nine-year-old girl and sexually assaulted her. He stabbed a woman on the street. And finally he tried to run down police, who shot him in the leg.

This was the major news of the day in Easton the

morning of June 15. The weather was fair, seasonally warm and sunny.

Richard Allen Deemer, an equipment operator with the city of Easton's highway department, had been laboring near a place commonly called "the falls," a spillway behind a gravel parking lot and an unoccupied park-system building known as "the old canal museum."

It was about one o'clock and Deemer's crew had just finished up at the site for the day. The crew had parked its John Deere front-end loader outside the gate between the parking lot and the falls. It was a great spot to be working this time of year, especially on a fine spring day.

A coworker remained below, in the fish hut by the falls, when Deemer himself began locking up the two steel beams that swung together to form a gate to keep motor vehicles out of the falls area. He would recall being in the middle of shackling the gate, the hush of the water tumbling down behind him, when a red Honda Accord pulled off Route 611 and into the parking area of canal park.

The events that unfolded next would mark the beginning of an episode in Easton's history that would shock, stun and sadden the tight-knit city for many months to come. But Deemer had no way of knowing what was in store when he looked up from the gate.

Michelle and Keary were running out of places to look. Last night had been a long night, and neither had slept.

Now it was almost one o'clock in the afternoon.

They were traveling Route 611. Michelle had the wheel. The falls loomed up ahead. It was a park along the canal where the water tumbled over structures called fish ladders, creating a waterfall effect.

The falls held special meaning. One of them had suggested it to the police last night. Maybe the cops had looked there already; maybe they hadn't. No harm in the girls checking for themselves.

Michelle's vodka had worn off many hours ago, and now she looked spent. She flicked on her blinker ahead of the parking lot, approached slowly and swung the red Honda into the gravel lot.

There it sat. The silver Pontiac Sunfire.

"I could kill her!" Michelle shouted. It was so like Devon to do something like this when she drank. Pass out somewhere, and have everybody up worrying all night.

"This is the last time she's going to do this to me," she swore to Keary.

Michelle pulled up close behind the other car. The girls got out.

"Go talk to her," she told Keary. "Go see what she's doing."

Keary got out, circled around the front of the Sunfire and called out, "She's not in there."

"What do you mean she's not there?" Michelle retorted.

Keary shrugged and went back for another look. She couldn't see very well through the windows. She tried the door handle, but the car was locked. She put her face to the glass and saw something.

Michelle did not go to the car right away. She spotted a man bending over the gate between the parking area and the falls. She approached him, calling out questions.

Richard Deemer looked up as the slim blonde neared.

"Do you know how long that car has been sitting there?" Michelle asked, referring to the silver Pontiac.

Deemer squinted past the big yellow John Deere.

"No," he said. "I don't."

"It belongs to a friend of ours," Michelle explained. "We've been looking for her."

Now Keary was calling out to Michelle.

"It looks like she's sleeping in the back!" An edge of panic crept into her voice.

Keary dug for her own key ring. It had a set of keys to the car. She found the Pontiac key and slid it into the lock.

Michelle left Deemer to join Keary.

Keary opened the car door. Michelle took a step back. Something smelled bad. She put her hand over her mouth.

Keary reached into the back.

"Baby, are you OK?" she asked.

She shook her friend, who was curled up on the backseat.

"Michelle! She won't wake up."

Keary saw that her friend's lips and eyebrows were discolored.

"She's purple!" she called over her shoulder. The panic had grown full-fledged now, bordering on hysterics. "We have to take her to the hospital!"

Michelle stepped closer and looked into the car, where Keary was cradling their friend's hand. That smell again. She backed away and doubled over, retching.

Keary broke out into sobs.

Deemer would recall at future proceedings that Keary "started to panic," screaming, crying and shouting that Devon wasn't moving. At that point Deemer himself went up to the car to see what the trouble was. Both doors were open, and Keary was on the driver's side of the car and Michelle on the passenger side.

"They were frantically panicking," he said. "They were screaming, crying, 'She's not moving. Is she breathing?'"

As hysterical fear overcame them, Deemer tried to calm the girls.

"They were just frantically crying, screaming, 'Is she

alive? Is she breathing?' I just told them both to back away
from the car, calm down."

Next, Deemer said, he looked into the car himself,
ducking between the open door and the car with both
hands raised.

"At that point I proceeded to look into the car. Now, when
I went in between the door and the car itself, I had both
hands in the air, because I didn't want to touch nothing."

It was only a quick glimpse, but it was enough to persuade him that something was seriously wrong with the
woman in the car. Her face looked yellowish.

"I believed that there was a serious problem," he said.
"The discoloration told me that she was probably not alive
or at least that she was not breathing."

The sobs coming from the two young women were
softer now, but persistent. Michelle stood near the car.
Keary stepped back and sat on a landscaping tile. Deemer
urged them to move away from the car.

As he began to make the emergency call to county dispatch, he remembered Michelle wanting to call 911 herself from her cell phone. He convinced her to let him
make the call. Being a city worker, he knew he could establish two-way communications directly with county
emergency dispatch and the call would be recorded,
which might prove important later.

Easton patrolman David Beitler was alone in his patrol
car at the heart of the city, Centre Square, where the
cheery sounds of a children's sing-along featuring rhythm
instruments and made-up lyrics had been punctuating the
traffic noise since noon. A call came over the radio, dis-
patching him to the old canal museum on Route 611 to
check out a report of a body found in a vehicle.

Beitler, who'd been with the Easton Police Department

(PD) since 1997, made note of the time: 12:55 P.M. Weaving through the lunchtime traffic snarls, he piloted the cruiser out of Centre Square and down toward the river and Route 611. Because he was already mobile when the call came, he made good time, being the first law officer to arrive.

Arriving at the park, he recognized city worker Rich Deemer in the parking lot, along with two young women. He pulled his patrol car behind a silver car on the left side of the lot, seeing that the passenger door was open.

A yellow John Deere front-end loader sat to the right of the car and a red Honda Accord was off to the rear.

Beitler got out of his car and approached Deemer, who quickly pointed him in the direction of a silver car parked just ahead of the patrol car, facing the river. Beitler approached the car from the side of the open passenger door, bending so he could see inside. A key ring dangled from the ignition. A woman lay in the backseat.

He crouched lower, trying to see around the front seats.

The woman wasn't moving.

As first responder, it fell to him to check for signs of life, so he leaned the passenger seat forward and ducked behind it.

The woman was curled in a fetal position, facing the trunk. Some kind of green jacket covered her upper body. He noticed what looked like grass or mud stains on her lower back, legs and sneakers.

The patrolman reached back delicately, careful not to disturb anything. At this early stage, he could not know what kind of situation he was facing, but if it turned out that a crime was involved, everything and anything might be crucial evidence. It was imperative that evidence remain uncontaminated.

He touched her, pressing his fingertips to her skin. It was cold, lifeless.

Beitler retreated from the dim, stale interior of the silver car, stepping out into the daylight and fresh air coming off the river to contact his supervisor, who would, in turn, assign detectives to come on down and start the investigation.

It wouldn't be long now before the detectives, rescue personnel and other authorities, such as the coroner and district attorney, arrived.

While he waited, Beitler went to gather information from Deemer and the two young women. Deemer told the patrolman he'd been in the area since the morning and hadn't witnessed any suspicious goings-on.

Beitler took the names of the two girls for the report he'd have to write later. The shorter of the two was a nineteen-year-old South Side girl, Michelle Hetzel, of West St. Joseph Street. Her companion gave her name as Keary Renner, her age as nineteen and her address as the Mineral Springs Hotel, a tavern and rooming establishment up the river in Forks Township.

The girls told Beitler that the person in the car was a friend of theirs who'd gone missing the night before. The last time they'd seen her was just after midnight.

Michelle Hetzel said they'd been out looking for her all night, and they'd reported her missing at 3:00 A.M. to Forks Township PD. She was teary.

Beitler glanced around, alert for any stray details he might have missed, anything that might prove significant later on. He thought the skinny blonde looked nervous. He took in the scene, the people, the vehicles. Something on the red Honda caught his eye: a narrow, rectangular rainbow decal. Just like the one on the silver car.

Maybe it didn't mean anything. Maybe it did. In any case, it was another detail that would go into his investigative report. It was something to point out to the detectives, who were just starting to arrive.

3

Three cities anchor the corners of Pennsylvania's Lehigh Valley, and each has its own claim to fame. Allentown became a household name after the release of Billy Joel's 1982 song by the same name, about the death of the steel industry (although the title is a misnomer—the song more aptly describes the nearby city of Bethlehem). Bethlehem is known far and wide as "the Christmas city," for its annual holiday celebrations and elaborate Christmastime festivities. And Easton, though the smallest of the three cities, lays claim to nothing less than its very own heavyweight champion of the world.

Boxing great Larry Holmes owns the city of Easton the way he once owned the blood sport of boxing, cutting a distinct profile and boasting the most universally recognizable name in town. The open-air deck at his popular Ringside Restaurant & Lounge commands the city's most dramatic view, overlooking the violent crashing together of two formidable forces of nature: the Delaware River, descending from upstate New York and severing the state of Pennsylvania from neighboring New Jersey, and the Lehigh River, tumbling down from below Scranton through coal country and the Blue Mountains of Pennsylvania.

This confluence of waterways, colloquially called "the Forks of the Delaware," is a place equally beautiful and deadly, a God-made climactic marriage of opposing powers. It is at once furious, noisy, raging, restless, soothing, tranquil and inspiring—a centerpoint of natural beauty that rivets the attention because it at once repels and attracts.

On Thursday, June 15, like most fair-weather days, there was activity out on the water at the Forks, a favorite recreation spot for Pennsylvania and New Jersey anglers, boaters and nature lovers, despite its treacherous crosscurrents, annual boating mishaps, heroic river rescues and periodic drownings.

It was about one in the afternoon. White ceiling fans whisked the air over Holmes's open deck. The lunch crowd was light. Straight ahead, beyond the red deck rails and across Larry Holmes Drive, sat a tidy corner of bright green grass, outfitted with park benches and a historically significant cannon. Pedestrians often stopped to lean against the railings atop the bluff along the river and gaze out over the water. It was easy to see why the little park was a favorite of painters and photographers seeking to capture the picturesque drama of the Forks.

To the left, a lone cyclist traversed the gothic-detailed Northampton Street Bridge to the town of Phillipsburg, New Jersey, a place that briefly served as the childhood home of one Vera Jayne Palmer, the precocious beauty who would eventually achieve Hollywood stardom as a blond bombshell by the name of Jayne Mansfield. To the right, the expanse of a black railroad bridge stretched across an open span of sparkling silver water.

Directly across the water, beyond where the two rivers collided, sat another park, belonging to the Delaware

Canal State Park system. Locally, most people referred to the spot as the old canal museum. Most summer days, this bucolic spot, looking out on structures called fish ladders built to help fish swim over the dam, served as a starting point for joggers, cyclists, mothers with strollers and high-school sweethearts setting out for a walk down the canal path that followed the Delaware south.

But today, virtually no one without a badge had been able to get near the park since the fleet of cop cars and emergency vehicles swarmed the lot. Now police had it cordoned off with yellow tape. A two-door Pontiac Sunfire sitting in the gravel parking area received intense scrutiny. Two young women, red-eyed, weeping, talked to police around the silver car. The chirp and squawk of emergency radio chatter punctuated the steady roar of the rivers pouring together below the dam.

People observing from various points along the river traded theories on what might have happened. In town, shopkeeper gossip and bystander speculation ran the gamut, but anyone could tell that when the news came out, it would be bad.

A handful of reporters with notepads shuffled on the perimeter of the park, watching, scribbling, eavesdropping. News photographers climbed and ducked, framing shots, looking for clean angles on important faces, which included heavy hitters such as Northampton County district attorney (DA) John Morganelli and coroner Zachary Lysek.

As the time ticked by, a sense of gravity, of inevitable loss, depressed the mood among onlookers, the way a sobering feeling overcomes motorists passing by a wreck from which no driver could have walked away. Even the jaded journalists grew somber, waiting for word to come.

A cluster of people moving with frantic urgency arrived at the park and was gingerly ushered through to where the silver car sat in ominous isolation. The two crying girls, who had been talking to police, consoled the new arrivals.

There was no consoling some.

A woman howled.

"No!"

The cry was anguished.

"She's not dead!"

It was the cry of a mother whose only daughter just six days ago turned nineteen years old, and today lay lifeless in the back of a car.

Easton detective William Crouse Jr. pulled into the canal museum lot off Route 611 while the officers who arrived before him were still stringing yellow tape to preserve the crime scene. He had twenty-seven years with Easton PD under his belt—twenty years on patrol and the past seven as a detective—and he more than knew his way around town. Today he was the day-shift detective, officially on the clock from 8:00 A.M. to 4:00 P.M.

He responded to the scene at the request of other officers, and all he knew when he got there was that the call had come in as a "DOA in a car." During a quick briefing by Lieutenant Steven Parkansky, head of Easton's criminal investigation division, Crouse was put in charge of the case.

He looked across the lot. He saw a silver Sunfire, and right behind it a red Honda Accord parked close enough to be included in the taped-off crime scene.

He approached the silver Sunfire, leaning inside for a look.

It was going to be a long day.

He stepped away from the car to coordinate with the other detectives coming to the scene and to hash out with his lieutenant what their duties would be.

* * *

Across Route 611 from the old canal museum, from the loading dock of Easton Plating and Metal Finishing, a handful of people had been observing the goings-on with the idle curiosity of workers killing time on coffee and cigarette breaks. One of them was Thomas Reinbold, whose shift had started at three o'clock that morning. Reinbold told police that when he'd arrived for work, he'd noticed the silver car parked in the lot at the canal museum. It didn't strike him as strange, because the lot was sometimes used by early birds who came in the predawn hours to jog the canal path or fish along the river. Walking back and forth inside the workshop, he'd looked out a number of times throughout the course of the morning and noticed that the car never moved. It was parked in the same place when police arrived as it had been when he showed up for work that morning. Reinbold's coworker, Michael Yudisky, who had arrived for work at four or four-thirty that morning, agreed with him.

To further corroborate the time frame, police called Donald Bachman, superintendent of the city of Easton's Bureau of Highways, and asked him to come down to the canal museum. Bachman had been to the site between eight and eight-thirty that morning to begin setting up fireworks for the city's upcoming "Heritage Day" celebration. He'd had to open up a barricade so that a city truck could get across the canal and down to the area where the Lehigh River and Delaware River meet, to a spot where the fireworks would be set off. Looking out from his pickup truck that morning, he, too, had noticed the silver car parked in the gravel lot. He hadn't bothered to look inside.

This information helped bookend time of death for investigators. The two girls who found the body said they'd last seen their friend a little after midnight. Reinbold put the Sunfire at the canal museum at 3:00 A.M. This narrowed the window for time of death to somewhere between around midnight and 3:00 A.M.

A detective walked over to talk to Keary and Michelle, who had been consoling Devon's family members while choking back sobs themselves.

"Is she alive?" Michelle sniffled.

The detective told her that Devon was not.

Keary borrowed Michelle's cell phone and called her mother, who didn't answer, so she called her sister. Michelle herself used the phone to dial Ashland Chemical Co., a plant in nearby Glendon, a couple miles upriver from South Side, where her husband, Brandon, worked as a chemist. When somehow the call got disconnected, she changed her mind and phoned her mother's house. It was the second time that day that Mary Hetzel had heard from her daughter. Michelle had called her early that morning, telling her that Devon Guzman was missing.

Now Michelle was calling to break the unthinkable news that her best friend was dead.

The phone rang at the Hetzel home on West Nesquehoning Street in Easton, one block over and two blocks down from Michelle and Brandon's house on West St. Joseph Street. Mary answered.

"Mom," Michelle sobbed. "They found her body."

Neither of Michelle's parents had looked favorably on their daughter's relationship with Devon, but what could Mary say now?

"Can you come down?" Michelle pleaded.

"Where do I go?"

"The canal museum on six-eleven," Michelle told her.

It was a mile or less away. Driving there meant weaving a few short blocks out of South Side's one-way streets, traveling down a hill to the river, turning left up 611, and then making a right into the park. The trip could be made in less than five minutes.

Mary Hetzel arrived a short time after her daughter's call. Michelle was visibly shaken. She was crying, sobbing. There was little her mother could do.

"Michelle was upset," she would remember later, testifying in court. "She was talking with the detective. And then the detective said that he was going to take her down to police headquarters for questioning. I asked if I could go along, and the detective said no, so I went home."

When Mary got home, she recalled putting in a call to Ashland Chemical. Brandon himself remembered it that he, having received a message from Michelle, tried to reach Michelle and couldn't get through, so he called his mother-in-law to find out what was going on. In any case, the two connected by phone. Mary let him know that Michelle's friend Devon, the one Brandon had griped about to her so vehemently on the phone last night, was now dead, and that furthermore, Michelle was going to police headquarters to be interviewed.

Brandon told her he'd come by the house after he finished his shift.

In the meantime, Michelle handed off her car keys to Lieutenant Parkansky before being transported downtown to the stationhouse.

At 1:13 P.M. on June 15, Lieutenant Steven Parkansky, head of Easton's criminal investigation division, put in a call to Northampton County coroner Zachary Lysek, requesting his presence at the stone parking lot of the canal museum on Route 611. Lysek left his office in the

Northampton County Courthouse, which was just a few blocks up the steep slope of Washington Street from the site in question.

Because he was what is known as a "lay coroner," meaning that he was not a physician or forensic pathologist, he would rely on someone trained in those specialties to conduct an autopsy, if one was needed. However, certain statutory duties under state law belonged to him. Among them were officially confirming the identity of the deceased, leading the investigation to determine cause and manner of death, determining whether an autopsy or toxicology tests were warranted and notifying next of kin, if that had not already been done. These were the duties he set out to perform.

Throughout the region Lysek was well-regarded for his work as county coroner, a position he'd held since April 1992. An ambitious, hardworking former police officer, with two bachelor's degrees to his name, he had served as Northampton's deputy coroner, worked as a deputy medical examiner and also put in time as a forensic pathology assistant. In addition, he was a member of the American Academy of Forensic Science, and had attended training in crime scene reconstruction, evidence collection, crime scene interpretation and blood pattern analysis, some of which had been conducted by noted criminologist Herb MacDonnell, who testified in the O. J. Simpson case. Lysek would need to draw upon all of these areas of expertise in the weeks and months to come.

When Lysek got to the canal museum, there were several police cars, numerous people standing around and yellow police tape surrounding several vehicles. He took a quick scan of the layout. To the right, a red Honda. To the left of that, the John Deere front-end loader. Next over, a silver Pontiac. And beside that, a small pickup.

"My initial reaction was to assess exactly what type of scene we had," Lysek later recounted. He started off by talking with Lieutenant Parkansky and the other police officers regarding how the call came in and what had transpired since then. Then Lysek went for his camera to photograph the scene. First he approached the Pontiac from the passenger side, and saw the body through the window. He noted that the woman was lying on her left side. It was a simple detail that would prove very significant later on.

From the driver's side, he pointed his lens, photographing the buttocks region. From the passenger side, he snapped a photo of the upper torso, and another of the head and shoulder region.

A green jacket lay over the upper body. Before moving the garment, Lysek examined it carefully for any hair or fiber evidence that might be lost if it were not removed with care. The jacket was upside down, with the collar near her hip and the bottom portion near her head. It had a small amount of blood on it. After a thorough examination, he peeled off the jacket and placed it into the waiting hands of an Easton police officer to be logged as evidence.

With the green jacked removed, the coroner saw no visible injury, but he did note a "large amount of blood on the back surface of her body." He snapped a photo of the bloody shirt the victim was wearing.

Then he zeroed in on her hand. It held a knife. A wooden-handled knife. Another photo. He removed the knife carefully, so as not to destroy any potential evidence.

He also found a Motorola pager. Curiously, it was not clipped to her clothing, but rather it was "pushed under the waistband, and it was pushing the underwear down."

Next to the pager was another curious find: a small syringe containing a granular, yellowish orange liquid that Lysek described as looking like the soft drink Crystal

Light. The syringe brand was Terumo, a maker of insulin syringes, and it had no needle or cap on it.

Lysek turned the knife and syringe over to Easton police before waving over an assistant to help prepare to remove the body from the car. The next steps would be to closely inspect and carefully remove all clothing from the body, and preserve each piece of attire as evidence just the way it was found at the scene. The reason for removing the clothing now, before the body was transported to the city morgue, was to maintain the integrity of the evidence. If the body were to be transported with clothing on, blood could escape the body and create patterns on clothing that might mislead investigators.

While authorities were going about their jobs at the canal museum, Keary Renner placed a call to Devon's father, Rick Guzman. Her voice broke up and her words tumbled out incoherently, but she managed to bluntly convey the terrible news.

"I got a call from Keary saying Devon was dead," Rick remembered. He'd just returned from taking his girlfriend for a doctor visit. The rest of what Keary told him was "inaudible ramblings." Reeling, he hung up and dialed his mother, who worked in the county courthouse as a translator with the public defender's office.

"Come over, I have to talk to you," she told her son. She'd already received word.

"I went to my mom's office at the courthouse, and we had to go downtown," Rick related. When they arrived at the canal museum, Devon's body had not yet been removed from the car. Police at the scene saw him coming and tried to keep him away.

"Her body was still in the backseat of the car. I tried to get toward the car, see what the hell's going on, but they didn't let me," he recalled. "I was this close to bull-rushing them, but I still had some sense, you know, that maybe I didn't want to see it."

He relented about trying to see his daughter, but he couldn't stand for being kept in the dark about what had happened to her. "Is there anything obvious?" he demanded of the preoccupied investigators. "Shotgun wound, stab wounds, what?" No one offered any information. It was about four o'clock now, and Devon had been found just before one o'clock.

"I said, 'You guys have been here for three fucking hours with her! You gotta know something.' And they were still taking pictures of her, of the crime scene and everything."

Rick said he might've snapped, if not for the fact that the first detective to talk to him was Steve Parkansky. The two men had gone to school together, and Parkansky had a calming effect. "If I didn't know him, I may've jumped the line, just to go get a peek. But seeing that we went to school together, there was comfort in knowing somebody I know was on it."

It was one of those moments Rick would look back on, and be thankful for his family and the fact that his love and respect for them kept him from doing something he might regret.

"You couldn't love and respect your mom more than I love and respect mine," he said, and at the time his mother was beside him, trembling with stress and emotion. "I didn't want to add to that," he said. "Even though I was faced with the most devastating news in my life, you know, I still had respect for my loved ones."

It was this respect that helped him keep a grip on sanity, however tenuous, at this terrible moment, as well as in the months ahead, when it felt like nothing mattered, or when he itched to take matters into his own hands and "go shake some trees" to get the answers he craved. The support of his family was invaluable. "They helped me stay out of trouble," he said.

As Coroner Lysek performed his grim tasks, police investigators combed the riverbank and ground beneath a nearby railroad bridge in search of possible evidence. They had many more questions than they had answers regarding the disturbing death of the petite, nineteen-year-old brunette by the name of Devon Guzman. They knew she'd disappeared just after midnight, and that she was last seen by her friends. They knew also that somewhere between the time she disappeared and the time Tom Reinbold showed up for work at Easton Plating at three in the morning, something terrible had happened.

But what? Where had Devon gone after leaving her friends, and what had happened to her? How did she wind up at this park?

Was her death drug-related? Anyone familiar with Easton's law enforcement issues had to consider the possibility. A major portion of the city's crime problems had something to do with drugs. It wouldn't be the first time a teenager had gone to a spot like this and succumbed to an overdose. When the dispatch call had first gone out, drugs had certainly seemed like a plausible explanation.

But if drugs were the answer, what about the knife? Did it point to a suicide? And if it was a suicide, where did the dirt and grass stains on her pants come from? A visible linear pattern to those stains suggested that she might have been dragged. This fact by itself raised the possibility that Devon did not meet her death alone. If true, who was with her? Was it a stranger or a friend? Was she carjacked at a stoplight on the empty streets of Easton? Had she pulled over and picked up someone she thought she could trust?

The questions were numerous. Was it an overdose as the syringe might suggest, a suicide as the knife might suggest, or something else? Did the victim die here, in her car, or elsewhere, as the drag marks might suggest? These were the questions that presented themselves before the body of the deceased had been removed from the car.

When the time came for the body to be taken out of the car, two of these questions were answered in a swift and dramatic fashion that left observers aghast.

District Attorney John Morganelli was among the observers present, and the memory of what he witnessed that day, when the body of Devon Guzman was lifted from her car and placed on the ground outside, remained vivid and troubling, seared in memory even years later.

"My recollection of that day was when they put Ms. Guzman down on the ground and turned her over, my initial reaction was that her [head] just almost fell off," Morganelli later recalled. "She had been cut so deeply from front to back that it was almost a decapitation. I was shocked, obviously, by what I saw."

Only then, when the body was out of the car, was Coroner Lysek able to see the full extent of the young woman's injury. A dark, gaping cut stretched across the front of her neck about four inches wide, and so deep that it nearly reached her spine.

After examining the vicious slice, Lysek sought out the DA to convey three preliminary conclusions in which he had complete certainty.

It was definitely a homicide, he informed Morganelli. That was his first conclusion. The second was that the car at the canal museum was a secondary crime scene, not the primary one. When Lysek compared the relatively small amounts of blood evident in Devon's Sunfire with the voluminous amounts an injury like the one to her neck would have produced, it left no doubt that Devon had been killed elsewhere. This led to the coroner's third conclusion: the crime scene they were looking at had been staged. A number of things just didn't add up. Whoever had placed Devon's body here at the canal museum had taken pains to mislead investigators into thinking it was something other than what it was: a homicide.

Morganelli listened to what the coroner had to say. An autopsy and crime lab analysis on evidence collected from the car would provide more information. For now, there was not much more that could be determined.

"At that point there were no suspects in mind, necessarily; no one knew what happened," the DA later recounted. So he went over to the police investigators and told them, "OK, well, process the scene and keep me abreast of what's going on."

After that, the case was in the hands of detectives.

The DA had been going out to crime scenes going on ten years now, and it still wasn't easy seeing the things his job required him to see. "I remember my first body that I went out to the crime scene and saw, there dead, you know, lying in the bushes, killed. It was very disturbing, you know, and it's still not pleasant to see human bodies dead in that condition, blood usually and sometimes, you know, eaten up, and et cetera. It's very difficult. But usually I get there and I look at it, I see what the situation is. My focus generally then goes on trying to get the person who did this."

He hardly noticed the two friends of the victim's, Michelle and Keary, crying among the shocked and grieving at the canal museum. "At that time I did not pay any attention to those girls," he said.

4

Easton detective Barry Golazeski knew that there was a death to be investigated, but that's about all he knew. He hadn't been to the scene or received any detailed information from the first responders yet. It had been less than an hour since the girl's body was found in the car at the canal museum.

Golazeski, an eight-year officer with the department, claimed the rank of second in command of the criminal investigation division. He was also assigned to an FBI violent crime task force, in charge of investigating federal organized crime violations in eastern Pennsylvania's Lehigh Valley.

But today he was at the Easton police station, charged with assisting with interviews regarding the death investigation. The body had been discovered at 12:55, and now it was almost three o'clock in the afternoon. Golazeski had nineteen-year-old Michelle Hetzel, one of the young women who'd discovered the body, in a small interview room off the main area of the criminal detective division. Detective Howell Storm accompanied him. Hetzel looked like she hadn't slept, but otherwise nothing appeared out of the ordinary about this young, blond-haired woman with long, manicured nails. After a little informal conversation, Gozaleski turned on a tape recorder and began the formal interview.

"Michelle, you understand that you're not under arrest, correct?" he asked with the tape rolling.

"Correct," she answered.

Golazeski asked her to start at the beginning, recounting how she had met up with Devon the night before and what had happened after that.

"She called me," Michelle began. "She was at her dad's house, and she asked me to come over. And I drove over to her dad's house. Her aunt Candy was there before I got there, and her dad and her dad's girlfriend. They were drinking vodka when I walked in. Then Candy left, and then Rick and I and Devon went to the Twenty-fifth Street liquor store to get another bottle of vodka. And we went to the mall and we got some CDs for Rick. I drove. And we went back to Devon's dad's house and we drank."

Michelle said she and Devon left around 9:00 or 9:30 P.M. "And then when I got home, I was feeling pretty sick. I drank a lot, and I passed out on the couch. And my husband had spoken to Devon and told Devon, you know, that I wasn't feeling well, and her and Keary were not OK at that point in time. So Devon and Keary came to my house approximately twenty minutes after my husband had spoke with them. Keary waited in the car. Devon was in my doorway. My husband didn't want any fights because Devon and Keary have a past of fistfights. And Devon was drinking, which was really going to antagonize her to fight more. So my husband said if Devon wanted to come back, she could, or Keary, just so they're not there together."

"Just one at a time?" Golazeski asked.

"Right."

Michelle said Devon took Keary home and called to say she was coming over. About a half hour went by and she hadn't shown up. "I called Keary. I thought Keary was lying to me and Keary didn't let her leave."

After waiting an hour and a half, she and Brandon drove to Keary's, waited awhile, then called 911. "I originally called the cops to see if there was any accidents in the area. And then I asked if I had to wait twenty-four hours or if I could file a report now. And they sent a cop over, two cops. And then after that, me and Keary just sat up and waited. Then I took my husband home, because he had to go to work. So I took my husband home and then came back."

"About what time did you take your husband home, approximately?" the detective asked.

"Before five."

After dropping Brandon off, she picked up some food at McDonald's and returned to the Mineral Springs sometime before 10:00 A.M. She and Keary ate, and then they went looking for Devon. Michelle said she called police from the car to give them her cell phone number in case Devon turned up.

First they drove by Servpro on Ferry Street, where Devon worked. Her car wasn't there, so they proceeded along Ferry Street to Devon's mother's house, but her car wasn't there, either. Next they checked Rick's house. After that, they went to a placed she called "the bridge" on Industrial Drive. It was a place Keary and Devon would go to sort out troubles in their relationship, Michelle said. "When they'd fight, that's where they'd go," she explained. After that, they continued down Route 611 to a place she, Keary and Devon referred to as "the waterfalls."

"That's what we called it, in the park. And we used to sit on the little ledge, a little ledge overlooking things."

Golazeski asked, "Is this by the canal museum? Is that where you mean, the waterfalls?"

It was. "We saw Devon's car in the parking lot, and we were both very angry because we figured that she was drunk and passed out. So, you know, we were all geared up to yell at her and have Keary drive her home so we can interrogate her some more."

At first Keary said no one was in the car. "I walked over. Keary has keys to Devon's car, opened up the car. Devon was in the backseat and it smelled. And alls I remember Keary saying is 'Devon's purple.' Then I got sick. Keary started crying, and the guy got in his truck and got on the CB and he called the police and the ambulance to come."

Golazeski asked how it was that Keary hadn't seen Devon in the car at first.

"I think that she was standing in the front of the car. And I think that she just glanced in the car and she said that nobody was there. And then I said, 'What do you mean that nobody's in the car?' And then I ran over and she opened up the car. And then I remember her saying that she sees blood. And I only looked at the back of Devon's body, and it was all bloody and I just got sick."

"When Devon and Keary came to see you last night, OK, and your husband told them to come back one at a time, how long of a time frame were they gone before—before you heard from Devon again? She did call you on the phone?"

"Yeah. It was less than an hour. Less than an hour, I believe."

"You were sure that she called from Keary's place?"

"I don't have caller ID, but, yeah, I guess."

"But you thought so. And Devon and Keary were having a fight?"

"Yeah. I guess Devon pulled out some of Keary's hair."

"Well, they had a relationship," Golazeski reasoned. "You said they'd also—they had had some sort of physical altercation that night?"

About a week ago, Michelle said, when she and Devon got back from St. Croix, Keary was threatening to kill herself, and Devon went to grab the knife from her and got cut on the hand or thumb. Michelle said she didn't know if Devon had needed stitches, but she did go to the emergency room.

"OK. But you and Devon used to have a relationship a while back?" the detective asked, trying to keep it all straight.

"Yeah."

"About how long ago was that?"

Two years ago, Michelle told him.

"Were you two, like, getting together again?"

She said no. "Sometimes when Keary would fight with Devon, I would fight with Brandon. It was never really—like we never slept together like that. That was just basically we hang out together. We'd drink together. We'd basically go to Rick's like every—at least four times out of the week. That's basically when Devon gets off of work, that's all she really wanted to do."

"But how did Keary view the two of you hanging out four times a week?"

"Um, well, being that Devon—"

"Did she know that you had a relationship with her in the past?" Golazeski pressed.

"Right. Devon would sneak around Keary's back and she would tell Keary she was just going to her dad's. And she would tell Keary that I'm not there. And she'd tell Keary that she told me to get out of her life and leave her alone and whatever. And I'm just like, 'She didn't say that.' I mean, Devon—Devon's the kind of person where she can't be alone. And when she is, she gets very angry and sometimes—basically, she would never really tell Keary. She would let Keary—Keary would have to find out for herself that I was with Devon 'cause Keary—Keary, you know—I don't know if Devon was afraid of her or not."

"Well, how did you feel about Devon?" Golazeski asked. "Did you want to get back together with her?"

"No. My family doesn't like her, but she was always really good to me and we were always really close. We had a lot in common."

"You said she was your only friend?"

"Yeah, in high school."

"Now, how about Keary? Were—you and Keary ever have a relationship?"

Michelle told him they were best friends for four years, until Devon moved back from Arizona, coming between them.

Now that he had some background, it was time to get down to business. "Well, what do you think happened last night?" Golazeski asked. "Do you have any idea? Can you think of anybody who wanted to hurt her?"

"Hurt her?" Michelle echoed.

"Yeah."

"No, not Devon. No, Devon has . . . Devon has a lot of friends. She has a lot of friends. And she's . . . Devon gets along with everybody, really. The only time she kind of gets stupid and out of her mind frame is when she's drinking, because then, like I said, she does drink a substantial amount of vodka."

"How about her and Keary when they have these fights?" he asked. "Is it possible that something could get out of hand, I mean, especially if they were both drunk? You said that she got jealous of you hanging out with her?"

"Possibly. I'm not going to say it's . . ." Her voice trailed off.

The detective let it go for the moment.

"When you got to Keary's house last night, OK, how did the place look?"

"Ransacked."

"Ransacked?"

"A mess. There were tables turned over. She had newspapers on the floor. There was like a whole bunch of crap on the floor. There was dishes thrown, um, just on the countertops that, you know, like—and the place was a mess. Like you really couldn't walk without stepping on something, and she said that Devon did that."

The detective kept silent.

She continued: "She said that Devon turned over the tables and Devon started throwing things. I mean, I don't know that to be true. I don't know if Devon really did do that or Keary did that. Because I know Keary's very—has a temper and so does Devon. They both could have had a part in it, but I don't know. Keary told me that it was Devon."

Golazeski switched gears a moment.

"And Keary doesn't have a car, right?" he asked.

"No. Her dad took it away from her, so she—Devon transports—transports her to and from work." Michelle said Keary worked as a security guard at a nearby hospital.

The detective resumed the previous line of questioning. "When you were at the house, did you see any blood or anything around the house?"

"No, but I—"

"Just overturned stuff, just looked ransacked?"

"Just looked a mess. It just looked like that they were having a bad fight. And then Keary showed me a clump of her hair, so then obviously something—something had to [have] happened."

That got the detective's attention. "That happened last night that her hair was pulled out, that big clump?"

"Right."

"Is that still at the house?"

"Should be. Unless Keary threw it out. I know she was starting to straighten up things."

"She was straightening up things while you were there? Was she cleaning up?"

"Right before the cops came, she asked me if we could . . . if we could help pick the stuff up off the floor and—"

"Before you filed the missing person's report?"

"No, after we did."

"After you did?"

"Yeah, we ran around the house and we put the stuff on the tables, because it was a pigsty. So we just . . . I mean, it really . . . It was still a mess when the police got there, but, I mean, at least they could step."

Golazeski explored a possible scenario. "From where Keary lives to the canal, how long of a walk would that be approximately? Is it a long distance?" he asked.

"May take her half an hour, forty-five minutes," Michelle replied.

"How much time from when you last spoke to Devon until you went up and actually met up with—"

"Keary?" Michelle offered.

"Yeah, with Keary. About how much time had passed?"

Michelle said about an hour or an hour and a half went by, but she'd been talking with Keary every twenty minutes or so.

"From when Devon called and said, you know, I'm coming to your house, you didn't see her for like a half hour, right? And then when you called back, you get Keary, and what does Keary say?"

"Well, I was hysterical, Keary's hysterical, and I just said, you know—I said, 'Keary, if she's there, just tell me.' And Keary said she's not there. I said, 'You're lying.' She was like, 'No, I'm not.' She goes, 'Come here and see for yourself.'"

The detective sprung a direct question: "When was the last time you and Devon were intimate?"

"It was—you mean like sex?"

"Yeah."

Now it was on the table, the unspoken issue. Michelle seemed taken aback. She waffled, coming short of any kind of outright admission.

"A long time ago," she said. "I mean, I hugged her and kissed her, but we . . . Her and Keary did that thing. Um, I—"

Golazeski eased off. "Well, the reason I'm asking is Keary, it appears to me, that she was very jealous of you, OK?"

"Right. I mean, well, Keary is very jealous of a lot of people."

"OK. Well—"

"I knew her long enough never to take it personally."

"You and . . . but you and Devon were close, so—"

Michelle agreed that they were close, but said Devon always called when Keary wasn't around, or when she was in the shower or at work.

"How was Devon?" Golazeski asked, digging further into Michelle's relations with Devon. "Did she want you to get back together, if she was having trouble with Keary?"

"Devon was a very confused person," she said, adding that she had trouble choosing among various boyfriends. "And you know, with me, with Keary, she was like very confused. She didn't know which way to go, which person to stay with. She always felt really bad for Keary, because she would pay Keary's rent and bills, and like Devon . . . and Devon was very, very confused, yes. She just had a lot going on."

At the conclusion of the interview, Golazeski asked, "Do you have anything else that you would like to add at this time?"

"I guess I just want to know what happened," Michelle said.

"All right. That's what we're here to find out," Golazeski said. He turned the tape recorder off at 3:22 P.M.

Michelle said later that she was asked if she wanted to get back to the canal museum to get her car, since she'd come to the station in a police vehicle. She said she declined the offer, asking instead to be taken to her mother's house.

5

Given what Michelle had told Detective Golazeski about Keary and Devon's volatile relationship, detectives assigned to the case had good reason to want to talk to Keary, as well as ample excuse to get inside the Mineral Springs apartment the two women shared to have a good, hard look around.

Detective William Crouse tackled the task of applying for a search warrant for apartment 3 at the Mineral Springs, wasting no time in accomplishing his mission. Well before the day was out, he was on his way north out of Easton, snaking up along the Delaware River on Route 611 with several other officers, search warrant in hand.

The Mineral Springs Hotel is a three-story establishment rising right up from the winding river road and overlooking a picturesque stretch of the Delaware. Behind it towers an abandoned railroad bridge boarded up to keep thrill-seekers off the dangerous span. The hotel is an establishment with a storied past, though its 175-year history is obscured in local legends and half-truths. It is said to have once served as a stagecoach depot, and rumor had it that some unfortunate soul there once fell victim to a poisoned cup of coffee.

As the investigators rifled through the contents of the apartment that Devon Guzman and Keary Renner had shared, they did not yet know that a woman living right across the road had had an unsettling encounter with one of the occupants of that apartment just the night before.

Audra Maynard, whose residence on North Delaware Drive was the first house up on the northbound lane from the Mineral Springs, remembered the evening clearly. After spending most of Wednesday night at home, at about 11:30 P.M. she decided to head over to the Mineral Springs bar for a change of scene and some company. Maybe she'd drop in on a friend who lived up above the bar in one of the second-story apartments.

She sauntered through the blue-black haze of the June night, across the road and into the familiar, cozy atmosphere of the Mineral Springs tavern. A loose string of five or six people wrapped around the bar. The jukebox supplied background music, its sounds filling the large, empty space to the right.

Maynard ordered a drink from the server behind the bar and started to make herself comfortable. It was only moments before she became aware that some kind of commotion was going on upstairs.

Later, she would describe hearing "very loud thumps," punctuated by abrupt "slamming" coming from above.

Thump, bump, thump, bam!

The noises were loud enough to rise over the pounding beat coming from the jukebox.

Thump, bam!

She winced and looked upward, unsettled by the violence of the impacts above.

"The ceiling tiles were shaking," she would recall. "That's how loud this was; that's how much percussion there was to this."

What the heck is that? she wondered.

She put the question to the bartender, who shrugged helplessly. "The two girls . . . ," the server said, referring to the occupants of the apartment directly above.

The violent ruckus continued for twenty minutes, maybe half an hour, Maynard remembered. Once it stopped, there was quiet above for about an hour.

Around 1:00 A.M., she got up from the bar to go upstairs and say hello to her friend. She went past apartment 3, the one above the bar, from which all the noise earlier had been emanating.

Behind a screen door, the interior door to the apartment stood open. Maynard could see inside, right into a shocking wasteland of the night's domestic squabble.

"It was a mess," she recalled.

So much so, that she remained in front of the door for a longer look.

The wreckage of that loud, long brawl she'd heard from below when she'd first arrived at the bar was strewn from wall to wall.

"There was glass broken on the floor. There was, like, overturned furniture, a table that was broken, just everything was a mess."

Suddenly Maynard was face-to-face with one of the occupants of the apartment.

"Want help cleaning up?" she offered to the tall figure.

The young woman declined.

Maynard had never met her before, but she would soon learn that the woman's name was Keary Renner, and that the roommate she'd fought with that night had been found murdered the next day.

When investigators came to talk to Audra Maynard, she would tell them about the drawn-out fight that rattled the ceiling tiles over the bar. She would tell them about the shattered glass, the smashed table, the overturned furniture. And she would tell them about something else she saw, too, while she was peering through that screen door into the demolished apartment.

"I saw something on the couch with a blanket covering it," she said, "a green comforter."

While investigators worked furiously to gather as much information as they could about what had happened to Devon, news that the fiery nineteen-year-old had been found dead traveled quickly by word of mouth, through Easton and surrounding communities, among those who knew her.

After Holly Ronco received the shattering news that her boyfriend's daughter, Devon, was dead, she might have had reason to recall an ominous conversation from the night before. It was shortly after Devon and Michelle had ripped out of Rick's house in that mad fury that the house phone had rung. The caller was Michelle. She told Holly that Devon had gone home to Keary, and that she was worried something might happen to her.

At the time Holly didn't know what to make of the call. She was sure Devon would be fine. What could she do? Nothing, really. Devon had played Cupid and had introduced Holly and Rick, but she was Rick's daughter, she was an adult and she was on her own. And this was how these girls related. Like typical teenagers, everything was volatile, dramatic and emotionally wrenching. Why should tonight be different from any other night?

But it had been different. Somewhere along the line, things had taken an evil turn.

And now Devon was gone.

It was unthinkable. An unimaginable, unforeseeable tragedy.

Or was it?

Because Michelle seemed to have predicted it. Had she been right to fear for Devon in Keary's hands?

6

When Brandon arrived at his in-laws' home on West Nesquehoning Street, Mary Hetzel would recall in court, he seemed to have one thing on his mind: Michelle's red Accord. It was the thing he asked about when he first came in, Mary said.

"Where's your car, Michelle?" Brandon wanted to know.

At the canal museum, she replied.

"Oh, shit! We have to get that car" was his response, she recounted in court.

Mary recalled that her daughter was too upset to leave the house, so Brandon turned to her for help.

"Will you drive me down to get the car?" he asked.

She agreed, and left with Brandon for the canal museum. On the way she remembered him emphasizing that it was important that he retrieve Michelle's car.

When they arrived, there were people around. Brandon told her to turn around and go home, which she did.

Back at the house, Brandon's concern about the car did not diminish.

"He asked me to call the police and see when we could get the car," she recalled. "So I called and I talked to a Lieutenant Riley, and he said the car was on a rollback."

When she told Brandon that Riley had said the car was on a tow truck, he urged her to take him down to the canal museum a second time. When they arrived, the place was still crowded with people; so they turned around a second time and returned home.

Back at the house again, Brandon spent some time asking Michelle what the police had questioned her about, Mary said. Later, he returned to his own house, the one he shared with Michelle, two blocks away on West St. Joseph Street.

Around 9:00 P.M., Brandon's evening was interrupted by a knock from Easton lieutenant Steven Parkansky, who headed up the criminal investigation division, and Detective David Ryan, who was assigned to help with the Guzman case. Michelle and Keary, who'd spoken with police earlier in the day, were also at the house. Now it was Brandon's turn to come down to the station and tell investigators what he knew.

Despite the June warmth, Brandon was wearing a dark, long-sleeved sweatshirt when he left with the detectives. The long sleeves covering his arms may not have raised eyebrows at the time, but soon enough they would.

David Ryan, a detective assigned to the criminal investigation division who had taken a statement from equipment operator Richard Deemer earlier at the canal museum, now handled the interview with Brandon Bloss. It began at about 9:15 P.M. on Thursday, June 15, at Easton police headquarters, where Brandon's wife, Michelle, had been interviewed by Detective Golazeski earlier that day. Michelle's interview had been tape-recorded, but Brandon's was not. Something was wrong with the recorder. Ryan recalled that Brandon gave the following account of the previous day and night:

Wednesday, June 14, had begun as a normal workday for Brandon. From his South Side home, he headed out to work at nearby Ashland Chemical, where his bachelor's degree in chemistry and math, along with a year and a half of credit toward a degree in chemical engineering, had secured him employment as a chemist.

His shift at Ashland ended at three in the afternoon, when he returned home to take care of Sadie and the other pets. From four to nine o'clock, he worked at his second job, tending bar at the Rice-Ebner American Legion Post in South Side on Davis Street, which runs perpendicular to West St. Joseph, about six blocks down from his home.

Around nine, he finished up at Rice-Ebner, arriving home shortly after to an empty house. Michelle showed up a half an hour later, at about 9:30 P.M., appearing exhausted and intoxicated. (Phone records would establish that Michelle probably arrived home a little after 10:00 P.M., but at the time of the interview, Brandon recalled it being earlier.)

Brandon asked Michelle why she was in the condition she was in, but received no satisfactory answer.

Suspecting that the situation had something to do with her best friend, Devon Guzman, with whom Michelle often went out partying, Brandon told the detective he decided to phone Devon and ask her to come over and help figure out what was wrong with Michelle.

Reaching her by phone, Brandon got Devon to agree to come. About ten minutes later, she arrived at the front entrance of the house.

Brandon met her at the door.

He told the detective that she'd brought along her roommate, Keary Renner, who was not welcome in his home. He didn't specify why she was not welcome, but he said that he wouldn't let Devon inside his home while

Keary was present. He told Devon she'd have to take Keary back to her place and come back without her to see Michelle.

Devon agreed to this request and left with Keary.

Half an hour passed without Devon's return. It should have taken her no more than twenty minutes to drop Keary off and come back, so Michelle then placed a call to Devon and Keary's place at the Mineral Springs to see where Devon was.

Brandon said he didn't know the specifics of that conversation regarding Devon's whereabouts, only that Michelle had placed a call to the Mineral Springs trying to find out where Devon was.

Another half hour went by. Still no Devon.

Michelle called again in search of her.

Devon still had not come back to the house when Brandon went to bed around 11:00 P.M., he told Detective Ryan.

He slept until 2:00 A.M., at which time Michelle came into the bedroom, woke him up and asked him to drive her to the Mineral Springs to check on Devon.

Brandon agreed, accompanying his wife in her car up to the riverside hotel and remaining in the car while Michelle went inside.

Next, Brandon told the detective, he fell asleep, and remembered being awakened by Michelle and Keary at about three-thirty in the morning. They told him that they had called the police to report Devon missing. Michelle then drove Brandon home so that he could at least get in a couple hours of sleep before having to get up for work.

Brandon left the police station after telling Detective Ryan that he didn't see or hear from Devon again that night, and in fact had not seen or heard from her after she left his house with Keary.

Later, when investigators sat down to compare notes,

they would find that Brandon's account of the activities and events of June 14 into the early-morning hours of June 15 agreed very closely with the account given by Michelle during her interview with Detective Golazeski seven hours earlier that day.

The following day, June 16, Detective Ryan also interviewed Keary Renner at Easton police headquarters. Her version of the previous night's events was in rough agreement with Michelle's and Brandon's. The point of distinction was that Michelle and Brandon claimed to have last seen Devon leaving their home with Keary. Keary maintained that she last saw Devon when Devon dropped her off at the Mineral Springs and departed for the couple's house alone.

7

On Friday, June 16, the newspapers reported on how a cheerful crowd of hundreds had turned out the day before at the Easton Area Public Library to welcome home the city's flag. The flag had spent the past three months in Keedysville, Maryland, where a textile preservation company had restored and framed it. The flag had been in possession of the Easton library since 1821, and its true age was a matter of debate among local historians. They believed that the flag, featuring thirteen white stars on a blue background, was either flown in 1776 during a reading of the Declaration of Independence at Easton's Centre Square or was something that had been given to troops from the city who fought in the War of 1812. In any case, the textile preservation people in Maryland said it was the oldest flag they'd ever worked on. Apart from its historic value, one of the main reasons the flag's return garnered such a good turnout was its sentimental value. It had been displayed in the city library for as long as anyone could remember. Children had grown up counting the flag's fading stars as they came and went from the library. It was more than a symbol. It was a piece of American history, a piece of Easton, and it had a place in the hearts of many who'd grown up in the city.

But not all of the day's news was rosy. The Easton Block Watch Association chided city officials for not doing enough to improve the state of Easton's neighborhoods, complaining of drug dealers hanging out at neighborhood pay phones, loud music blasting, absentee landlords and houses with code violations. The Boys and Girls Club of Easton and local police were encouraging support for a "Silence the Violence" walk that weekend to make a statement against violence in the community. And Northampton County councilman Ron Angle, a showman politician with his own Saturday-morning talk show on local radio, had handed out bogus $100,000 bills from his breast pocket at the county Government Center in protest of the $110-million bond endorsed by his political rival.

"Here at the county, we just pass out money," he declared to passersby. "Take some for your friends; it's only money."

He was protesting the big bond that rival politician Glenn Reibman had endorsed in print in Thursday's *Morning Call.* Despite Angle's antics, the bond passed by a vote of 7 to 2, after raucous debate in a jam-packed courtroom. During the debate Angle informed the crowd that it had a "filthy, rotten, corrupt government."

With the funding approved, $22 million would go toward expanding the county jail, and $35 million would be used to build on the courthouse, both of which were overcrowded. Some $700,000 would go toward cultural improvements at the State Theatre in Easton.

But by far, the most disturbing news of the day had nothing to do with money, politics or the local war on drugs. It was the simple, shocking fact that a nineteen-year-old girl had been found dead in her car at the canal museum by the river. That kind of thing just didn't happen in Easton, and it didn't sit right.

The headline above the story in the *Express-Times,* an aggressive local daily whose style of coverage harkened back to newspapering days of old, ran the width of the front page: FORKS WOMAN, 19, FOUND SLAIN IN CAR. A photo of Devon's Sunfire next to the big John Deere accompanied the story. Three people were peering into the car through the driver's-side door. Despite the big play the story received, officials had little of substance to say about the crime. Coroner Zachary Lysek was quoted as saying the death was "clearly a homicide," a statement that was simple enough but may have been pointedly crafted for the purpose of letting the guilty know that the staged crime scene had fooled no one.

An autopsy is simply an examination done on a person who has died to determine why and how that person expired. Dr. Sara Funke performed more than three hundred such examinations a year, which averaged out to a little more than one each and every working day. Over the course of her career as a forensic pathologist, she estimated that she'd performed about twenty-five hundred.

On Friday, June 16, 2000, the purpose of her inquest was to determine how and why this thin, five-foot four-and-a-half-inch girl named Devon Guzman was lying cold, cut and bruised on her autopsy table at Easton Hospital instead of being out in the world somewhere, earning spending cash at a summer job, or making plans to go tubing down the Delaware or spend a week at the Jersey Shore.

Funke, who owned a private-practice group specializing in forensic pathology, had trained long and hard for the privilege of doing just this type of work. She'd gone to medical school at Temple University School of Medicine in Philadelphia, graduating in 1987. From there, she served an internal medicine internship at Lehigh Valley Hospital in Allentown, Pennsylvania. Next, she transplanted to the West Coast, trading temperamental Northeast weather for sunny California and four years of pathology residency training at Harbor UCLA Medical Center in the Los Angeles area. From there, she went on for a final year of specialized training in forensic pathology with the Los Angeles County Coroner's Office. Her training complete, she was now a medical doctor certified by the American Board of Pathology in anatomic and clinical pathology, as well as forensic pathology. She'd worked in the Los Angeles area for a while, before returning East in 1995 and joining the private-practice group here.

Much of her work was done on behalf of area coroners, acting as the coroner's pathologist when it was decided that an autopsy was needed. Such was the situation with Devon Guzman. Northampton County coroner Zachary Lysek had phoned Funke's office to schedule an autopsy.

When Funke arrived at Easton Hospital, Detective Crouse was there to observe and photograph the proceedings. Before beginning her examination of the young woman, whose weight she estimated at no more than ninety to a hundred pounds, she received the standard briefing regarding the individual she was about to examine, along with the circumstances of death, to the extent that they were known. She was told that the subject was a nineteen-year-old woman last known to have been alive around 11:30 P.M. or midnight on June 14, reported missing around 3:00 A.M. on June 15, and found dead in her car, about ten hours later, on the fifteenth.

With that in mind, Funke set out to determine the why and how of her death—the cause and manner, in law enforcement terms, with cause referring to the particular bodily dysfunction that resulted in death, and manner referring to how that dysfunction came about. For cause of death, the possibilities were myriad; for manner, there were only five options: natural, accident, suicide, undetermined and homicide.

The body was cold when Funke began, because it had been refrigerated in the hospital morgue overnight. The state of rigor mortis, a term literally meaning "stiffness of death," she described as "full and fixed."

Funke began with an external examination, viewing the body, part by part, making notes, keeping an eye out for identifying characteristics, such as hair and eye color, scars or tattoos. Special attention was paid to any and all injuries, down to the smallest of bruises or scrapes, making sure that photos were taken and that each injury was measured and accurately documented in notes.

The pathologist immediately identified a number of obvious injuries to Devon's body. The most glaring was the four-inch cut across the front of her neck. In addition to that, there were scrapes on her face, as well as something Funke recognized as petechia, tiny red dots of pinpoint bleeding under the skin.

Leaning for a close look, Funke noted that the petechia covered the face of the deceased. She lifted the eyelids. The petechia appeared on and underneath them, as well as on the lining of the eyes and on the whites of the eyes. She opened the mouth. The petechia appeared there, too.

This number of petechia, distributed in this widespread manner, was clear evidence of one thing: asphyxia. They told Funke that in addition to being bruised and cut, the victim had been deprived of oxygen before she succumbed to death. But they didn't tell the story of how asphyxia occurred. The possibilities included manual strangulation, a ligature around the neck, a choke hold, an arm bar or pressure on the chest that was heavy enough that she couldn't breathe—such as the weight of another person sitting on her chest.

Lifting the right arm, Funke spied a large pink bruise on the right upper portion. On the back side of the arm, she noted a corresponding large dark pink contusion. By the elbow was another bruise, and another by the right wrist. Other small bruises and scratch marks, possibly from fingernails, clustered around the wrist. A scrape on the back of the third finger of the right hand had done some bleeding.

Moving across the autopsy table to the left arm, Funke located a series of five round brown bruises on the forearm, as from the fingertips of a hand gripping the arm tightly enough to leave marks.

Progressing to the lower body, Funke found a series of small round bruises on the back of the left thigh and the front of the right thigh, and more bruises on the knees and over the shins. A number of bruises on the right leg extended from the thigh to the midcalf. The doctor also noticed some scraping on the knees.

Tallying up the bruises, there were seven on the right arm, seven on the left arm, nine on the right leg and five on the left leg. Twenty-eight on the arms and legs alone. Devon Guzman did not go down without a fight.

A prominent smudge of dirt marked the right ankle, around which was tied a black cloth anklet. Funke cut it free and held it up. It was a friendship-type band with the words "Puerto Rico" spelled out across it.

Turning the body over, the pathologist noted dirt and vegetation across the back. On the back of Devon's neck, Funke discovered what is called a poke wound. It was a small injury, about a quarter of an inch in size, of the type that can be produced by a knife stick, or when some other sharp object is jabbed into the skin, just piercing it.

Down from that, along the spine, ran a series of four

oval abrasions that differed from most of the other injuries the victim had suffered in that these had been inflicted postmortem. They were arranged in a linear fashion, forming a pattern whose meaning and significance escaped Funke. She could tell the injuries occurred after death, because when an injury is inflicted on a living person, the heart is beating, keeping blood pressure in the system, which will cause bleeding and swelling at the site of any injury. When an injury is inflicted on someone who is dead, there is no heartbeat, no blood pressure and no bleeding at the site of injury. It doesn't swell or turn red. The result is obvious visible differences between premortem and postmortem injuries. Those inflicted after death appear orange, dried out.

To confirm her conclusion, Funke picked up a scalpel and slid the blade over the skin to make a shallow incision. There was no bleeding underneath, as there would be with a premortem wound. She also took a small biopsy and examined it under a microscope. Together these tests confirmed that this strange pattern of bruises had occurred after death. Beyond that, Funke could not tell much else. She could not say what made them. Something blunt, scraping over the skin, was the best guess she could hazard.

In addition to the petechia, the injury of most interest was the massive cut across the neck. Just above it were an abrasion and a shallow cut, and there were a number of scrapes on her face, including two scrapes on the right cheek that could have been caused by fingernails, and a number of scrape marks on her chin. There were also some scrapes on her nose and earlobe.

The gaping wound across her throat measured four inches from side to side and was centered across her throat. It was a deep wound, reaching not quite to the spine, but almost. The slice had completely severed the tongue, separating it from the rest of the throat structures. After the cut was made, Devon would not have been able to speak. It also cut the right carotid artery and jugular vein in half.

These vital channels are sometimes called the great vessels of the neck because of their importance in sustaining life. The carotid artery brings oxygenated blood from the heart to the brain, while the jugular brings it back to the heart for circulation. Both of these were severed, but only on the right side, leading Funke to conclude that Devon's head had to have been turned to the left when the cut was made. With her head turned to the left, the left-side vessels would have been shielded while those on the right would have been vulnerably exposed.

The cut was an even slice. The edges appeared precise and neat, rather than notched or torn. This told Funke that the mortal wound had been caused not by sawing, but by a blade that had been drawn across the neck in a single forceful stroke. With no bone to stop it, the knife had only to slice through soft tissue and muscle. The instant it passed through the carotid artery, a huge outpouring of blood, under pressure from the pumping heart, would have spurted forth. The blood would have sprayed anew with each heartbeat, the volume decreasing each time, as the blood pressure suddenly plummeted and the victim started to die.

This much Funke knew, simply from the nature of the injury. What the gaping wound did not tell her was about the weapon that caused it. A sharp instrument, yes. A cutting instrument with a fairly sharp edge. But what kind? There was no way to link a wound of this nature to any particular blade, the way some bullet wounds may be connected to a particular type of bullet, and a bullet in turn can be matched to a particular gun. A stab wound would be different. A stab wound told a lot about the weapon that caused it—how wide and long the blade might have been, what type of cutting edge it had. But this wasn't a stab wound. It was a neat slice, and the weapon that caused it could have been two inches long or eight inches long. It could have had a single edge or a double edge. There was no way to tell.

And that was not a good thing for detectives investigating the murder. Over the course of the investigation, knives would be found, both on suspects' property and near the canal museum where Devon's body was found. But there would be no way to match any of them to the cut that killed Devon Guzman, no way to use a knife to link that fatal cut across her throat to a particular killer. In other words, if and when a killer was found, there probably would be no definitive murder weapon to present to a jury in the case, and putting on a murder trial with no murder weapon would certainly amount to a hurdle for prosecutors to overcome.

When Funke had completed her external examination of Devon Guzman's scraped, battered and bruised body, she proceeded to the internal portion. Overall, she found that the organs and internal structures of the body were healthy. During this portion of the autopsy, she collected blood and urine samples that would be sent out to a toxicology lab to be tested for alcohol, drugs of abuse, such as heroin and cocaine, and a variety of other substances.

When those results came back, they would show that based on a sample of blood taken from a leg vessel, the victim had a blood alcohol level of .12 percent, which meant that she had been over the state limit for legal intoxication. No other findings of significance emerged from the toxicology testing. Despite the fact that a syringe had been found with Devon's body, her body bore no evidence of needle marks.

During the autopsy Funke also noted two areas of bleeding under the scalp, but determined that they were not the result of any skull fractures or injuries to the brain.

When the autopsy was completed, Funke spelled out her conclusions as to the cause and manner—the how and why—of Devon Guzman's death. The cause of death she determined to be asphyxia and sharp-force injury to the neck. The manner of death, homicide.

After completing the autopsy, Funke wrapped up her examinations by accompanying Detective Crouse over to the Easton police station to look at the clothing that had been removed from Devon's body and now was hanging up to dry.

What she noticed was that on the T-shirt and sweatshirt Devon had been wearing, there was heavy bloodstaining on the right-hand side. This fact proved significant, because Devon had been found lying on her *left* side in the back of her car. Blood on the right side meant that while she was dying, she had been lying on her right side, the blood from her neck wound flowing downward with gravity, soaking into the right side of her clothing. If she had been on her left side when she died, the blood would have pooled on the left side of her garments.

It seemed perfectly obvious now. Nothing more than common sense. But it was something the killer or killers hadn't considered. If they had, they would have put her on her right side in the car, which would have made the staged death scene a little more plausible. But as it had been arranged, it was impossible for Devon to have died that way. It defied the laws of physics.

This gave investigators some important clues about the perpetrator or perpetrators of this murder. It told them that once this vicious killing had been committed, whoever had murdered Devon had mustered enough self-preserving presence of mind to cool off and devise a way to cover up the tracks. It told them they were looking for someone calculating and intelligent, but perhaps not criminally sophisticated.

The reality of what had happened had not sunk in when Rick Guzman left the canal museum the day Devon's body was found. After an interview at police headquarters, "I just went home, sat on the couch," he said. "It didn't really hit me until the next day."

But a day later, when it did begin to hit, he needed to do something about it. Michelle and Brandon's house was among the last places Devon was seen, so that seemed like a good place to start asking questions. He went outside and got into his car, but the engine wouldn't start. He got out and saw why. His spark plug wires were scattered on the ground. Someone had pulled them out.

"My brother whipped the wires, the spark plug wires, off my car," Rick explained. It was one of those instances where a family member was looking out for him, looking to keep him from harm, to protect him from himself, if necessary.

But Rick was not one to be so easily deterred. Car or no car, he would find out what happened to his daughter. The police weren't telling him anything. And they still had her body, and might keep it as long as a week, so he couldn't even begin to make funeral arrangements.

Rick had injured his shoulder in March and undergone several surgeries since then. The injury had not yet healed. But injury be damned, he lugged out his bicycle, heaved himself upon the seat and began pedaling furiously toward South Side.

Family members had come to the house to try to keep him calm, but how could he be calm? He'd spoken to Keary Renner, the girlfriend of Devon's he was never particularly fond of, and she'd been very forthright with him. But he'd also spoken with Michelle, and her unusually reserved manner gave him reason for concern.

"Michelle called me the next day and was very matter-of-fact about it," Rick said, referring to the day after Devon's body was found. He found her to be "lacking emotion," which was very uncharacteristic of her. "She was always an excitable kind of personality, you know. She was very emotional. When she was happy, she was happy, so if she was sad, you'd know it." Talking to her after Devon's death, it was this emotion that he found lacking, "like she was being . . . strategic, I guess, if you will."

If Michelle's demeanor was unsettling, so was the fact that one of the last places Devon was seen was at Michelle's South Side home.

"The last place she was seen was at Michelle's, so I wanted to get over there," Rick recalled. He was determined enough to get the answers he sought, and if gritting his teeth while riding a bicycle with an injured arm was how he had to get them, so be it.

But despite his determination, he didn't get far.

A little incline on Freemansburg Avenue, a scant few blocks from his home, sent him tumbling off the bike into a woman's yard, unable to see through blinding tears.

"I crashed on Freemansburg Avenue," he recounted. "Cops found me. I was just laying there. I couldn't see 'cause of the tearing so bad. And I guess my family from my house called police, and then I guess the lady who owned the yard I crashed in [called police and said], 'Hey, there's a man in my front yard, crashed a bike. He's just laying there, I think he's hurt.'"

It would be years before he could see any humor in it.

8

Mary Hetzel woke up early the morning of Friday, June 16. She was leaving on a trip to Missouri the next day, and had things to do to prepare for the trip. On her list was an 8:00 A.M. nail appointment. But before that, she picked up the phone and dialed over to Michelle and Brandon's house, telling them she would be dropping by for a cup of coffee. It was about 7:00 A.M.

The drive from her corner house on West Nesque-honing to West St. Joseph Street took no more than a minute or two. She parked at the little house and went in through the front door. Michelle was in the kitchen, Brandon in the living room. He wasn't going in to work at Ashland that day, which was understandable, given the trauma of the day before. Mary said good morning, received her coffee and joined Brandon in the living room, while Michelle went off down the hall to shower.

The house looked normal that day, Mary would later recall. Nothing about the place seemed out of the ordinary. The one unusual thing she did notice, however, was a mark on Brandon's arm. A "nasty" mark. It looked sore, and the injury looked bad. She voiced her concern about it to her son-in-law.

"I burned it at work," he said, explaining away the ugly injury.

Mary Hetzel could boast of a close relationship with her son-in-law. They spoke often, with Brandon freely confiding in her about his marital problems and other issues. She might well have expected him to confide in her now, perhaps about how Michelle was coping with the shock of Devon's death only a day old.

Mary knew full well that her daughter had lost more than just a friend. She knew that Brandon's gripe of two nights ago, a common gripe of his that Michelle was running around with Devon, wasn't just about two nineteen-year-old girls out partying, celebrating their youth and independence.

It went much deeper than that.

She knew that Michelle was bisexual, and that despite being a newly wedded wife still in the honeymoon phase of her marriage, she was having a love affair with Devon Guzman. Devon, meanwhile, had a girlfriend of her own, Keary Renner, with whom she lived, and that relationship had become a bone of contention for Michelle.

It had been eating Michelle up, torturing her—Devon being with Keary, living with her. And all of that angst took its toll on her marriage to Brandon.

Mary would recall Brandon's having told her that he and Michelle would never be happy as long as Devon was around. He had no love for Devon. In fact, Mary would one day testify to having heard him say of Devon that he could "just kill her," because he was so furious with her for interfering in his marriage.

Still, none of what had come before in her daughter's young marriage or her relationship with her hardworking son-in-law—a college graduate, no less—could have prepared Mary for hearing what she alleged to have heard next.

Sitting alone in that West St. Joseph Street living room early that Friday morning after Devon Guzman's murder, while most of South Side was still sleeping or just getting up for work, Mary Hetzel would claim to have heard a most chilling and horrifying tale from the mouth of Brandon Bloss.

And yet, in spite of the gravity of the tale and the severity of its implications, it was a story that she would keep close to the vest for a long time to come. When she spoke to Brandon's mother, Pauline, by phone later that day, she would not breathe a word of what Brandon had allegedly told her. Nor would she speak of it to any of the detectives who would come to her home over the coming weeks in search of clues to help solve Devon Guzman's murder.

In truth, the fact that such a conversation ever took place between Brandon Bloss and Mary Hetzel would remain hidden from investigators for many months, only coming to light more than a year later, in October 2001, when the case went to court and on the seventh day of trial Mary Hetzel was called to the witness-box to testify under oath.

Also testifying under oath that same day in October would be Michelle Hetzel, who would recall a version of events transpiring that Friday morning after Devon's death that closely echoed her mother's.

Michelle said she went to bed the night of Thursday, June 15, with no idea of who could possibly have murdered her best friend, a girl she'd known since she was twelve and had been romantically involved with since age sixteen. The morning of Friday, June 16, she awoke to the sound of her husband screaming, she said. She got out of bed and went down the steps from the second floor, encountering a bizarre sight. Brandon was holding something to his arm and yelling in agony. It was a cigarette lighter. He was holding the lighter up to his arm, she claimed, searing his own flesh with the flame.

"What are you doing?" she demanded.

At first, Brandon didn't answer. Then, a few minutes later, he began ominously:

"I need to talk to you about something," he said.

The things she alleged he told her had to do with Devon, with Wednesday night, with what had happened while Michelle herself was dozing on the couch or on the telephone. It wouldn't be the last time he would speak of these things. He would bring them up several more times; only every time he did so, he would say something different, according to Michelle.

9

Detective Michael Gibiser had six years as a street officer and five as a detective with the Easton police—eleven years in total with the department, and hundreds of investigations to his credit. On Friday, June 16, at 10:00 A.M., he joined the growing number of officers involved with Easton's highest-profile investigation, the murder of Devon Guzman. He had been assigned to head over to the police garage on Bushkill Drive in Easton to process the victim's car.

The task entailed examining the vehicle inside and out, photographing it, searching and vacuuming it with special filters for evidence, tagging and bagging the evidence and compiling an inventory of anything he collected.

It wasn't a big car, but the task took a good two hours. Looking over the exterior, he noted some damage to the driver's door and mirror, and a dent in the right rear body panel. Gibiser got out his camera and started shooting. It was ten-thirty before he started logging pieces of evidence into his inventory.

By four minutes before noon, he'd collected a total of eighteen items, which included swatches of suspected blood from the driver's-side door rail, right rear passenger seat and seat belt, along with control samples for those blood swatches; a plastic bag with suspected blood from the left rear passenger floor; an extra-large green polo shirt from the left rear passenger floor; an empty jerky wrapper with suspected blood on it from the right rear seat; a CD case and paper with suspected blood from the rear seat; two packs of Marlboros from the rear seat; a 3M evidence vacuum filter; trace evidence from the lower driver's-side rail, picked up with an evidence vacuum filter; a photograph of assorted negatives found in the trunk; an envelope of photo negatives in the glove box; and a Radio Shack cell phone and charger in the glove box.

The green sweatshirt said SERVPRO SPECIAL CLEANING AND RESTORATION, an establishment in Easton that performed specialized cleaning services, particularly in cases of smoke or water damage. The photographs appeared to have been taken during a tropical vacation.

After the detective had filled out orange evidence tags for each of the items, logged them on the inventory and packed them up, he headed back downtown.

Back at headquarters, it was just before two o'clock when a strange phone call came in. The man on the line wanted to talk to someone about the Guzman murder. His call got routed to Detective Gibiser.

The man identified himself as George Vine, and he had a bizarre claim to make relating to Devon Guzman, which he wanted to pass along to police.

"I'm coming to see you," Gibiser told him. He wasn't about to handle this by phone.

Vine gave the detective his address. Shortly after, Gibiser rolled up to the place on Line Street in Easton, an address in the southwestern quadrant of South Side.

* * *

At two o'clock in the afternoon on Friday—almost exactly twenty-four hours from the time Devon's body was first found—the family of the nineteen-year-old convened at the canal museum for a somber vigil in her memory. The gesture had been organized by members of Devon's extended family as a measure of assurance that Devon would not be forgotten. Throughout the remainder of the day, a purple vase, white candle, cards and a photograph stood in the park above the falls, a makeshift memorial that caused anglers, cyclists and other curious passersby to stop and crouch to examine the assembled items and try to decipher the meaning and story behind them.

Some of them could not help wondering about the pretty young brunette in the picture that was propped against the vase. They studied this girl, leaning against a railing with a waterfall behind her, smiling. Some of them had to feel a tug, a slight empathetic ache of grief and loss in their hearts, when they read the messages that had been left, obviously by loved ones of the girl in the picture, and realized that she was gone now, that this world was going on without her. They had to know that not far from here were people who loved her, who built this memorial because they were reaching out for her, struggling to say something, anything.

Anything but good-bye.

When Detective Michael Gibiser left the Line Street residence of George Vine, the man who'd phoned police headquarters claiming to have information about the Guzman case, he did not leave empty-handed. Because once Vine had told his story, the detective immediately had him sit down and write out and sign a statement reiterating what he'd said, in print, for the record.

Vine, a thirty-seven-year-old conveyor systems assembler with a company just down the road from his home on Line Street, did as he was told. He scrawled a brief, choppy note that outlined what amounted to an unbelievable allegation. The allegation went back about two or three months, to a turbulent, troubled night when Devon, Keary and Michelle were all hanging out at Vine's house. Previously Vine had given Devon a key to his place, and the girls often met there to hang out and drink. Sometimes Vine was present, sometimes he was not. Often he was a witness to jealousy and fights among the girls. Sometimes the fights turned physical, which had been the case on the particular night of which Vine told Gibiser.

But it was something that happened after the fighting, in his kitchen that night, that burdened Vine's conscience now. He hadn't reported the incident to police at the time because he hadn't taken it seriously. But now he did. Now he certainly did, because Devon was dead, and now George Vine was seeing what had transpired that night in a stark new and ominous light.

He was tormented by the thought that if he had only mentioned it to Devon, she might still be alive. Whatever friendship or loyalty he might still feel toward the others involved would have to take a backseat to a larger concern: the pursuit of justice. A girl who'd been a friend for three years was dead. And not just dead, but murdered.

He thought back two days, to Wednesday night. Keary had woken him from a sound sleep around midnight with a phone call looking for Devon. Vine paid little heed to the call, thinking it was just the result of another fight going on between them. Then Michelle had rung his phone around 4:15 A.M., saying that Devon was missing and wondering if Vine had seen her. When he said he hadn't, Michelle had hung up quickly.

Now today, after finding out about Devon's death and

hearing things about whom she was last with before her death, he'd started piecing things together in his mind. And the conclusion that he came to was that the information he possessed belonged in the hands of the police. They would have to figure out what it meant and what to do with it.

Gibiser, for his part, had to know that if Vine's allegation proved true, the case had just taken a most sinister turn. It meant that they weren't looking at mere manslaughter, or even third-degree murder. It meant that they could be looking at a clear-cut case of murder in the first degree, and that was something that District Attorney John Morganelli would want to know about right away.

Vine's allegations, if true, also said something about the killer, something that investigators would certainly have to keep in mind as they went about trying to build up sufficient probable cause to make an arrest. They spoke of a daring, manipulative and very dangerous mind.

10

On Friday evening a baseball game was taking place at Easton's Hackett Park. Brian Otto Sr., Devon's uncle, and his son Brian Jr. had come to watch, when Tony Nauroth, a tenacious veteran reporter with the *Express-Times*, caught up with them. Father and son looked weary and emotionally drained.

Police had not yet publicly uttered a word regarding a suspect or suspects, but Otto, an outspoken forty-three-year-old, was helping with Devon's final arrangements and had taken on the role of Guzman family spokesman in the dark days after the murder. He confidently assured the reporter that he had strong feelings about whom police were looking for. He said he believed the culprit would be caught soon, and vowed that Devon's family wouldn't miss a day of her killer's trial, when that time came.

Otto spoke warmly of his niece. He noted that she left Easton Area High School after completing eleventh grade, opting not to return for her senior year because she wanted to "get out and explore the world" and "see what life was all about."

He explained that three months ago, Devon had left home to live with a friend at the Mineral Springs, not to break away from her family, but to pursue that holy grail of teenage life, independence. Despite her newfound freedom, Otto told the reporter, after Devon took up residence on the river, she kept in touch with her mother back on Ferry Street in Easton on a daily basis.

Otto described the extended Guzman family as a close-knit clan, with relatives from as far as Las Vegas and Puerto Rico now coming into town to be near the immediate family. In truth, it was about the only solace to be had in such a situation, being in the company of others who also loved that person who is now gone. Others who felt that same gaping void as the living world spun away in one direction and the dead retreated in another, leaving the grieving adrift in limbo with nothing but unanswerable questions running circles in their heads, and the weight of their loss crushing the breath out of them.

Whereas Devon's grandmothers made sure everyone kept eating, Otto supplied the emotional sustenance during this time, serving as a pillar of strength and a shoulder to cry on. He was someone to pick up the phone and handle the practical duties that had to be carried out. He spoke to the press, insulating those too fragile, angry or unresponsive for the task. He helped to pull Devon's mother and father through the awful, unavoidable reality of organizing Devon's funeral and making other final arrangements.

The one thing he hadn't done was to grieve himself. It would be almost a luxury at this point to allow himself that kind of emotional break while his sister was enduring such unimaginable suffering—Otto, himself the father of five, couldn't comprehend what she must be going through—and so putting off grieving became a matter of practicality. It was something that would have to wait, maybe until his brothers got to town, he told the reporter. In the meantime, he was concerning himself with insulating Devon's mother, Melody, from a world that had destabilized with the sudden and terrible loss of her only daughter, a girl Otto recalled as "peppy," that rare type of person whose very presence illuminated a room.

He remembered her as someone who was always on the go, concerned with the welfare of family and friends, and someone with plenty of encouraging words and hugs for troubled souls. He said she was close to her brother, three years her junior, and the two confided in each other often about their lives.

The crack of a baseball bat shattered the evening stillness, bringing the interview to an end. Otto excused himself and his son, trudging away up the hill to watch the pitcher hurl strikes from the mound.

That same night, Detective Gibiser, who in the morning had painstakingly searched and inventoried evidence from Devon's car and in the afternoon had taken a statement from George Vine, departed on a drive to the nearby city of Bethlehem, to the office of Magistrate Nancy Matos-Gonzales, with applications for two search warrants beside him in the car. The disturbing statement from Vine had helped provide grounds for the warrants.

The first warrant was for the South Side home of Michelle Hetzel and Brandon Bloss. The second was for Michelle's red Honda Accord, which had been taken from the canal museum crime scene on a rollback and was now sitting in a secure bay in the police garage on Bushkill Drive.

The magistrate signed off on the warrants just before 9:00 P.M. About an hour later, at nine-fifty, Gibiser and a crew of fellow officers arrived on West St. Joseph Street. Gibiser entered through the front door, using a key obtained from his supervisor, who had gotten it from

Michelle's father, who in turn had given it over voluntarily to police.

The little two-story home was quiet. No one was home when the investigators entered. The procedure guiding the search was that different officers were designated to search different areas of the house. Photos would be taken when officers both entered and left the residence. Any items collected as evidence would be logged on an inventory list.

Gibiser and the other investigators took their time over the next 2½ hours, methodically photographing, searching, and combing through the house as well as the property on which it sat. It was after midnight when they wrapped up. Seventeen items had been logged as evidence.

Item one on the list was a pair of women's Tommy Hilfiger jeans, size five, found at 11:00 P.M. in a first-floor washing machine in the rear of the house. The washer was half-full of soapy water. Gibiser had reached down into it and fished out the sopping denim. It was the only thing in there. He wrung the jeans out just enough to keep from leaving a puddle behind as he packed them away into an evidence bag.

Item two on the evidence list was a vacuum bag from a Hoover vacuum in the living room. Number three was three personal letters found torn up in a trash can. Number four was a water sample from the washing machine in which the jeans had been soaking.

Other items included water samples from the kitchen and bathroom sink drains, a dirt sample from the backyard, dog hair from the dog pen out back, hairs and trace evidence lifted off the living room couch, a swab and a hair sample from a first-floor tub drain, fireworks found in a second-floor storage room and dirt and grass samples from the yard on the east side of the house.

The remaining items that police confiscated were

knives, plenty of knives. They collected five from a kitchen drawer, four from a wood block, one from the kitchen sink and six from the drying rack next to the sink. When Brandon and Michelle returned home, they'd have trouble finding something to cut with.

What all of this evidence would amount to was anyone's guess at this point. Nothing on that evidence list was overtly incriminating. There was no indication anywhere in the house or yard that a life-and-death struggle had taken place there, or that a brutal and bloody murder had been committed.

So it would be up to the forensics people, the people with the tools to see what the human eye could not, to evaluate the evidence now. The jeans, water samples, hairs and trace evidence were sent to the state police crime lab for testing and analysis.

11

The front page of Saturday's *Express-Times* led with the headline: FAMILY WANTS ANSWERS, followed by the subheading of DEVON GUZMAN'S UNCLE PREDICTS AN ARREST SOON. The story was written by Tony Nauroth, the reporter who'd interviewed Otto and his son at the ball field the night before. Next to the story ran a photo of four individuals—three with crossed arms and bowed heads, one staring sidelong at the news photographer—standing at Devon's memorial, the one constructed at the canal museum at the confluence of the Delaware and Lehigh rivers.

The image contrasted sharply with the one just below it, a picturesque bird's-eye view of canoeists paddling down the Lehigh on a seventy-eight-canoe river sojourn. The story accompanying that photo waxed poetic about a leaf drifting with the current, speculating philosophically about how something so routine can take on such meaning and significance, about how the uniqueness of a simple thing in this world can be cause for wonder and celebration.

It was an appropriately uplifting story for Saturday-morning news readers to peruse with coffee, but in light of such sentiments, the death of Devon Guzman stood out all the more poignantly. Devon's photo appeared in the upper right of the page, and the nature of that photo further enhanced this impression. It was a partial profile, capturing her face from the right side. She wore a V-neck top and her hands were raised, sweeping her hair up off the back of her neck. Her eyes danced under dark brows, and her smile had a slightly devilish twist. It was a playful photo with an enigmatic side, the kind that made observers wonder what was going on when it was taken. What was the secret reason for her smile? Was she posing for an admirer? Primping with girlfriends? Teasing a family member?

Sometimes a photo captures a person in such a moment and such a way that it seems to capture her essence, and this was one of those shots. Whatever was going on at the time imbued the picture with something beyond just an image. It caused the camera lens to capture also the hint of a spirit, the spirit of this person's life, and so this striking photograph brought Devon Guzman to life that Saturday morning, if only in just the smallest way. It was a photo that would appear again and again in the months to come as the news story surrounding her murder progressed, and it might have been one of the reasons why Devon's death touched so many so deeply and personally. Because it was more than just youthful beauty that came through. More than that, it conveyed a glimpse of the joy with which she might have lived her life, this girl who lit up rooms, gave hugs freely, loved children and dreamed of getting out and experiencing the world on her own.

For family members, the fact that this dream had been cut short left an urgent need in its wake, the need to find out why. Why was Devon not permitted to live out her dreams? Who would do such a thing? Who could commit such an atrocious and final deed?

While Devon's uncle made no secret of the fact that he had some theories of his own, the police and other authorities were keeping confidential any information or suspicions they had. Coroner Zachary Lysek revealed to newspapers only that the initial results from Friday's autopsy established that Devon died of asphyxiation and a "sharp force entry" to the neck. He offered no information about what type of weapon might have been used. He also told reporters that he was awaiting toxicology tests, and wouldn't say whether any drugs were found or if the victim had been sexually assaulted.

Saturday was Keary Renner's twentieth birthday. The weekend before, she and Devon had celebrated Devon's nineteenth birthday by going away on a camping trip. All week, Keary had been expecting Devon to come up with a birthday surprise for her this weekend. But now this birthday was no cause for celebration. It had been the most devastating few days imaginable. Just two days ago, she'd lost her roommate, closest friend and lover. And now, amidst her sorrow, she was starting to get the awful feeling that certain people suspected her of murder.

The police investigators who'd searched her Mineral Springs apartment didn't think the murder took place there, but that didn't mean Keary was by any means free of suspicion. The fact was that she could be construed as having had both motive and opportunity to kill Devon Guzman.

As for motive, there was the jealousy factor that Michelle Hetzel had made so abundantly clear during her interview on Thursday with Detective Golazeski. Michelle had painted a picture in which Keary was a jealous and possessive lover, while Devon was confused, conflicted and liable to play the field. On top of that, the two were prone to physical brawls. Michelle had made it clear, without expressing it in so many words, that she thought it quite possible that an eruption of violence between Devon and Keary could have led to Devon's death. Lending weight to that scenario were letters and notes found in the Mineral Springs apartment detailing a history of romantic attachments and surreptitious breakups between the two. Certainly it wouldn't be the first time that the wild ups and downs of romantic jealousy had finally culminated in murder.

As for opportunity, Keary was the last person to have been seen with Devon alive by someone outside the circle of friends, this person being Joseph Welsh. No one disputed that Keary had left Michelle and Brandon's house alone with Devon, in Devon's car. That fact suggested that Keary could have had an opportunity to go somewhere with Devon, kill her, place her body in the back of the car and leave the car at the park.

In addition to motive and opportunity, there was some tangible evidence pointing to Keary's possible guilt. Although no direct evidence of murder was found in the Mineral Springs apartment, police did collect a handful of suspicious items, which they logged as evidence to be sent for testing.

One of these items was a floor mat from Devon's car. It was found in the shower stall at the apartment. Keary's explanation for why it was there seemed a little fishy. She claimed that the reason the mat found its way into the shower was that when she and Devon had gone camping the week before, some pickled-egg juice had spilled on it. When they returned from the trip, they put the mat in the shower to wash it off.

But why, police wanted to know, was it still there, almost a week later?

Because Devon liked to watch soapsuds foam up in the mat while she showered, Keary had told them.

It was a strange explanation.

A simpler one might be that some evidence of the killing had wound up on the mat, and so it had been brought inside to the apartment so that the evidence could be washed down the shower drain.

12

Sunday, June 18, was Father's Day. For Rick Guzman, it was the first one in nineteen years on which he wouldn't be able to look upon his daughter's face, hear her laughter or feel her strong, skinny arms around his neck. It was the first of many such days to come, in which he would be forced anew to contemplate his loss. It was a cruel irony, this day of all days coming with Devon's death still so fresh, a new source of pain for this father already undergoing the ultimate agony a parent can bear. In place of a sappy greeting card that morning, Rick Guzman had his daughter's obituary to read in the newspaper:

> *Devon N. Guzman, 19, of Easton, died Thursday, June 15. She was a cleaning technician for Servpro of Easton. Born June 9, 1981, in Phillipsburg, she was a daughter of Rick Guzman of Palmer Township and Melody Otto Guzman of Easton. She had attended Easton Area High School. . . .*

The obituary listed survivors who included two sets grandparents in Easton, a great-grandmother across the river in Phillipsburg and a great-grandmother in Puerto Rico. Funeral services were to be held at Ashton Funeral

Home, and Devon would be buried at Northampton Memorial Shrine, a tranquil hilltop cemetery.

It was, as necessitated by the nature of obituaries, such an unsentimental and inadequate summation of the life and contributions of a vibrant young woman. And yet who could express what her life was about, what she had meant to those she touched? Who could put into words, now that her life was over, what impact her too-brief existence here on earth had wrought? Certainly her father could not. Not now. Not yet. Maybe not ever.

So his sister, Candy, who lived in the nearby city of Allentown, gave voice to his feelings that day in a letter published in the *Express-Times*. "Rick Guzman has suffered a loss no parent wishes to contemplate," she wrote. "He, along with Devon's mother, have been consumed by overwhelming grief at the tragic loss of their daughter."

She observed how family members were trying to provide consolation at a time when there could be none. She wrote, "Rick Guzman adored his little girl and loved her unconditionally. How does a Daddy deal with his worst nightmare? At what point is it possible to begin the transition from shock to acceptance? How does a father accept that he won't ever again see the grace of his daughter's brilliant smile, the gift of her sweet embrace or the sincerity of her love?"

She also wrote of the inscrutable role of providence in human events. "Devon knew that her Dad would move heaven and earth to keep her from harm. But as we all know, God's will supersedes and transcends human logic. Instead of moving heaven he must learn, along with the rest of the family, to accompany her to heaven's gate, deliver her with pride to God's kingdom, and commend her spirit to a more peaceful and perfect existence."

* * *

Detective Gibiser spent his Father's Day morning at the police garage on Bushkill Drive, doing the same thing he'd done twice already in this case, first to Devon Guzman's car and then to Brandon and Michelle's house: conducting a methodical, painstaking and time-consuming search for evidence.

This time, the subject of his search was Michelle Hetzel's car, the red Accord that had been transported to the police garage from the crime scene the day Devon's body was found. On Friday night, Gibiser had obtained Magistrate Matos-Gonzales's signature on a warrant to search the car. Now he was ready to begin.

He followed the same base procedure as he had the other times, starting by examining and photographing the outside of the car. He noted some minor damage to the driver's-side bumper.

Moving on to the inside of the car, the detective collected a handful of items of interest. These included a brown paper bag, a 3M evidence vacuum filter from the front floor area, and from the rear seat, an envelope with a résumé and cover letter belonging to Michelle. Nothing particularly earth-shattering.

But when Gibiser opened the trunk of the car, the case suddenly took a whole new turn.

Inside, in the center of the trunk, sat a plastic bag. And inside that bag were everyday items that amounted to the first major evidentiary break in the case. It was amazing to think that the car had been sitting in the police garage since Thursday, three whole days now. And while investigators had been running around interviewing everyone connected with Devon, scouring the canal and riverbank by the old museum, combing through Devon's car, Keary's apartment and Michelle and Brandon's home, the most compelling evidence to be found was sitting right here, under their noses, in their very own garage.

When Gibiser lifted the bag from the trunk and opened it up, he had to know he was holding something big. He reached inside and, one by one, removed the following items: a large black sweatshirt, a pair of black Lee jeans, with a thirty-two–inch waist and thirty-two–inch inseam, a medium white T-shirt, a pair of red-white-and-blue boxer shorts, a pair of size-eleven white Nikes and a pair of white-and-gray socks.

Six items that in total comprised an entire outfit, down to the underwear, for a tall, skinny man with a build like that of Brandon Bloss. The clothes would have to be sent to the lab for testing, but even without forensic proof, it was clear that they bore stains that looked highly incriminating. The detective held up the black sweatshirt. The midchest area and another spot down by the waist were stained with what appeared to him to be dried blood.

And that wasn't all. Along with the clothes in the bag were four rubber gloves.

It had been a good day's work: four rubber gloves and a bunch of bloody clothes inside a bag in the trunk of a car that had been parked at the crime scene. It was about as close to a smoking gun as this case was likely to see.

Around midafternoon that Sunday, Father's Day, Joe Welsh glanced across West St. Joseph Street to see the young couple just across the street arriving home together. This time, thankfully, there was no ugly scene like there had been between them the other night, Wednesday night it would have been, when the young wife had thrown herself on the ground, hysterically demanding to know what her husband wanted of her.

Today their arrival home had been uneventful. Welsh noticed that Brandon spent several hours that Sunday afternoon out in the little yard situated behind and to the left of the house. Brandon's wife was not with him as he went about doing whatever it was he was doing back there.

Meanwhile, a mile or so away at the canal museum, a makeshift memorial for Devon grew steadily with each new mourner who stopped by. The assemblage stood silently over the river as the evening cooled. At nightfall, a white mist lifted off the river and ghostly strains of music from the "Rhythms of the River" concert drifted south from Riverside Park, just the other side of the Northampton Street Bridge.

13

At 11:00 A.M. on Wednesday, June 21, Devon Guzman was laid to rest during a wind-whipped burial at Northampton Memorial Shrine, a cemetery across from a school on Green Pond Road in the township of Palmer, where her father lived. Mourners came by the hundreds, and the wind tore at their clothing and snapped the fringes of the tent that covered the burial site as her silver casket, which had been borne by the young men of her family, was lowered into the earth. Police officers assigned to protect the family's privacy made sure that the newspaper photographers and reporters who turned out to cover the service kept their distance.

"The funeral was really something else," Devon's father recalled. "There was a lot of people there. *A lot.*" Michelle Hetzel and Keary Renner were not among them, having been informed that they were not welcome.

The funeral home had agreed to lead the procession of mourners down Northampton Street, Easton's main thoroughfare, around the Centre Square circle, and back up Northampton Street toward the shrine, where Devon was to be buried, but too many people turned out to do so. "There was so many people there, it would've caused gridlock through the whole city," Rick Guzman recalled. "By the time we got to the shrine, there was still people leaving the funeral home."

So many people attended the funeral, "it took an hour and a half to park them all," Rick said. Once everyone had walked up the slope where Devon was being laid to rest, final words were spoken. A giant photo collage created by Rick's sister, Candy, stood on a tripod next to the casket, a testament to the shining person Devon had been.

"She was such a bright star," her father recalled.

The profound sadness of the occasion extended its reach well beyond the gathering of family and friends around the grave. It weighed down neighbors around the cemetery, and struck at people just passing by. Anyone around who read a newspaper knew about this nineteen-year-old girl who had been mysteriously murdered, and many of them recognized that this somber send-off was for her. There was an undeniable sense that with her death, everyone had lost a little something.

Meanwhile, over at the canal museum, the memorial started by her family had grown steadily day by day. It now included letters and notes, flowers and candles, toys and trinkets, a strange collection of innocent little things, each thing signifying yet another aching heart.

Police, for their part, were now conducting a round-the-clock investigation to find Devon's killer. Although they were tight-lipped about their progress, DA John Morganelli emerged from a meeting with lead investigators the day Devon was buried to reveal that in the week since the killing, a total of fifty people had been interviewed.

"We're making progress," he assured reporters.

However, he disappointed media representatives, who were hungry for information about the case, by declining to reveal any details about the investigation or any possible suspects police might have had.

As a result, there arose a growing feeling of helpless-ness and vulnerability around Easton, an unsettling sus-picion that maybe authorities weren't discussing their leads because they had none. Furthermore, some people grumbled that if something like this could happen to an innocent girl like Devon, just mere minutes from the police station, well, then, it could happen to anyone. Maybe everyone had better start looking over his or her shoulder just a little bit more often, they groused.

The day Devon Guzman was buried, Brandon Bloss went to see a lawyer for advice regarding his status as an apparent suspect in the young woman's death. The police had searched his house and seemed to be keeping an eye on him, and he needed a professional opinion on what to do about it.

Brandon had a fresh injury on his arm, and the lawyer sent him to see an expert whose specialty included exam-ining such injuries. This expert took a look at the mark, then went on to trace, measure and photograph it for his files. Presumably, Brandon had undergone this visit for exculpatory purposes, hoping the examination would in some way help establish that he did not murder Devon Guzman.

14

It had been about two weeks since the murder when Brandon and Michelle went to visit Brandon's mother, Pauline, at her home in Hellertown, a short drive from Easton. His older sister, Natalie, was there.

Michelle recalled that at a certain point during the visit, she was asked to leave the room, so she went outside to the back porch and had a smoke. Soon after, she and Brandon, along with Pauline, left the house and went to the home of Pauline's ex-husband. From there, Pauline and her ex went to the bank and returned with money. The next thing Michelle knew, travel plans were being made, and soon after that, on July 1, she and Brandon were on a flight out of Philadelphia, en route to Cancun, Mexico.

The flight included a stopover in Houston, Texas. Michelle recalled that it was during the Houston stop that she had a disagreement with her husband.

"I don't want to go any further," she insisted. "I don't want to go to Mexico. I have no reason to go to Mexico. I want to go home."

But Brandon wanted to continue on, she said, and in the end, his will prevailed.

* * *

Meanwhile, back in Easton, as two of their prime suspects jetted off to sunny shores south of the border, homicide investigators were toiling furiously to build their case in the murder of Devon Guzman.

In addition to the high-tech forensic work being done behind the scenes at the state police crime lab, the investigation had come to rely heavily on nothing fancier than good old-fashioned detective work. Cops had gone door to door, doggedly interviewing scores of people who had known Devon and her friends. Grueling round-the-clock surveillances had been conducted on the West St. Joseph Street home of Brandon and Michelle. And Detective Golazeski, who'd taken over as lead investigator when Detective Crouse went on vacation, had voluntarily assumed the role of garbage picker.

On a hunch Golazeski had instituted weekly "trash pulls," meaning that in the dark of night after Brandon had lugged his trash to the curb for pickup, Easton's finest swooped in and snatched it up. Then Golazeski picked through the rubbish in search of anything that might point to a killer.

It was thanks to one of these trash pulls that Golazeski found out the couple had gone to Mexico. Some packaging for airline tickets through Continental Airlines turned up in the refuse. Also turning up in the trash were a parade of used bandages and ointments. Golazeski scrutinized each new bandage that appeared. He stared at the stains and the imprints left in the gauze as if they might tell him a story. As if they might speak for the dead young woman who could no longer speak for herself. And then, all of his poring over the bandages paid off. Suddenly, coming to him in a moment of inspiration, the bandages did speak. He was sure he knew what the imprints were saying. Only he would need someone to confirm it. He needed an expert. The person who came up was a specialist named Dennis Asen. Golazeski brought the bandages he'd accumulated from his trash pulls to the office of Dr. Asen, a dentist and forensic odontologist.

"Could these be bite marks?" he wanted to know.

Asen examined the oval pattern in the gauze and said they could be.

But more pieces of the puzzle were needed to complete the picture. One of those pieces was the human specimen who'd worn the bandages, so Detective Golazeski obtained a warrant to photograph Brandon Bloss, and specifically the wound on his arm. He served the warrant and snapped the photos himself. Afterward, when he returned to Asen's office with the photos in hand, the dentist had a curious reaction to them.

Asen told the detective that a young man had come to see him about a week before to have a wound on his arm examined. The dentist said he'd traced and photographed the wound. When Golazeski obtained the photos from that visit from Asen's files and held them next to the ones he'd taken himself, he saw that they were a perfect match.

Asen confirmed the detective's hunch that the wound on Brandon Bloss's arm was a human bite mark. Brandon had been bitten, and police had statements from witnesses that would put the occurrence of the injury at or around the time of the murder.

The question was, by whom had Brandon been bitten? Was it Devon? To find out, investigators would have to see if the marks on Brandon's arm and the imprints on the bandages he'd used matched up with Devon's teeth. The only way that could be done was to exhume Devon's body and compare her teeth to the bite pattern left behind in Brandon's arm. Upon returning from Asen's office, Golazeski got busy completing the paperwork necessary to authorize the exhumation. It was going to take some time to make all the needed arrangements.

15

Most people never meet a single murder suspect their entire lives, but the night of July 17, Cara Judd was about to meet two of them. One was her girlfriend's younger brother, Brandon, and the other was his wife, Michelle. Cara had heard a fair amount about this couple since she began dating Natalie in March, but had not met either of them until tonight.

Brandon and Michelle, back from a recent trip to Mexico, were coming by to celebrate Michelle's birthday. The gathering was taking place at the home of a friend of Natalie's mom's.

Of late, Cara had heard plenty about Brandon and Michelle. Natalie had told her that they were suspects in a murder committed in Easton in June. When Cara and Natalie got to the house, Brandon and Michelle were already there. It felt weird to meet them finally.

A few days later, she encountered the couple again at the Hellertown home shared by Natalie, her mother, a foster child, and now Cara as well. Cara and Natalie, both women in their midtwenties, had met at a bar in March. They'd hit it off right away, quickly becoming friends, and more. Cara had moved in with Natalie not long after they met, staying just about full-time at the Hellertown home.

At the home that night in Hellertown, the conversations grew more intimate than they had during the previous gathering. At about 10:00 P.M., Cara remembered, she went to the kitchen for a drink, and from there headed into the bathroom, where she unexpectedly ran into Michelle. She didn't look good.

"Are you OK?" Cara asked her.

Michelle shook her head. She said she was sad. Sad, and didn't feel good, because she was pregnant.

"Do you want to sit and talk?" Cara asked, taking pity on her, wanting to do something. "Do you need some water?"

Cara found herself alone with Michelle, back in the laundry room. She remembered that she was sitting on the drying machine and Michelle on the washer, when Michelle began talking about Devon, the girl who'd been murdered, and how she missed her.

Then the conversation set off down a dark road.

"Well, Michelle and I were sitting on the dryer and washing machine," Cara would later testify. "Then she started telling me about the night that girl Devon died. She was telling me how much she loved Devon and missed her. She told me everything."

Cara recalled that Michelle told her she and Devon had been out that night and were both drunk. They got into a fight before going their separate ways. When Michelle got home, she felt crummy and wasn't in the mood to talk to her husband. She wanted Devon to come over, and so a call was made to ask her to come.

When Devon showed up with Keary, Michelle told Cara she "couldn't handle it." She grew furious and yelled at Brandon not to let her in the house.

A while later, Devon returned to the house alone. She

and Michelle began arguing in the living room. The fight escalated into a battle of pushing and hair-pulling.

Brandon jumped between them to intervene. He grabbed Devon, holding her back to protect his pregnant wife, Michelle had said.

Devon struck back, clamping down hard with her teeth.

Brandon was hurt, and mad.

He wanted to know why the two women couldn't talk like human beings. He said he didn't want to deal with the situation or continue to watch them fight.

A suggestion was made to take the argument outside. On the way out, Michelle grabbed a wooden-handled knife from the kitchen. She told Cara that she knew Devon carried a black-handled knife.

When Michelle had finished telling the rest of her chilling story, Cara recalled that the young woman sitting on the washer became a little teary-eyed, but not the way she would have expected of someone in such a situation. Cara didn't know what to say.

Later, she would relate Michelle's story to Natalie and her mother.

A few nights later, on July 29, Cara Judd had a second intimate encounter with Michelle Hetzel, again at Natalie's house. It was about 10:00 P.M. when Michelle announced that she didn't feel good, and went upstairs to lie down.

A little while later, Cara walked past Natalie's mother's bedroom on her way to the bathroom and saw Michelle sitting on the bed, crying.

"Are you OK?" Cara asked. She felt some apprehension about getting involved. But she couldn't turn her back. She entered the bedroom and sat down to talk.

Michelle confided that it was Devon that was troubling her. She missed her so much. Loved her so much.

She opened her hand, displaying a gold-and-diamond ring. "This was from Devon," she told Cara. She toyed with the ring in her fingers.

"I loved her so much," she reflected. "I mean, I love Brandon, but it's not the same as I love Devon."

Cara said Michelle went on and on like that, alternating between past and present tense when referring to Devon, reiterating how much she loved and missed her. She said she wished she had married Devon.

After that, Michelle went on to say some strange things that Cara really couldn't follow. She did commit these things to memory, however, so that she could record them in her journal because the encounter was so bizarre and shocking.

"These people think they're so smart and just keep checking my house," she recalled Michelle saying. "Well, go ahead; what do I care?"

Cara also heard her say, "My jeans were soaking for so long that they'll never find any blood from them."

And then something about her garage, some sort of leak in her garage, and something about Brandon hosing it down.

The bizarre thing was, one minute Michelle was talking about hosing down a garage and the next she'd moved on to the subject of shopping. She complimented Cara's Tommy Hilfiger outfit, telling her that she wished Hilfiger made maternity clothes.

Cara Judd hung out with Michelle and Brandon a number of times after this. During one of her conversations with Michelle, Cara recalled Michelle assuring her regarding the murder investigation: "I'm gonna come out of this smelling like a bed of roses."

Another time, maybe a week or less since their first meeting, Michelle announced that she was pregnant with twins no less, and asked if Cara and Natalie would serve as godparents. Cara took the request to heart. She and Natalie made a shopping trip to Unclaimed Freight, a discount store for salvaged goods, and purchased a bookmark that read "no. 1 godmother."

16

DA John Morganelli credited Detective Golazeski with giving the investigation its major direction. "Barry Golazeski—who was the lead investigator, one of the guys who was big on the case—he started to formulate some theories early on in the case, and started to put the relationships together."

Once Brandon's bloody clothes were found in Michelle's car, it was clear he was on the right track. "And so Golazeski started to focus in on Hetzel and Bloss pretty early in the case. There was some discussion about the other girl there, Keary Renner, and she was certainly in the mix as well, as to whether they were involved, or one of them, or all of them. But the investigation started to focus on that three, and then Barry sort of kept me informed over the months," Morganelli said.

As the summer progressed, Easton detectives began to focus their investigative work tightly, directing their efforts to several main avenues of inquiry. One of these avenues involved taking the necessary steps to include or exclude Keary Renner as a suspect. This proved a frustrating task, since the evidence produced elusive answers and ambiguous conclusions.

The mat from Devon's car found in the shower at the Mineral Springs Hotel had been tested and the shower stall sprayed with the blood-detecting chemical luminol. Luminol is a simple chemical compound that emits a greenish blue glow when it comes in contact with blood, reacting to hemoglobin, an oxygen-carrying protein in red blood cells. Luminol is so sensitive, it can detect blood at one part per million. With the help of this chemical compound, evidence of blood was found in the Mineral Springs shower. However, the possibility that the blood was the result of menstrual bleeding could not be discounted, so the blood testing was of no help.

Seeking some definitive resolution regarding Keary's innocence or guilt, police decided to ask her to take a lie detector test. Keary submitted to the polygraph, but the results were inconclusive. Some might interpret that to imply a hint of guilt; however, in truth, the inconclusive results were just that. No conclusions could be drawn from them—one way or the other—so the polygraph was of no help, either.

However, as the weeks passed and the evidence mounted, Keary Renner, who had started off as the strongest suspect, began to look less and less like a suspect at all.

Sure, it was true that there had been a history of violent fights between Keary and Devon, and that by some accounts she was the last person seen with Devon alive. And there were Michelle's not-so-subtle nudgings to police that Keary could be guilty. There was the knife incident that sent Devon to the hospital, and the tavern patron who'd seen a blanket covering up a lump on the couch after Keary and Devon's big fight the night of her death.

However, the problem was that Keary lacked one practical item needed to commit the crime. She lacked a car, and this was crucial because in any scenario that could be envisioned, it would have been impossible for Keary to have disposed of Devon's body at the canal museum and then walked the 7½ miles home to the Mineral Springs in time to receive Michelle's call looking for Devon. The time frame was too tight for Keary to have committed the crime without a car or a ride.

No witness had reported giving anyone of Keary's description a ride that night, and police made sure she didn't have a car of her own. They knew that the car she'd once driven had belonged to her father, and that he'd taken it away from her. Just to be certain Keary didn't have a car hidden somewhere, Detective Golazeski ran her information through the motor vehicles database, and turned up no vehicles registered to her name.

Investigators had entertained the possibility that she'd somehow acted together with Michelle and Brandon to commit the murder (it hadn't escaped attention that the night they picked up Brandon for an interview, Keary was at the couple's home), but no evidence of that had surfaced, either. In fact, as evidence went, although police were having trouble putting together what it all meant, virtually all of it—including the syringe full of mysterious liquid found on Devon's body and a Motorola pager that had been tampered with and shoved into her waistband—pointed in only one direction: the house on West St. Joseph Street.

By August 1, Easton homicide investigators had collected most of the physical evidence they were going to find in the Devon Guzman murder case. Blood, hair, fiber and other trace evidence collected from the victim's body and her Sunfire, from Michelle Hetzel's Accord, from the South Side home shared by Michelle and Brandon, had been forwarded to the state police crime lab. The next steps in the investigation were to tie those pieces of evidence to a particular suspect or suspects.

To that end, Detective Golazeski obtained warrants for hair and blood samples from Michelle Hetzel and Brandon Bloss. On August 1 at 1:30 P.M., Detectives Gibiser, Crouse and Storm teamed up to serve those warrants.

The three lawmen met Hetzel and Bloss at a walk-in medical facility called RediCare, located in a shopping center in Palmer Township, just up the highway from downtown Easton.

Both suspects were taken to exam rooms. Gibiser accompanied Michelle, observing while a nurse and a physician's assistant trainee went about taking exactly the samples called for in the warrant. These were two tubes of blood, which were capped off with purple tops, along with hairs plucked from five locations on her head—front, top, back, left side and right side—five hairs from each location.

In Bloss's exam room, a physician's assistant and a doctor collected a similar set of samples. Two full tubes of blood and one partial tube, again capped with purple tops. Five hairs plucked from each of the same five locations as they had been from Michelle, plus about twenty-five chest hairs.

When they were done, the purple-capped tubes of blood and the collections of hairs were passed over to Detective Gibiser, who brought them back to the police station. For the time being, he stowed the tubes of blood in a refrigerator and the hairs in an evidence cabinet. Soon they'd be on their way to the Pennsylvania State Police Lab. If they came back a match to the evidence found at the crime scene, an arrest or arrests wouldn't be long in coming.

* * *

That same day, while police were plucking hairs and extracting blood from Brandon and Michelle, a renowned forensic odontologist by the name of Richard Scanlon was diligently at work in the morgue at Easton Hospital, taking dental impressions from Devon Guzman. Based on Dr. Asen's and Detective Golazeski's efforts in identifying the wound on Brandon's arm as a human bite mark, a judge had signed an exhumation order, and Devon's body had been removed from its burial place at Northampton Memorial Shrine specifically for this purpose. Scanlon had traveled three hours east from his home in Lewiston, Pennsylvania, to conduct the inquiry. It was the first time he'd ever done such work on an exhumed body. Police investigators had good reason to await his findings anxiously. No small stakes were riding on them. The results could be damning, or they could render weeks of careful detective work to obtain what looked like a key piece of evidence entirely irrelevant.

17

Inside the state police crime lab located in Bethlehem, Pennsylvania, serologist Carol Ritter was about to put her biochemistry background to work. She pried open a vacuum filter submitted by the police department over in Easton from a police evidence vacuum. The filter contained whatever the vacuum had picked up from the driver's side of Devon Guzman's Pontiac Sunfire. Inside the opened filter, she looked through the contents for any hair or fibers lurking among the dirt and dust particles. She began her search with the naked eye, then put her magnification light over the entire contents of the filter. She found an assortment of hairs, which she mounted on slides and examined under a microscope. Four of the hairs proved to be human hairs, and several others animal hairs. In this homicide case, the Easton police had submitted what was called a hair standard—sample hairs plucked from known people—to which she was to compare any hair found in the filter. The hair standards had come from four people: the victim Devon Guzman, her roommate, Keary Renner, her friend Michelle Hetzel and Michelle's husband, Brandon Bloss. Ritter's analysis of the hairs police picked up in the filter against the hair standards submitted by police determined that three of the hairs were consistent with Devon's and one most closely matched Brandon's.

Ritter conducted the same procedure on a filter from the passenger side of the Sunfire. It contained six human hairs and an assortment of animal hairs. Four of them most closely matched Devon's, and the other two matched Brandon's.

Ritter continued on in this fashion, examining the clothing Devon wore, the men's clothing found in the trunk of Michelle's Honda Accord and the vacuum filters taken from the Accord.

Following standard laboratory procedure, she had another analyst review her analysis and her supervisor confirm her conclusions. When she was done, she tagged the analyzed items with the time, date and her signature, and sealed the evidence with PENNSYLVANIA STATE POLICE evidence tape.

Ritter also unpacked a green coat with the word SERVPRO on it. Before examining it for signs of biological fluids such as blood or semen, she collected all of the trace evidence— hairs and fibers—that could be found on the garment. Comparing the hair she found to the hair standards supplied by police, she determined that four hairs most closely matched Devon's and one matched Michelle's. She also found fifteen dog and cat hairs. She used no specific test to identify them as such, but her trained eye could tell what they were by looking at the root.

After collecting all of the trace evidence from the green jacket, Ritter began her search for biological fluids by simply looking for red stains. If it had been a darker item of clothing, on which a red stain might be easy to miss, she would've sprayed it with luminol, turned out the lights and looked for spots that glowed in the dark. But on this green jacket, the stains stood out. She found one on the right cuff and labeled it with the letter *A*. Then she moistened a sterilized cotton swab, swabbed the stain and then dabbed the swab with drops of a clear reagent. The swab turned a pinkish purple/magenta color, which meant the stain was possibly blood. The test was called a presumptive test; a positive result meant that further testing was warranted.

A confirmatory test came next. This would confirm that the stain was definitely blood, and that the presumptive test hadn't been wrong, which could happen. Certain vegetables, or even just oxidation from the air, could turn the swab magenta, producing what is known as a false positive. A confirmatory test was needed to rule this possibility out. It was exacting, step-by-step work, dictated by the rules of laboratory procedure. Ritter continued on through the items supplied to her by the Easton police, analyzing each one in a similar fashion and documenting all of her findings.

When she got to a pair of women's jeans, she went through the pockets, finding a small item in the back left pocket. It was a small plastic cap with a white substance in the bottom. She packed it up for forwarding to Easton police.

In addition to performing her own analyses, Ritter turned over the blood samples taken from "the knowns," meaning the victim and known suspects, to colleague Kenneth Mayberry for a DNA profile analysis. She also forwarded swatches cut from the clothing the police had sent in, along with certain hairs collected from the various garments they'd collected as evidence.

In the clinical confines of the crime lab, Mayberry performed the DNA analyses, reviewed the information the computer spit out, made a chart of the results and handed it to his secretary to type up. What use would be made of these results would be up to the Easton police and the Northampton County DA.

18

District Attorney John Morganelli was elected Northampton County's highest-ranking law enforcement official in 1991 with about 60 percent of the vote in the primary and general elections, defeating a three-term incumbent for the position. In mid-August 2000, he was on his way to becoming the longest-serving DA in Northampton County history. Since his election, he'd won two subsequent four-year terms, running unopposed both times because no candidate was strong enough to challenge him. During his years in office, he'd built a reputation for fairness, impeccable courtroom preparation and political drive. He approached his position as DA with a well-formed professional philosophy.

"I believe that it's my job to protect the public from violent criminals," he said. "I believe strongly in punishment. And I think that people who commit violent crimes should be locked up and warehoused for long periods of time. I also feel that the district attorney's office can be a very strong bully pulpit for influencing criminal legislation that helps protect the public. I've been a pretty outspoken DA on a lot of different issues."

Morganelli was also a family man, married and raising

three teenage children. Outside of work and home life, his interests included golfing, running and politics. If things had gone differently in the spring, he would have been preparing to run in the fall for attorney general, the highest law enforcement office in the state. However, he'd been edged out in the spring Democratic primary by Jim Eisenhower, a former federal prosecutor and distant relative of Dwight D. Eisenhower. Now Morganelli was watching from the sidelines as Eisenhower prepared to challenge Tom Corbett for the state of Pennsylvania's top law office. It was going to be a noteworthy race. Eisenhower was a strong candidate, and his famed surname alone lent interest to his candidacy. However, Morganelli knew that in the end, it was unlikely Eisenhower, or any Democratic candidate, would prevail. The state attorney general's office had been an exclusively Republican stronghold for two decades.

But even without an election campaign to run, Morganelli had his hands full with the business of criminal justice in Northampton. In addition to the day-to-day cases handled by his office, the murder caseload was mounting. The slaying of Devon Guzman was one of three murders in three weeks in Northampton County that summer, and in addition, Morganelli was preparing to prosecute Douglas Crist for the December 22, 1999, murder of his girlfriend's mother, Debra LaForm. That case was on the docket for October 2000.

But on Sunday, August 13, 2000, Morganelli had a more immediate matter for which to prepare. Blood and DNA test results had come in from the state police lab. Tomorrow morning at ten o'clock sharp, he'd be hosting a press conference regarding a couple of arrests that, to many in Northampton county, felt like they'd been an awful long time coming.

* * *

Rick Guzman had stayed overnight at his sister's house in Allentown the night of Saturday, August 12. He and Holly had gone there to watch movies that evening and wound up spending the night. An unexpected early-morning phone call woke him up. It was someone with the Easton police.

"We're gonna go in and bust these two bastards," he remembered being told.

He was in Allentown, a good fifteen miles from Easton.

"Can you wait?" he asked, wanting to be as close as possible when the long-awaited arrests went down.

They couldn't. "They set up their ducks, and before they busted them, they called me," Rick said. But they didn't want to delay any more than they had to.

Until that phone call, Rick said, police had divulged nothing to the family about their investigation. It had been hard to bear having two months going by without hearing any official word about who might've killed his daughter. In hindsight, Rick said the police investigators were very astute in how they handled the investigation. While Devon's family members were emotionally involved and unable to think clearly, the police remained detached and uninvolved from the emotional aspects, and focused on doing what they had to do to solve the case, even if it meant remaining maddeningly tight-lipped.

Rick remembered asking periodically during the investigation, "Can you at least tell me where you're at?" Each time he was rebuffed with the excuse that they couldn't discuss an ongoing investigation. "So they keep you in the dark," he said. Looking back, he saw it was the professional way to handle it.

The knock came at 7:30 A.M. on Sunday, August 13, at the West St. Joseph Street home in South Side, Easton. It was almost two months to the day since Devon Guzman had been murdered—two long, arduous months for police investigators operating under both public pressure and deep personal commitments to bring about justice for Devon. It had taken that long to gather and analyze enough forensic evidence and to interview enough witnesses, neighbors and friends to go forward with the arrests. They had been long months of painful, patient waiting for Devon's family. They had been two grueling emotional months for Brandon and Michelle as well. During that time Brandon had consulted with an attorney to discuss divorcing his wife. And Michelle was involved in legal issues of her own stemming from a charge of drunken driving.

When the door opened, police were standing on the concrete walk with warrants for the couple's arrest. Brandon was cuffed at the doorstep. Michelle was taken into custody on the second floor. Husband and wife were whisked away in the cool of the early morning, to be later arraigned by District Justice Matos-Gonzales on charges of criminal homicide and criminal conspiracy to commit homicide.

In the days to come, they would be spending their time in the overcrowded quarters of the fortresslike Northampton County Prison, where they would be held without bail. They'd have plenty of time in the months to come to contemplate how and why their lives and the lives of those they touched had taken this tragic turn.

19

In January 2000, Brandon Paul Bloss was a young man of whom great things might be expected. He had arrived in the Northeast after spending some of his younger years in Florida, and now he was among family. His mother, Pauline, and older sister, Natalie, lived in the area, as did his father, Charles, and his stepmother, Martha.

Brandon had attended the University of Pittsburgh from 1992 to 1993, completing a year and a half of studies in chemical engineering before deciding to continue his education closer to home, at Allentown College of St. Francis de Sales in Center Valley, Pennsylvania. In 1996, he graduated Allentown College with bachelor of science degrees in chemistry and math. The average student would have found the course load he undertook extremely challenging, but Brandon demonstrated a clear aptitude in these demanding technical areas. He excelled in courses that included analytical chemistry, biochemistry, advanced calculus, probability and statistics, and linear algebra. He also belonged to the American Chemical Society, the Sigma Alpha Chi chemistry fraternity and the college math club. Brandon attended school on an academic scholarship, and graduated with 4.0 averages in both chemistry and math.

While in college he also worked at Steel City Chromium Plating Co. in Hellertown as an assistant manager. Despite his young age, he supervised a crew of five workers assigned to projects with six-figure budgets. Proving himself a self-starter unafraid to take initiative, he took steps to advance his knowledge, independently completed five-figure-budget projects and implemented compliance with regulations from federal and state environmental protection agencies.

Upon emerging from college, Brandon described himself on his résumé as a "determined, self-motivated graduate" seeking a laboratory technician job as an analytical chemist. He was the kind of candidate virtually any employer in need of his skills would have been eager to hire. Ashland Chemical Co. in Glendon, a small borough a few miles up from Easton's South Side, certainly was lucky to acquire him for its workforce. Brandon often worked an early shift, completing his workday at 3:00 P.M. With time to spare in the afternoons and evenings, he took a second job, bartending at the Rice-Ebner American Legion Post in South Side, where his father-in-law served on the board and where Brandon was liked by the Legionnaires who socialized there.

In the year before the murder, Brandon began trying to rebuild a relationship with his father after a seventeen-year separation. His stepmother told the *Morning Call* that the year she and her husband had spent getting to know Brandon had been pleasant and that he had treated her and his father with decency. She said that she enjoyed being with him and that his father was glad to have Brandon in his life.

By all accounts, Brandon had a promising life and career ahead of him. He was educated, ambitious, well-mannered and intelligent. He had a strong work ethic, a likeable personality and the ability to earn his own way in the world, on his own or with a special someone.

Although Brandon was old enough to frequent any of the Lehigh Valley's popular dance clubs or party hangouts—Players, Diamondz or the Tally-Ho—it wasn't a connection he made in a club that led to the most life-altering romantic involvement of his life. Instead, it was someone he met closer to home. It was a blue-eyed girl by the name of Michelle Hetzel. Through a temporary foster-care placement, the reason for which has never been made public, she was living with Brandon's mother and sister in Hellertown, about twelve miles from Easton.

Thin and ladylike, with pretty blond hair and big eyes, she was the youngest child in her family by about ten years. She was truly the baby of the family—the only daughter Elbert and Mary Hetzel had conceived together, and Elbert's sole biological child. Timid as a child, she was known to be eager to please, though a little on the spoiled side and used to getting what she wanted. "Michelle had everything," her father told *Express-Times* reporter Rudy Miller. "We bought her cars, clothes. Money was no object."

Michelle had gone through a troublesome rebellious stage, and by age eighteen, she was ready to experience life on her own, away from the restrictions of parents and guardians. Practically speaking, it would be a challenge for her to make her own way. She'd dropped out of high school after eleventh grade, and life on one's own was expensive, even with plenty of education. However, meeting Brandon Bloss, an educated and financially independent young man, opened up new possibilities.

Brandon was twenty-five and Michelle eighteen—not old enough to drink alcohol legally, but old enough to marry. Before long, plans were being made and wedding dates were discussed. The couple found a little two-story residence in South Side, Easton, and began setting up house together. A wedding date of February 26, 2000, was chosen.

Perhaps it could have been the start of a fairy-tale life for this promising fair-haired couple, who would look so picture-perfect as they smiled for their wedding photos. But not everything was as it seemed. Some people suspected Michelle was marrying to please her parents. And linked to that suspicion was another issue, an issue some of those closest to Michelle hoped the marriage to Brandon would put to rest. It was the issue of bisexuality.

20

Young people today are recognizing their sexual orientation earlier than they have in the past, according to the American Academy of Pediatrics (AAP), and teens finding themselves to be something other than heterosexual face a hard road. They are often worse off physically, emotionally and socially than their heterosexual peers, mostly because of the social stigma and isolation that often go along with a nonhetero identity.

These hardships remain very real, despite the fact that society's understanding and acceptance of nonheterosexuality has evolved radically over the past thirty to forty years, to a more accepting stance. Until 1973, the American Psychiatric Association classified homosexuality as a mental disorder, but that year, the organization reclassified it as a sexual "orientation" or "expression."

The term "expression" might seem to imply the element of choice, but the current thinking is just the opposite: that one's sexual orientation is not a choice. Instead, it is believed that sexual orientation is determined by no single factor, but rather by a combination of them: namely, genes, hormones and environment. It is also thought that sexual orientation is usually established during early childhood. No evidence suggests that abnormal parenting, sexual abuse or other life hardships cause a deviation from heterosexuality.

Early studies in the field, from the 1930s and 1940s, reported that 37 percent of adult men and 13 percent of adult women had at least one consummated sexual experience with a same-sex partner, and that 4 percent of men and 2 percent of women were exclusively homosexual. More recent studies indicate that 3 to 10 percent of adults are gay or lesbian, and that the percentage that is bisexual may be even larger. One survey of sixteen- to nineteen-year-olds found that 6 percent of the girls and 17 percent of the boys had at least one sexual experience with a member of the same sex.

"Profound isolation and fear of discovery" can permeate the lives of adolescents struggling with an emerging nonheterosexual identity, according to the AAP, and this can interfere with their ability to develop healthy self-esteem, a strong identity and intimacy skills. Nonhetero youths are often the victims of harassment and violence, with 20 percent of lesbians in one survey reporting that they had been verbally and physically assaulted in secondary school because of their sexual orientation.

Nonhetero teens are more likely to drop out of school, get kicked out of their homes and face life on their own at an early age. They're more apt to smoke cigarettes, drink alcohol and use drugs at a younger age as well. And they're more likely to have sexual intercourse, to have more partners and to be forced into sex against their will. Lesbian teens also face high risk for sexually transmitted diseases because they are likely to have had intercourse with males. And high schoolers who identify themselves as gay, lesbian or bisexual, or engage in sex with same-sex partners, or admit to same-sex attractions, are more likely to be victimized in some way, to become substance abusers and to attempt suicide.

According to the Triangle Project, a group that promotes understanding of sexual diversity, gay teens face an array of challenges that heterosexuals don't. Attempting to develop a healthy bisexual identity is a "draining, secretive, anxiety producing and lonely task" for most, says the group.

The development of a nonhetero identity generally occurs in recognizable stages, outlined by researchers in the 1970s and 1980s. These stages chart a progression from confusion to exploration to integration. The best-known model names six stages: confusion, comparison, tolerance, acceptance, pride and synthesis.

In the confusion stage, an adolescent experiencing same-sex fantasies or attractions begins questioning her assumed heterosexual identity as feelings of intimacy and physical attraction toward members of the same sex arise. The question she may be asking herself is: *could I be gay?* Denial may be the main coping strategy.

In the comparison stage, she slowly begins to accept the possibility of homosexuality, sometimes saying to herself, *I might be gay,* and other times rationalizing away the possibility as just a phase, or by telling herself that the person she is attracted to *just happens to be a girl.* The idea of bisexuality may enter her mind at this stage, allowing her to indulge both heterosexual and homosexual attractions, fantasies and possibilities. Social alienation becomes a factor as she begins to see herself as different, someone who does not belong.

In the next stage, the toleration stage, she admits to herself that she is probably gay. This ends some of the internal wrestling, easing some confusion and turmoil, but widens the gulf between herself and others in the process. For girls with a big need for approval and acceptance, this can be a very tough time, resulting in keen ability to "mask," or pass as heterosexual.

This could explain why some bisexuals marry young, wanting to please their parents and others by appearing to have become a "normal" heterosexual adult. The price of successfully masking, however, can mean keeping a separation between "public" and "private" self, as well as sacrificing genuine relationships with family and friends who can't know the whole truth about her.

"Contacting other gay, lesbian, and/or bisexual people becomes a more pressing issue to alleviate a sense of isolation and alienation and to provide the individual with the experience of being accepted for their whole being and not just for their mask," states the Triangle Project.

The remaining stages involve making peace with homosexual feelings, integrating these feelings into one's self and identity, taking pride in this identity and finding one's place in society as a nonheterosexual. But in order to make it to the emotional wholeness of the healthy later stages, one must first safely navigate the perils and pitfalls of the earlier phases, which can be fraught with confusion, denial, self-doubt and deception.

21

With her wedding approaching, Michelle Hetzel had many exciting new days ahead to look forward to, but already a problematic aspect of her past was threatening her chances of future happiness with Brandon. That part was her relationship with Devon Guzman, whom she'd first met back in grade school.

Devon Neireda Guzman was born just across the Delaware River from Easton, Pennsylvania, in the town of Phillipsburg, New Jersey, on June 9, 1981. She was the first child of Ricardo Guzman and Melody Otto, who'd conceived her not long after high school. Her middle name was bestowed in honor of her paternal grandmother.

Rick was born in Brooklyn, New York, one of four children, two brothers and a sister. The Guzman family left Brooklyn and began moving westward in 1969, when Rick was eight years old, settling first near Clinton, New Jersey, a picturesque town centered around a historic woolen mill, which stood as a symbol of early-American industry and claimed to be the most photographed spot in the

Garden State. In 1972, the family moved west again, this time to Easton.

"I grew up basically right here in Easton," Rick said. He attended Easton High School, and just after that, he met Melody Otto, a petite and bubbly redhead who was the sister of Rick's sister's boyfriend. "That's how we met, back in '79," he said. "Devon was born in '81."

Rick Guzman is a straight-talking truck driver who speaks his mind with a flair that's impossible to forget. "As you can see, I'm not your average individual," he said during an interview. "I have quite the personality. Point is, Devon was like that. So she was really vibrant."

Even as a young girl, she displayed the free spirit and vivacious personality that would make her a popular teenager and a much-remembered personality among family and friends. The sparkling character is something that runs in the family. "My parents are that way, all my brothers and sister," Rick said. "We're just kind of personalities that you just don't forget."

Some of the outgoingness was in the upbringing, Rick believed. "Some people, they grow up being timid. Depends the way you bring them up. Suppress them, they'll be shy. Encourage them, they'll shine." Devon was encouraged, and she certainly shone, growing into a good-humored, active and athletic girl. She was nimble on her feet, loved to be on the go and participated in karate and other activities.

Three years after Devon was born, in 1984, Melody gave birth to a son, Derick, and she and Rick married the same year. Marriage and family life held its ups and downs for the young couple, and twelve years after the birth of their first child, in 1993, Rick and Melody divorced. Immediately afterward, the children lived with their mother, while Rick moved into a rented town house in Forks

Township, remaining nearby to continue doing his share
to raise the children.

Two years later, in 1995, Rick was ready for a change
of scene. He had some savings put away and a bonus
coming to him from his trucking job. One of his brothers, who lived in Phoenix, Arizona, offered to take him
in until he got settled in the West. Knowing he'd have no
problem finding a job driving a truck in a big city like
Phoenix, he made the move, happy to be able to take the
children with him.

"I thought, what a great idea—a fresh start, somewhere totally new," Rick said. Devon was fourteen years
old, a difficult age socially to be uprooted from friends
and family and moved across the country. And it wasn't
easy for Rick, either, a single father raising two children
during the challenging preteen and early teen years. But
he relished the idea of supervising his children and pro-
viding stability and structure through these vital years of
their lives. Having family close by eased the transition.

The difficulty of long-distance custody arrangements
strained family relations at times during those years, but
overall the children thrived in Phoenix. The move was
imbued with the wide-open freedom of a clean start and
a feeling of adventure. "We went out there with no furniture," Rick recalled. "We took a tube ride down the Salt
River and we kept the tubes at the end of the ride. We kept
them for furniture. It was fun, you know. She was fourteen,
he was eleven. They were doing great."

Looking back, it was a happy, fun-filled time. "The
kids were excelling in their academics, their attendance,
their attitude," Rick said.

Rick, Devon and Derick spent two years in Phoenix
before family matters brought them back East, in 1997.
Now sixteen years old, Devon entered Easton Area High

School, where a familiar face was there to welcome her: Michelle Hetzel.

Devon and Michelle had first become friends when they were schoolgirls. "They were little," Rick recalled. "They were still in grade school. Michelle had a newspaper route when they met. They were still pretty young yet."

The friendship had lapsed during the years Devon was in Arizona, and the girls had no contact with each other during that time, but it quickly resumed when Devon returned.

"So we came back and they started hanging out again, and you know, they were young ladies now. They were sixteenish, seventeenish," Rick said. Referring to Michelle, he said, "I never did see anything crazy coming from this girl."

Rekindling their friendship in the halls of Easton Area High School, Devon and Michelle were drawn together right away. The connection was so natural, it was as if Devon had never left. However, adolescence had introduced a new and troubling factor into their relationship that had not existed in their more idyllic girlhood friendship.

This factor evidenced itself through competition over Michelle's close friend, a towering blonde by the name of Keary Dehaven, who had moved into South Side around sixth grade. By high school Keary had developed statuesque proportions and a striking glamour that occasioned one observer to describe her as "model material." Michelle, on the other hand, possessed a more understated beauty, and was described as proper or even "prissy." Keary was Michelle's close friend, but once Devon entered the picture, a three-way tug-of-war dynamic ensued. The girls were close and devoted, but the competition drove a sharp wedge in the friendships.

Part of the reason for this wedge may have been simple

adolescent jealousy, favoritism games or jockeying for best-friend status, but another part was romantic competition. Michelle may have been less forthcoming about the fact that her developing sexual identity was at odds with that of the majority of her boy-crazy peers in the hallways of school, but Devon was more open. She understood herself to be bisexual, and she shared this fact about herself with her close family.

Rick preferred Michelle over Keary, who was less polished than Michelle and occasionally "manhandled" his daughter. He admitted that not everyone shared his fondness for Michelle and that "women's intuition" told at least one person close to Devon that Michelle was trouble. But Rick didn't see it.

"I actually liked her. You know, she always came by and she was a finer breed. Nicer clothes, nice car, nice family," he said. "But she had the wool over my eyes. I never would've thought. Never."

Dealing with an alternative sexual identity could not have made the year or so they spent in high school together an easy experience for Michelle, Devon or Keary—all three of them dropped out without graduating.

In the year that followed, free of school schedules, classes and homework, the girls entered into commitments that seemed designed to set a new course for their future relationships. Michelle found Brandon, and their relationship moved quickly to the engagement stage. Keary also met a man and married him, changing her name from Dehaven to Renner, but they quickly separated while he went off to basic training for the army. In his absence Devon and Keary took their relationship to a new level. Keary moved into Devon's mother's house on Ferry Street in Easton. Then, in October 1999, Devon and Keary set a wedding date of their own. It was to be June 11 of the coming year, and it marked the anniversary of their relationship together, the day they began telling people that they really were a couple.

On the surface the fierce three-way jealousies involving Michelle, Devon and Keary appeared to be dissolving as the girls moved through their eighteenth year. They embarked upon paths that promised eventually to disentangle them from the close-knit triangle they'd formed in high school and propel them into adult lives and relationships of their own, apart from the jealousy-plagued threesome they had become.

But the fact was that under the surface, the tension that had always existed still existed. Only now, with Michelle engaged to Brandon, and Devon committed to Keary, it had been forced underground. The love triangle had not gone away, but rather it had become a secret, and the feelings engendered gathered force in the confines of secrecy. If before, these feelings had been merely destructive to healthy friendships, now they were growing dangerous.

22

The first evidence of the intense and irrational love/hate relationship growing ever fiercer between Michelle Hetzel and Devon Guzman made its way into the public record at the end of January 2000. About a month before Michelle's wedding, Michelle marched into the office of District Justice Sandra Zemgulis and filed a private criminal complaint of harassment against the girl she often described as her closest friend, her only friend.

Though Devon had pledged to marry Keary, she had not given up on Michelle and took bold steps to keep from losing her. Michelle's father told *Express-Times* reporter Rudy Miller that before the wedding day, Devon called him.

"I love your daughter," she declared.

"Good," he replied, and hung up.

He said his thought was "Michelle is getting married. This is over."

Michelle claimed that as her wedding day approached, Devon drove past her house and phoned repeatedly to cajole and threaten, to profess her affection, to try and reclaim Michelle for herself. When it became too much, she filed the harassment complaint.

In backward-slanting print, she wrote: "Defendant drives by my house numerous times and stops right in front and beeps horn." Michelle continued, writing that Devon harassed her parents and told Michelle's mother Michelle was gay. "I have my own home and she calls there and harasses me," the complaint continued. "Sometimes she calls to say she loves me and she wants to marry me, then she wants to see me." Such behavior was common whenever Devon broke up with her live-in girlfriend, Michelle wrote.

"She thinks it's a game, she claims she can't be alone. She threatened to show up at my wedding. I've had my number changed twice and she always gets it. She calls my work and yells at me and continuously calls." The last incident occurred on January 23, 2000, Michelle wrote.

As usual, however, the dispute was intense but short-lived. On February 11, Michelle called the office of District Justice Zemgulis and withdrew the harassment complaint, saying she and Devon had reconciled. She drove to Devon's father's house and told Devon she'd dropped the complaint. Later, she would say that Brandon had put her up to filing the charges.

If the fact that Michelle was not over Devon had escaped the notice of her fiancé, it did not go unnoticed by those close to him. Although Brandon had asked his sister and brother to take part in his wedding as members of the wedding party, according to a family friend, both of them withdrew as the fateful day approached. It was clear that Michelle was locked in some inscrutable entanglement with Devon, and that she was sneaking around with her despite the impending marriage. Brandon's siblings may have felt that she should choose—Brandon or Devon— before she went ahead with the marriage. If Michelle couldn't make up her mind, Brandon shouldn't marry her. Brandon's brother was even said to have offered him money to call off the wedding, but Brandon refused the offer.

The wedding went ahead as planned on February 26, 2000, and nineteen-year-old Michelle Hetzel and twenty-five-year-old Brandon Bloss became husband and wife. After the ceremony, and a reception at the local Ramada Inn, the couple retired to an upstairs suite, room 252, for their nuptial night together.

Devon Guzman, for her part, had watched the wedding from afar. Seeing Michelle in her wedding dress must've twisted her heartstrings. "I remember Devon telling me about how she snuck over to wherever they were getting married," Rick Guzman remarked wistfully. "It was outside somewhere, but she got to see it from a distance, and she was remarking how beautiful she looked. You know, she liked her."

After the wedding Michelle and Brandon began married life together in their quaint, two-story house on West St. Joseph Street in South Side, Easton. The street was a quiet, narrow one-way, running east to west, almost to the edge of South Side, with the Delaware River just beyond its westerly end. The convenience of a small neighborhood shopping center was just up the street. The house had a good-sized lot behind it, with plenty of room for their dog, Sadie, and other pets. An aboveground pool also sat in the backyard, the rear of which was bordered by a garage structure that ran the width of the lot. Michelle's father provided her with a sizable savings account to help her get started in her new life.

Serious trouble began in April. Hardly more than a month had passed since the wedding when Michelle reached out to her high-school friend Keary, telling her that Brandon was kicking her out. Though many things had happened over the months to strain her friendship with Michelle, Keary was not one to turn her back on a friend in need. Michelle needed a place to stay. Keary agreed to share an apartment with her at the Mineral Springs Hotel, where rents were comparatively cheap.

The Mineral Springs wasn't the oldest inn ever to have served the Easton area—LeFevre Tavern and the Bachmann Publick House both went back to the 1750s and later became popular stops for Revolutionary War soldiers reporting to George Washington—but the Mineral Springs was certainly one of the oldest lodgings around. It went back a full 175 years, to 1825, and in its heyday, it enjoyed a booming trade with travelers journeying up and down the thoroughfares that followed the Delaware River.

The Mineral Springs sits at the place where North Delaware Drive, the river road out of Easton, meets Fruchey Hill Road, a steep, winding country farm road with a green patchwork of sloping fields to either side occupied by occasional clusterings of dilapidated farm buildings and a handful of still-active farms. Here can be found what remains of real Pennsylvania farm country in the easternmost reaches of the state. These pastoral oases are isolated anachronisms among myriad new residential developments—a few fields, the rusting hulls of farm tractors, the smell of manure spread as fertilizer in the spring and the dusty Ford pickups bouncing over the back roads laden with hay bales and the like.

At the time Keary and Michelle went to the Mineral Springs for a room, alliances had shifted. Neither was on talking terms with Devon, and Keary and Michelle had found some common issues over which to commiserate. Both were out on their own. Keary's fledgling marriage had foundered just as quickly as had Michelle's. Her husband was off in basic training, while Keary remained behind in Pennsylvania to sort through her feelings and face an uncertain future.

It was a confusing time in her life, and she was undecided about who it was that she loved and whom she wanted to be with. On one hand, she'd found a man who'd swept her off her feet. On the other, there was Devon. Keary and Devon had matching key chains and love charms. For Valentine's Day she'd given Devon a ruby ring with diamonds. They'd had a license plate made that said "Keary and Devon." It had been around Thanksgiving, 1999 that Keary and Devon had moved into Devon's mother's house. But though they were supposed to be a couple, Michelle was always in the picture somewhere. So Keary and Devon had struck a deal stipulating that if Devon would stop seeing Michelle, Keary would leave her husband. But somehow that had not completely come to pass.

And now here was Michelle, caught, just like Keary, between Devon and the man she had married. It was a dubious alliance, but nonetheless it made sense in the context of things. The girls secured the keys to a second-story apartment at the Mineral Springs, and Michelle began moving clothes and other things in right away.

But just as quickly as the arrangement took shape, it disbanded without warning. Three or four days after moving in, Keary came home to find Michelle's stuff gone. It might not have been a big surprise, given the circumstances.

Despite the marital problems, there were some incentives for Michelle to make up with Brandon and return home rather than face life on her own. There were benefits that came with a hardworking husband who was liked by your parents. There was the nice, two-story home on St. Joseph Street, with all the amenities of a home of one's own and the ample yard behind it for pets. There was another person to see that the bills got paid. Michelle had gotten a job of her own, doing clerical work in an oncologist's office, but the fact was that after getting married, she worked little—only maybe three weeks in the first four months of her marriage. She needed money to do the things she liked to do—drive her new car, get French manicures during the day, go out partying at night.

Once Michelle and Keary's short-lived rooming arrangements fell apart, Keary found herself on her own at the new Mineral Springs apartment, creating an opening for Devon to reenter the picture.

An even keel seemed to have been reached as spring turned to summer. Devon was working at Servpro, the cleaning and restoration business in Easton. Keary worked at Warren Hospital, over on the Jersey side of the Delaware, as a patient transporter and also in security. The two lived at the Mineral Springs and shared the new Pontiac Sunfire that Devon had purchased. Michelle and Brandon were living in South Side, with Brandon working at Ashland Chemical in the morning and bartending at the American Legion Post in the evening.

But under the surface, problems brewed. Michelle was not content in her marriage and she wanted Devon in her life. Because she could not call Devon directly without incurring Keary's anger, she often showed up at Devon's father's house and urged him to call Devon for her. Sometimes Devon would come, but sometimes Michelle waited there for hours, and Devon never showed up. Occasionally Michelle would come up with a surprise designed to woo Devon away from Keary. Once, she took Devon to spend the night in room 252 of the Ramada Inn, the honeymoon suite where she'd spent her wedding night.

Keary, whose marital situation remained unresolved, was torn between pursuing a life with Devon and a desire to win back her husband. She began writing him a letter, to which she would continue adding for weeks to come:

> *Please don't rip this up. I'm not one to admit that I was wrong, so please read what I have to say. I'm so very sorry for everything that has happened. . . .*

Pino's Pizzeria is a neighborhood pizza joint by virtue of its location, if for no other reason. It is virtually impossible to end up there by accident, situated as it is on Line Street at the far south end of South Side, in a shopping center with far more parking than it will ever need, next to the somber shade and tranquil quiet of St. Mary Magdalene Cemetery.

Inside, the pizzeria itself is just wide enough for a row of booths down each side of the interior. On an average day, ceiling fans dissipate the pizza oven heat, which rolls out in waves over the dining booths. The faint hint of cigarette smoke wafts out from somewhere in the back, behind the kitchen. A man in white pants and a red shirt spins a disk of dough on his fist, while another worker takes no pains to hide his suspicion of the rare stranger who enters. Pino's has its own personality, but, all in all, it is just like so many other pizza joints, a bare-boned but beloved staple of the American landscape. Chance reunions between old acquaintances or classmates take place all day long on a typical spring or summer afternoon. Three hungry-looking construction workers lean in the doorway, waiting for slices to eat on the short walk back to their truck. A pair of teen girls en route from school dine in gloomy silence, pocketbooks plopped on the table next to their paper plates and Styrofoam soda cups.

Pino's was one of the places Devon Guzman frequented after returning to Easton from Arizona, and it was where she struck up a friendship with an employee named George Vine, whom she soon introduced to Michelle and Keary. Vine was a bachelor in his midthirties with his own pad. Though some would question his motives for befriending the three young women, people who knew him described him as a Peter Pan type, someone who liked the company of the girls because he himself wanted to stay young, to keep living like a teenager forever. His middle name was Arthur, and the girls knew him as "Art." During the course of their friendship, Art Vine gave Devon a key to his place, which became a kind of haven for the girls, a private hangout with empty beer cans and dishes in the sink, where they could go to let loose and be themselves, free of obligations or supervision. Free of worry about gay prejudices. Often they would drink while they were there; sometimes Vine hung out and drank with them, and sometimes they used his place while he was not there. Since Devon had a key, they could come and go as they wished. Vine liked their company, and the girls enjoyed the use of his place. He took them to New York for fake IDs, and they transported him places when he needed a ride. It was a happy arrangement.

By the spring of 2000, Art Vine had known Devon about three years. She came into the pizza place just about every other day, and he considered her a friend. He knew she was bisexual, and he'd witnessed the up-and-down relationships she had with Michelle and Keary, whom he'd gotten to know both at the pizza place and when they visited his house. Vine had also met Brandon Bloss when he'd come around on a couple occasions looking for Michelle.

It wasn't unheard of for fights to break out among the girls during the parties at Vine's place, and one night Vine decided to intervene in a disagreement. He got an unexpected surprise. He grabbed Devon to restrain her, but she wasn't so easily subdued, even by a grown man. With Vine's arms wrapped around her, she kicked off the nearest wall. Vine stumbled backward, tripped over a box and fell on his rear end. It was a lesson in how much toughness can come in a small package, a lesson he would not soon forget.

Sometime after that, another fight broke out at Vine's house. This one was between Devon and Keary. Vine had come home that night from work and had his usual beer or two. Devon, Michelle and Keary were there. Devon and Keary got into an argument, which turned into a fistfight, with the two exchanging blows back and forth. But even after all that fighting, when Keary left, Devon went with her. Michelle stood by and watched them go, though it got under her skin to see Keary win Devon away again, after treating her so roughly.

Their departure broke up the party, leaving just Michelle and Art. It was while they were alone together in his kitchen that night, after Keary and Devon's violent fight, that Vine said Michelle made an unlikely proposal.

Would he help her get rid of Devon?

She'd make it worth his while.

Vine considered Michelle a friend, and he viewed her as a nice person. Here she was, in his estimation, offering what—sex, money—in exchange for his help? She couldn't mean it, he decided, and he didn't take the offer seriously. Vine brushed off the request.

He didn't tell Devon about Michelle's proposal or report it to the police, either. Instead, he decided just to let it go. It was a decision that would haunt him. He would forever wonder: if he had spoken up, could he have saved a life?

23

With the approach of Devon's nineteenth birthday, June 9, 2000, Rick Guzman recalled that his daughter's life was headed the right way. For a time after quitting high school, she'd worked odd jobs, but now she was employed full-time with Servpro. She would be eligible for her own health insurance as of July 1.

"So you know she got the new car, brand-new, she was getting these gas credit cards, feeling a real part of the adult world, and she was going to have insurance. She was real excited about that," Rick said. "She was just going in positive directions."

Unlike many teens her age, she wasn't just "hanging and living." She was beginning to achieve things in the adult world, she had plans for the future and she knew that she'd want to move on from her cleaning job, which had some severe drawbacks. "She was on a job, she was telling me," Rick remembered. "Somebody blew their brains out. The guy had AIDS, so they had to go in there with the white suits and be real careful."

It wasn't the kind of job Rick wanted for his daughter's long-term future, so he encouraged her to get her general equivalency diploma (GED) as a step toward moving up in the world. "And I was dabbling in the realms of hypocrisy because I had quit school," he admitted. "So at that particular time, I was going through a course myself to get my GED. And with life's lessons, I guess, it was real easy." When he finished with the GED study books, he was going to pass them on to Devon so she could study up for her GED as well.

As Devon's birthday approached, so did Devon and Keary's June anniversary date, the date that many months ago they had decided on as the day they would get married, if conditions were right. Keary and Devon were also talking about moving away to sunny Arizona and having a baby. Michelle remained in the picture also, and with Devon and Keary's plans to move away, the competitive stakes were getting higher.

"And that was pretty much her life, those two friends," Rick said. "Now she's spending more time with this full-time job, which I thought was a positive thing for her. But by then, it was too late. The Grim Reaper had been called."

The first hints of summer were in the air as Memorial Day weekend approached. It was the last weekend in May, a big weekend for anyone devoted to river life. It was the time that people living along the banks of the Delaware got their boats, Jet Skis, water skis and life vests out of winter storage, wiped out the cobwebs, oiled and gassed up the engines and took them out on the river for the first outing of the season.

Up and down the Delaware, above and below Easton, it was a weekend of serious work and play, setting up docks, hosting barbecues and getting out to play on the water. Parking was at a premium along many of the skinny river roads dotted with what once were no more than fishing cottages and that had since been remodeled for year-round living. Fireworks popped, bonfires blazed, boats cut slapping wakes down the center of the Delaware and the telltale smells of marine fuel and barbecue smoke wafted back and forth across the river. It was the official beginning of summer.

And what better time for a vacation? Michelle had a surprise for Devon. Two plane tickets to an intimate getaway for two, departing from New Jersey's Newark Airport.

From Easton, Pennsylvania, the U.S. Virgin Islands—a popular Caribbean tourist destination comprising the islands of St. Thomas, St. Croix and St. John—are accessible in about four hours' flying time. San Juan, Puerto Rico, is the hub for most major intercontinental airlines flying to the region, serving as a main interconnecting point for travelers to and from the Caribbean. A number of major airlines fly jets into San Juan Airport, but within the Caribbean, small island-hoppers and turboprops are used to fly travelers to and from the various islands. Coming into San Juan Airport, the big jets arrive on the ocean end of the terminal, depositing their passengers directly onto the upper terminal level. From there, buses take passengers headed for the other islands to the fleet of island-hoppers and turboprops waiting on the tarmac.

San Juan Airport is typically a lively, swirling clash of international tourists on vacation and island natives traveling on more mundane business. At times, the mix can make for notoriously high levels of confusion and frustration. Tropical storms blowing through can create logistics problems for the turboprobs, which, flying at only ten thousand feet, must zigzag around the weather, rather than skip over it like the jets. The result can be delays, during which the tourists get anxious to get to their destinations and begin relaxing, while the natives get annoyed at having to battle armies of baggage-laden tourists just to get from one island to another. The frustration evidences itself in a stew of various people, cultures and attitudes making themselves known through a din of languages, including English, Dutch, Spanish, French and a host of island dialects. However, this frustration quickly dissipates once travelers are aboard their flights and on their way. It's hard to sustain a bad mood for long, amid such tranquil beauty and laid-back island ways.

From San Juan, flights destined for St. Croix arrive at the Henry E. Rohlsen International Airport, the only airstrip on the island. St. Croix is the largest of the Virgin Islands; at eighty-two square miles, it is bigger than St. Thomas and St. John together. Less touristy than the other two islands, it is sometimes called "the sleeping Virgin" for its undiscovered charms.

This onetime Danish West Indies capital has more of an old-world than new-world feel, thanks to its architecture, history and people. It is said that travelers choose St. John for its natural parks and St. Thomas for its vibrant nightlife and shopping, but that they come to St. Croix for something else, something less tangible. Perhaps it is the exotic sense of romance, or the way in which time and cares slip away amid the caressing trade winds, the hypnotic pace of life, the European charm and the landscape of beaches, rain forests, scrub growth and lush greenery.

When Michelle Hetzel and Devon Guzman arrived on St. Croix for Memorial Day weekend, the powerful spell of the island's charms must have done much to make the troubles and hardships of daily life in Easton, Pennsylvania, seem a distant memory.

Indeed, St. Croix was worlds away from the life they knew. Happy vacationers filled the streets. The sun shone brightly, tropical breezes ruffled their hair and the endless hues of the flora radiated all around. Yellow ginger thomas adorned hillsides and thickets, hardy hibiscus grew wildly along the roadsides and plumbago sprouted from planters around homes and businesses.

The activities available to the two eighteen-year-olds were practically endless—much more than could be squeezed into a few short days. They could scuba dive or snorkel in the island's sparkling waters. Walk the beaches, eat at a boardwalk bistro or a balcony café. Unwind under the straw roof of a beach bar or sip cocktails in style at Rum Runners on the Christiansted waterfront. They could take a table for two at one of the many restaurants where musicians played calypso, jazz or the steel pans. At night they could deck themselves out and go dancing to the sounds of reggae, rock and jazz that permeate Christiansted's Company Street around Club 54 or one of the town's other swinging nightclubs.

The island's two main towns are Frederiksted and Christiansted, and the two girls whiled away a portion of their getaway conducting a special shopping trip in Christiansted, where a myriad of boutiques display everything from fine china and crystal to French perfume, batik clothing and jewelry. Inside Zally Jewelers on King Street, Michelle purchased three gold-and-diamond rings, costing $1,044.60. Later, together on a beach, the tropical breezes in their hair, Michelle and Devon exchanged vows.

Afterward, while celebrating their happiness in the carefree ambience of a tropical bar, Devon and Michelle called Devon's father and excitedly spilled their news. They'd gotten married! They wanted to know if they could live with him when they returned home. Rick Guzman was happy for them, because Devon seemed so happy. Michelle's grand gesture—thousands of dollars on this trip, secreting Devon away, the expensive rings— had won out at last. Her wild extravagance had wooed

Devon away from everyday life with Keary, and now Devon was pledging herself to a future with Michelle.

Still, Devon must have been at least a little torn, because in the midst of all the excitement of the trip, she had not entirely forgotten the partner she'd left behind. Instead, she phoned Keary from the islands to save her the worry of wondering where she'd disappeared to.

When Devon called Keary to tell her that she and Michelle had run off to the Caribbean together, it was stinging news. Keary and Devon were just weeks away from their agreed-on marriage date of June 11, but there was Devon away with Michelle, who was herself mere months into her own marriage and still well within what is usually the happy honeymoon phase.

After learning what had happened, Keary picked up the phone and called Brandon Bloss. It was an uncharacteristic thing for her to do. She did not really know him much at all, but this development was something that had to be shared. When Brandon answered the phone, she told him that Michelle and Devon had run off to the Virgin Islands together. At first, he didn't believe her. She'd told him she was going to San Francisco, and not with Devon. What Keary told him took time to sink in. When it did, he informed her he was going to file for divorce. "Devon can have her," Keary remembered him saying.

That weekend Brandon went to a Hetzel family Memorial Day barbecue. It was a gathering for Michelle's family, but he went anyway, even without his wife. He confided to his father-in-law that he'd learned Michelle had secretly disappeared on a tropical vacation with Devon. Michelle's father commiserated. He advised Brandon to kick Michelle out—maybe then she'd realize what she had to lose. And he told Brandon that if he wanted a divorce, he'd support him, even helping to pay if he had to.

Brandon had put up with plenty in the course of his short marriage to Michelle, but this was a new level of betrayal. Come the start of the workweek, he visited the law office of attorney Joseph Corpora and spoke to him about retaining his services to divorce his wife.

Wrongs had been done that could not be forgiven. The back-and-forth triangle that had started with Devon, Michelle and Keary—and now had come to ensnare Brandon Bloss—could not go on like this forever. Many could have predicted that when Michelle and Devon returned from the tropics, things would be different. No one would have predicted that in two weeks, Devon would be dead.

24

Michelle and Devon's Caribbean trip worked like accelerant on a fast-moving fire, inflaming jealousies back in Easton to new heights, catalyzing new depths of despair and inciting ever more extreme acts of desperation.

Michelle, having run up some $7,000 in credit card debt to pay for the trip, returned home to a husband who'd been pushed too far. She'd left without warning, lying about where she was going and with whom. By one account, she'd called him the day she was leaving and said she was going to San Francisco with the oncologist she worked for, regarding a lump in her breast, and then hung up on him. But Brandon had learned the truth from Keary, and now he wanted a divorce. He'd already seen a lawyer.

Michelle may have cared little, at first. Her plan was to be with Devon now. Soon the two of them could get back on a plane and return to the islands, where things had been so perfect. They'd find a way to live down there. It was just a matter of Devon making the break from Keary.

Upon returning from St. Croix, Devon told Keary she was breaking up with her. This touched off a disagreement, and when Keary grabbed a knife and threatened to harm herself with it, Devon intervened, suffering a cut in the process. Bleeding from the hand, she sought emergency care for the wound. When word got around that Devon had gotten cut during an argument with Keary, those who already feared for her in Keary's hands began to fear even more. However, Keary's extreme reaction to the breakup, or something else she said or did, had some persuasive effect on Devon. Although she and Michelle had obtained Devon's father's blessing to come live with him, the first days of June went by without her moving out of the Mineral Springs.

In fact, Devon's birthday weekend was approaching and she made plans to spend it with Keary and her family, going away on a camping trip. The following weekend was the weekend of Keary's birthday, and after having spent Devon's birthday together, Keary was expecting to receive a birthday surprise of her own from Devon. In addition to the birthday celebrations, the date Devon and Keary had agreed upon months before as a possible marriage date was upon them. The plans they had made to move to Arizona, get married and have a baby were still viable. In fact, Devon had just gotten approved for a credit card with a $10,000 spending limit, which was something that would help them make their plans a reality. Although Keary had seen the pictures of Devon and Michelle in St. Croix and knew they'd had a great time there together, she said that Devon had changed her mind about wanting to be with Michelle.

This wasn't news Michelle was likely to take well. After everything she'd staked personally and financially on the trip, it wouldn't be surprising if she saw Devon as rightfully hers. Devon confided to Keary that Michelle had indicated jokingly that she'd reached the end of her rope with the competition, declaring, "If I can't have you, Keary can't, either." But though Michelle may have made up her mind about which person she wanted to be with,

Devon was still caught between her two companions. She spent her birthday with Keary, but she still drove around with an envelope of vacation photos of herself and Michelle in her glove compartment.

In the meantime, Michelle and Brandon continued to coexist under one roof, despite the fledgling marriage crumbling around them. The same old fights raged on, with Michelle wanting to go off on her own, Brandon wanting her to stay home. One of these fights, which spilled over to the outdoors and was witnessed by neighbor Joseph Welsh, indicated the escalating frustrations in the newlyweds' household.

It was June 10, the day after Devon's nineteenth birthday and the day before Devon and Keary's June 11 anniversary. Devon was away camping with Keary for the weekend. It was early afternoon, and Welsh, tapping away on the computer in the front room of his house, heard Brandon's raised voice from across the street.

"You're nothing but a fucking bitch!" he heard the young man holler.

Looking out, he saw Michelle on her way to her car and Brandon calling after her, "Aren't you going to fold your laundry before you leave?"

Michelle cursed back at him and got into her car, which was parked in the lot next to the house. Brandon ran back inside, appearing in a side window with a pile of laundry. He told Michelle she had ten seconds to get back in the house, and began counting down from ten, ticking off the numbers, one by one. Michelle sat in her car and waited. When her husband reached zero, he tossed the clothes out the window. Michelle shifted into reverse and took off, leaving the clothes strewn in the lot.

About a half hour later, Michelle returned, disappearing inside the house. Shortly after, Welsh saw Brandon come out of the house, collect the laundry and bring it back inside.

It was a telling incident for two reasons. One, the profanity-laced standoff showed publicly the escalating tensions in the Bloss/Hetzel marriage. Two, the fact that Brandon took the conciliatory step of going out and retrieving the laundry showed an elasticity in the relationship, an ability to bounce between rage and reconciliation in a short space of time.

Could this have been the day Michelle chose to tell her husband she was pregnant? It was sometime after the Caribbean trip, but the exact time had never been determined.

Also around this time, Michelle's copies of the island photos of herself and Devon got torn in half and discarded on a shelf in the garage behind the West St. Joseph Street house.

Monday, June 12, ushered in the workweek and a return to the daily grind. Devon and Keary were back from their camping trip, and although their June 11 anniversary had come and gone without their having gotten married or run off to Arizona, the plan was not dead yet. Keary's birthday was coming, on Saturday, June 17, and she was expecting a surprise from Devon at the end of the week.

Wednesday, June 14, began as any other. Devon left for work at Servpro as usual that morning and returned to the Mineral Springs that evening around four-thirty or five. She and Keary sat together on the couch watching TV for twenty minutes or a half hour before Devon said she was going to her father's house for a belated birthday celebration. Keary, aware that Rick Guzman's house sometimes served as a clandestine meeting place, asked if Michelle was going to be there. Devon said no.

Had that only been true, things might have turned out differently.

25

A reporter from the *Morning Call* phoned Devon's mother's house the Sunday that Brandon and Michelle were arrested for murder, but Melody Guzman had no comment for the press. The two-month anniversary of Devon's death was at hand, and she still kept a memorial to her daughter displayed in her Ferry Street home. The tribute had been started at the canal museum and was later moved to her home. Now it contained a myriad of photographs, notes, stuffed toys, flowers and trinkets.

A reporter also called Brandon's father's home, but neither his father nor his stepmother cared to comment on his arrest. The arrests had been a long time in coming, but now that they had arrived, few people, even those who had been vocal before, seemed to know what to say or how they felt. It was good to see that the wheels of justice were turning, however slow their pace. It was comforting to know that if indeed these people were Devon's killers, at least now they were off the street. And for those who'd wondered if this young woman had been the random victim of a psychopathic killer who might still be lurking somewhere in Easton, the arrests permitted a slight sigh of relief.

However, for most of those close to the principals in the

case, there was little comfort to be found. Devon was still gone, and the pain of loss was fresh. If comfort was in short supply, understanding and insight about how this murder could have happened was even scarcer. Friends and acquaintances of both Brandon and Michelle were struck with utter disbelief at the notion that the people they thought they knew so well could actually be cold-blooded killers. Even Devon's father had always thought of Michelle as "the nice one" among his daughter's friends. And the impression among some who knew Brandon was that he was just too mild-mannered to have committed this vicious murder. And at least one of the couple's neighbors knew them as mostly quiet, civil, keep-to-themselves kind of people, certainly not the type anyone would suspect of murder.

Although no one spoke out publicly, there were whisperings among those loyal to Brandon that if either of them was the guilty party, it had to be Michelle; those closer to Michelle naturally believed the opposite to be true. For the time being, many people seemed to be holding their breath and holding their tongues, certain that in the end the truth would emerge and the right person or people would be exonerated.

Naturally, Devon's family members were among those most in need of the truth, and some of them attended the press conference at 10:00 A.M. in the district attorney's office on Monday, August 14, the day after the arrests, to hear the latest developments firsthand. However, even though arrests had been made, it became clear from the start of the news briefing that getting to the complete truth was something that was still a long way off.

The Northampton County District Attorney's Office was located on the first floor of the sprawling yet still overcrowded maze that was Northampton County Court-house, which sat on top of Gallows Hill, directly up the steep incline of Washington Street from the churning waters of the Forks of the Delaware. The complex spilled over the hilltop, encompassing not only courtrooms but also a myriad of public administrative offices and the county jail. On the weekdays it mirrored the tumultuous flow of the Forks, a churning confluence of activities in its own right, a hustle and bustle of civic activity.

Built in 1861, the current courthouse was not the city's original hall of justice. That one was built in 1765, three years after the founding of Northampton County, in the middle of town at Centre Square. It stood until 1862, and its claim to fame was that on July 8, 1776, the Declaration of Independence was read from its steps.

Despite the modern courthouse's relative newness, it was still in no way a new building. Rather, it was an aging city administration building whose original design was now largely obscured under years of construction, additions and security measures.

In spite of all the changes and modernizations, the facade still reflected classical architecture, with its stately columns and its lofty cupola rising three hundred feet over the city of Easton. Inside were still to be found occasional touches of the workmanship, grandeur and grace of bygone eras—soaring ceilings, marble trim, huge drafty wood-sill windows that swelled and stuck in the summer humidity, and waiting areas furnished with lacquered church-style benches, where attorneys paced and mur-mured into cell phones while their clients sat wringing their hands.

The office of the DA himself could be found at the end of a long corridor from the street entrance. It was a cramped, bustling space flowing with purposeful activity. Inside Morganelli's personal office, diplomas and other credentials clung in a matter-of-fact row across the wall behind the desk. Black file cabinets occupied the corner to his right, supporting a few cardboard boxes stacked on top.

His desk was wooden, serviceable and unpretentious: an array of photos crossed the front. There was a 3-D wood carving of the name "John," a family photo, a small American flag standing up in a pen-and-pencil carousel that doubled as a four-sided photo frame. Judging by the desk, one could conclude that this was the workspace of a family man and a patriotic American.

Morganelli graduated Moravian College in Bethlehem in 1977 with a bachelor's degree in political science. Moravian, a liberal arts college in the heart of the Lehigh Valley, founded in 1742 by the Moravian Church, is recognized as America's sixth-oldest college. Morganelli was ranked fifth in his class of 305 students, graduating with highest honors and a 4.0 average in his major field of study. He went on to earn his law degree in 1980 from Villanova School of Law.

The degree in law was the fulfillment of a long-held ambition engendered at an early age by his fascination with the drama of the courtroom, something largely inspired by romanticized television portrayals of legal work. John Morganelli had set his sights on becoming a lawyer when he was about twelve years old. It was a goal from which he never wavered.

"I was interested in the law as a young kid, about eleven, twelve, thirteen years old. I saw a lot of lawyers on television shows and soap operas, and was sort of fascinated by the courtroom, the drama, and so, at an early age, I decided that I wanted to be a lawyer, around age twelve, and I never changed that thought."

Upon graduating law school, he entered private practice, honing his courtroom skills as a trial attorney and also engaging in the practice of civil law. At the same time, he served as Bethlehem's assistant city solicitor from 1981 to 1982, and then as Northampton County's assistant public defender from 1982 to 1986. From 1982 to 1984, he returned to Moravian as a part-time instructor of criminal law evidence and constitutional law. In 1991, he became solicitor to Bethlehem City Council, a position he held until 1991, when he was elected Northampton County DA. He was elected with about 60 percent of the vote in the primary and general elections, defeating a three-term incumbent for the position. He was reelected unopposed in 1995, 1999 and 2003.

Morganelli does not entirely look the part of the hard-nosed prosecutor he is. He has dark wavy hair, a ruddy complexion, and wears glasses. His smile is genuine and unexpectedly boyish. However, the strength of his presence lies in the form of a keen intellect and a driving ambition. He has a distinctive voice and forthright manner, answering questions quickly and simply, never at a loss for words—as would be expected of a man who makes his living thinking and talking on his feet. During conversation he occasionally elaborates upon an important point, but rarely deviates from concise, direct answers. His movement through the office is brisk and businesslike. He gives the impression of being someone who's always busy, who's always got a lot on his shoulders and a lot on his plate, which he does.

On Monday, August 14, Morganelli stood up to face the blazing lights of television crews and the faces of Devon's closest family members—father, mother and brother clinging close together—and announced that arrests had been made in the young woman's murder. Although the arrests had been two months in coming, Morganelli, who was joined by Detective Barry Golazeski, said that investigators had been on the scent of Michelle and Brandon from pretty early on, because it was clear that the information the couple gave to police wasn't entirely truthful.

Golazeski, whose dogged detective work was largely responsible for bringing the case up to this point, informed reporters that the investigation was still "far from complete" and acknowledged that the case against the couple had holes.

Some of those holes were, in fact, gaping voids. One of them was whether it was a crime of passion or if the couple intentionally worked together to lure Devon to their house for the purpose of killing her. The answer to that question would determine if charges of conspiracy and first-degree murder could be sustained.

Another major hole in the case was that officials did not know, and police had not asserted in the arrest affidavit, just who, exactly, killed Devon. Did investigators think it was Brandon or Michelle who cut her throat? And who was it that strangled her, causing the petechia on her face noted in the pathologist's autopsy? What part did each play in the fatal struggle? These details were nowhere to be found.

Morganelli asserted that prosecutors believed both Brandon and Michelle were "intricately involved" in the murder, but as far as who had actually committed the act itself or how, he hedged, saying that information was still coming in from various sources.

Another question to be answered was whether the knife found in Devon's hand was the murder weapon. Forensically speaking, Dr. Funke, the medical examiner, had not been able to say whether it was or wasn't, but the possibility still existed that other evidentiary links might be found to answer that question.

In spite of all officials didn't know, Morganelli commended the Easton cops and the investigative work done so far, saying that it had been a difficult case to bring to this stage, at which point enough evidence had been amassed to make the arrests.

What police and prosecutors did have were witness statements and forensic evidence that connected both Brandon and Michelle to Devon's death, and some of that evidence painted a bad picture for the South Side couple. The evidence against Michelle outlined at the press conference included the statement Golazeski had taken from George Vine the day after Devon's body was found. In that statement Vine asserted that Michelle had sought his help in killing Devon two months before the murder took place. The evidence also included the plastic cap crime lab analyst Carol Ritter found in the pocket of Michelle's jeans. It turned out to be a syringe cap that fit precisely over the syringe found with Devon's body.

Detailing the evidence against Brandon, Morganelli pointed to the bloodstained men's clothing found in the trunk of Michelle's car. Lab analysis had matched the blood on those clothes to the murder victim, and forensic testing had matched hair on the clothing to Bloss. The other major piece of evidence against Brandon was the bite mark on his arm, which the DA theorized had been inflicted by the victim in a "last desperate attempt to free herself from the attack."

All told, it was pretty strong evidence, adding up to the beginnings of a fairly solid circumstantial-evidence case. Despite the holes that remained, investigators felt justifiably good about the work they'd done so far; though at times it may have seemed to the public that they'd taken their time in putting the pieces together. But when the press conference was over, Devon's father took a few minutes to speak to reporters and thank police for their compassion and hard work. He said that even though nothing could bring his daughter back, the hope remained that justice would be done.

On the day of the press conference announcing the arrests, Keary Renner finally went public with the true nature of her relationship with Devon Guzman. Now that Michelle and Brandon had been charged with the crime, she could finally afford a long-deserved sigh of relief and the opportunity to speak out at last.

Immediately after the murder, she had been the hottest suspect on the cops' list, and even after Brandon Bloss and Michelle Hetzel replaced her as lead suspects, suspicion cooled slowly. Investigators wondered if somehow she had played a part, and Michelle had no small role in encouraging that suspicion.

But now that the arrests had put that to rest, Keary was in the clear. She had been freed of suspicion at last, and could afford to speak her mind and set the record straight. She made it clear to *Express-Times* reporter Tony Nauroth that Devon had been her girlfriend, her significant other. "First, I want people to know that we were not roommates," she said. "We were girlfriends."

She maintained that Devon's family had tried to hide her bisexuality, making her over to be something she wasn't. "They said she loved rainbows," Keary told Nauroth. "She hated rainbows." The reason Devon had a rainbow decal on the bumper of her car was because it was a symbol of gay pride, Keary said.

Keary also went public with her insights into how extreme jealousy over Devon may have driven Michelle to murder. In the months leading up to the murder, Michelle was intimate with both Brandon and Devon, manipulating both relationships and playing one against the other. Toward the end the love triangle arrangement deteriorated rapidly.

It reached a crisis point when Devon rejected Michelle's marriage proposal after the Virgin Islands trip and instead began to forge ahead with plans to move to Arizona with Keary.

Keary said Devon had told her that Michelle once insisted, "If I can't have you, then Keary can't have you, either." Something had to be done, and Brandon was so taken with Michelle that he'd do anything for her, Keary said.

The night of the murder, Keary said, she'd tried to look out for Devon by confiscating her car keys because she'd been drinking. But with Brandon's help, Michelle managed to manipulate the situation, crying wolf yet again to lure Devon to her home alone. She recalled Devon's final farewell. "She said she loved me and gave me a kiss. She said she'd be back later that night."

When suspicions of murder had begun to loom heavily over Michelle and Brandon in the summer of 2000, with police poking around their lives and confiscating various possessions, each of them had hired a lawyer. Brandon sought counsel from Phillipsburg attorney James Pfieffer, and Michelle retained Brian Monahan, of Easton. Following the arrests, however, the newlyweds claimed an inability to pay for their own defense and applied for public defenders, hoping to take advantage of the opportunity for a free legal defense on the long, costly road ahead. There was a problem, however.

Because Devon Guzman's grandmother worked as an interpreter in the public defender's office, the chief defender Leonard Zito balked at appointing any of his own for the job of defending the couple. He said it would be a conflict of interest to do so. A judge agreed, deciding instead to appoint them attorneys from what is known as the blue team, a roster of lawyers who accept court-appointed cases.

The court-appointed attorneys for Michelle were Brian Monahan, the same lawyer she had hired privately before her arrest, and Victor Scomillio. Both were local Easton lawyers. Two other Easton attorneys, Alexander Karam and Robert Sletvold, were appointed as Brandon's defense team.

The prospect of a defense team of four attorneys paid for at taxpayer expense outraged some, including an aunt of Devon's. In a letter to the *Express-Times*, she expressed "absolute disgust" at the arrangement. "Why do they need a team of four attorneys to represent them? They should only be allowed one lawyer between them," she wrote.

Her frustrations were palpable, and not an uncommon response from people who find themselves on the victim's side of the criminal justice system. The sentiments in her letter would be echoed in the months to come, and they symbolized the turmoil many of the victim's family members went through to come to grips with the fact that the civilized mechanisms of justice can feel inadequate and immensely unsatisfying in the wake of such a brutal death. The accused are awarded rights and considerations never to be enjoyed by the victim, and there would always be a certain chafing injustice in that.

The issue of court-appointed lawyers was only the first of many things that wouldn't seem fair over the road ahead. It wouldn't seem fair when the court approved thousands of dollars for the defense teams to hire private investigators to scavenge for evidence that might exculpate the defendants. It wouldn't seem fair when Michelle's request to leave jail to attend her grandmother's funeral was approved. For those who'd known the victim, there would be seemingly no end to the list of allowances that assured her alleged killers' constitutional and civil rights were not violated in any way.

Part of the feeling of unfairness had to come from all the attention lavished on the accused. The victim had been forever silenced, but the names and voices of the accused resounded still. The pursuit of justice became largely about the defendants. They got free lawyers. They got to tell their side of the story in court. It could be a maddening thing for a victim's family to watch, feeling one slap in the face after another. Most Americans understand the presumption of innocence and accept that protection of the rights of the accused is necessary to ensure the integrity of the justice system, but that is of little comfort to those who've suffered a terrible loss at the hands of a criminal. What was fair about how Devon was taken from them? They were beginning to learn that the road to justice could be a long one, with many bitter stops along the way.

At the end of August, Michelle Hetzel and her legal team obtained access to audiotapes of the calls she and Keary Renner placed in the early-morning hours of June 15 to report Devon missing and a call made after her body was found. Brandon's defense team, on the other hand, did not ask for the tapes, and this provided the first glimpse of the divergent strategies the newlywed codefendants' legal teams would employ in the proceedings to come.

Brandon's attorneys had no interest in the tapes, while Michelle's were keenly interested, describing them in court papers as "necessary and pertinent" to her defense. At this stage observers could only guess as to why, but two distinct possibilities stood out. One was that she hoped the apparent care and concern for Devon's welfare and whereabouts evidenced in the calls would suggest she was innocent of murdering her. Another possibility was that if someone interpreted the calls to police as merely a staged ploy intended to establish concern for the victim and deter future suspicion when she turned up dead, Michelle could point to the fact that hers wasn't the only voice on the tape; Keary had been right there with her making the calls. This might not mean much, but it could serve to create some suspicion or doubt, and a little doubt here and there was all a skilled defense team needed. Enough doubt could add up to an acquittal.

Police didn't stop investigating just because two suspects had been arrested. In the weeks after the arrests, their work went steadily forward, hand in hand with the efforts of prosecutors, to put together a case and find answers to the many as-yet-unanswered questions.

Although virtually all of the evidence police had collected pointed to the Bloss/Hetzel home, not all of it did. In particular, two unidentified fingerprints raised questions, and Detective Golazeski had an obligation to run them down.

One was a partial print obtained from the bulb of the overhead dome light in Devon's car. Mysteriously, although the car was new, the cover had been removed and the bulb taken out. The cover had been found in the backseat, under the victim's body, and the bulb turned up in the car's center console, between the two front seats. Golazeski processed the bulb for latent prints and came up with a partial. The print didn't match any of the suspects or other people, such as family members, who'd been fingerprinted for investigative purposes.

Since the Sunfire was a new car, Golazeski contacted Pontiac and found out that the headliner assembly had been manufactured in a plant in Ohio. He reached the plant manager and found out that the auto workers who manufactured those assemblies did not wear gloves, which meant the print could have belonged to whoever screwed in the lightbulb before the assembly left the plant. How many people had been on shift at the date and time Devon's particular headliner assembly had been put together? Twelve regular employees and twenty-four temps, Golazeski was told.

That meant the print could have belonged to any one of thirty-six auto workers out in Ohio. If it did, it was irrelevant to the murder, but tying up this loose end would mean fewer unresolved questions down the road. The problem was how to compare the partial print found on the bulb to three dozen people in Ohio, two-thirds of whom were only temporary workers and could have moved on to anywhere by now.

It was a losing proposition, but Golazeski went the extra mile just the same. He asked the police department in the locality of the Ohio manufacturing plant to obtain fingerprints from each of the employees who may have worked on Devon's car so that they could be compared to the latent print he'd found. He received back prints from only nine of the thirty-six workers, and none of the nine matched the partial. It was a dead end, an unexplained piece of evidence, a question without an answer. Frustrating as they are, every case has them. An investigator could follow one of these threads for weeks or months, only to have it lead nowhere. Sometimes the only thing to do was move on to the next piece of evidence.

In the Guzman case, Golazeski had another print to explain. This one had been lifted off a photo found on a shelf in the garage that ran the length of the Bloss/Hetzel property. The photo was part of a set that matched the ones found in Devon's glove compartment, taken during Michelle and Devon's Memorial Day trip to the Caribbean—only with the set in the garage, someone had torn the photos in half.

Golazeski processed the photographs for latent prints. In addition to finding prints from Michelle and Devon on the pictures, he developed one print he could not identify. He ran this print through the state police fingerprint identity system, an automated system that compares unknown latents against the prints of everyone it has on file: a match resulted. The owner of the print was Jerry Ronco, the younger brother of Rick Guzman's girlfriend, Holly.

Golazeski called Ronco in for questioning and, through a search warrant, obtained a blood sample. Although Brandon and Michelle had already been arrested, the detective had to find out whether they were the only ones involved. He resorted to a bit of a ruse to parse out the truth from Ronco. Sitting down with him, he said: "Well, there's something that I'm going to do; it's a little better than a lie detector test, actually. I think there's still somebody else involved that I haven't arrested yet, OK, and the only people who know that are right here, OK, and a few people on the DA's staff."

Golazeski displayed the photos. Ronco said he didn't recognize them.

So how did his fingerprints wind up on them?

Ronco concluded that his sister must've shown him the photos at some point. They weren't particularly meaningful to him, and that's why he didn't recall having seen them.

When lab results came back that showed Ronco's blood did not match any of the blood found in Devon's car, Ronco was eliminated as a possible suspect. Unlike the partial print on the dome light, this piece of evidence was now explained. It was one less thing that could cause problems later.

In the course of these continuing investigations, hard evidence of the love triangle involving Michelle, Devon and Keary emerged at last. It came out of a search at the home of Michelle's parents. Police went in with a warrant to search Michelle's third-floor bedroom. Her father, who had cooperated with police all along, asked them what they were looking for, and then helped them find the items on the warrant.

The search produced airline receipts, credit card bills and other records, but the most significant items were three gold rings. Two of the rings had channel settings, one with a row of two diamonds and the other with a row of four. The third ring had larger diamonds configured in a serpentine shape. They were the first tangible evidence of the volatile love triangle police had heard so much about, the first physical objects related to that triangle that police could actually hold in their hands. And physical things were important because they would carry weight in a courtroom. They were things a jury could see and feel.

Devon's family was not surprised at the finding of the rings. Her father said they stood for the wedding vows Devon and Michelle exchanged in St. Croix. When the news of this new evidence became public, Devon's mother spoke out publicly for the first time about her daughter's sexual orientation. Perhaps she also felt a need to answer Keary Renner's recent charges that Devon's family had tried to make her over after she died. "I love my daughter," she told the *Express-Times*. "She was proud of who she was. We never tried to hide the fact she was gay."

Keary Renner, for her part, scoffed at the significance of the rings, casting doubt on whether any kind of meaningful marriage ever took place between Devon and Michelle in the Caribbean. She saw the rings as nothing special, saying that they might have been the fourth set of engagement rings Michelle had bestowed on Devon.

Be that as it may, the three gold circles would make a strong statement for prosecutors. The fact that all three had wound up back in the possession of Michelle, in safekeeping at her parents' home, supported the argument that Devon had indeed broken off her relationship with Michelle after the Caribbean trip, rejecting the marriage proposal, returning the rings and leaving Michelle with a possible motive for jealous retribution.

In the days of early September 2000, District Attorney John Morganelli reported to work to face the strain of seven murder cases waiting to be tried in Northampton County. Seven of them were stacked up on the court schedule, the highest number lined up at any one time in recent memory for his office.

Even without any more killings taking place, that number could go up before year end, if the county grand jury produced any arrest recommendations out of the unsolved homicide cases it was currently reviewing.

The caseload presented enough of a problem that Morganelli elected to call attention to it at a news conference. "I can't remember a time in which seven active cases existed," he said, adding that the heavy load had already taken a significant bite into the personal time of the DA, his staff of five assistant district attorneys (ADAs) and his nine part-time staff members. In addition, it was taxing the DA's $1.8-million budget, especially the fund designated for paying expert witnesses.

The other problem was that the Morganelli staff had limited experience with the most serious types of murder cases. All five ADAs had previously prosecuted murders, but none had handled a death-penalty case, and several of those potentially loomed. Morganelli himself was the only one with capital murder experience, and he'd already committed himself to handling one of the capital cases, as well as personally prosecuting the Bloss/Hetzel case. Whether the young newlyweds would face the death penalty was something he had not yet determined.

On top of that, he had appeals in a dozen homicide cases to field. It was going to be a busy fall in the district attorney's office.

In mid-September, Michelle filed for access to records from an assessment of her by the county mental-health division, and a subsequent referral to a psychologist for treatment. The records dated back to a period of months in which Michelle was placed under supervision by the Department of Human Services. The details of and reasons for that placement have never been made public, nor have the results of Michelle's mental-health assessment, so little is known about this aspect of her past. In a published report, her father declined to elaborate on the reason for the court-ordered placement, other than to say it was something stemming out of her relationship with Devon Guzman. "She was there because she loved Devon. She wanted to be with Devon but she couldn't be with Devon," he told reporter Rudy Miller.

Devon's father recalled that Michelle had become more and more rebellious toward her parents as she approached her eighteenth year. She and Devon were an item, and her parents were against it. At one point Michelle asked about moving in with Devon and her dad. But the issue became moot shortly after, when she met Brandon.

At the time Michelle's attorneys requested access to her past mental-health records, the DA had not yet decided whether to seek the death penalty for Michelle and her husband. He still had months to examine whether the crime involved any of the aggravating factors needed to warrant capital punishment. If it was decided that these factors existed, any evidence of psychological problems that might be documented in Michelle's records could be used to argue against ending her life through lethal injection, if she was convicted.

In addition to seeking the mental-health records from Michelle's past, her defense team pursued new psychological evaluations of Michelle. The results of both the earlier psychological evaluation and any new ones ordered by her attorneys were never made public, so their conclusions are unknown. Whatever the contents, they never became a factor in her legal defense.

26

The preliminary hearing on Tuesday, October 10, 2000, was the time and place for a judge to decide whether the evidence detectives had collected and turned over to prosecutors was sufficient to hold Michelle Hetzel and Brandon Bloss over for trial.

Strategically speaking, District Attorney John Morganelli and his assistant prosecutors had the upper hand over the defense teams going into the proceedings. Morganelli, who spent the Monday before the hearing preparing, knew thoroughly well what evidence he had in his possession, and he'd had the luxury of deciding how best to present it.

The defense lawyers, on the other hand, could only guess for the most part at what evidence had been amassed against their clients and what kind of witnesses might be presented. They had to be on their toes that day, prepared to react to whatever prosecutors threw out. There was only so much preparation a defense attorney could do ahead of time to get ready. The information available to them was limited.

In reality, the general newspaper-reading public knew about as much about the Guzman murder case and the prosecution's evidence as the defense teams did at this stage. That information amounted to, in large part, whatever clues could be gleaned from the affidavit of probable cause and various other courthouse filings that had been submitted over the weeks, seeking access to this person or that possession. Those terse filings often gave a glimpse into what evidence investigators were after, but they provided little insight into why they wanted it or what it might mean. The cumulative result of piecing together the bits of information from such filings amounted to a rough image of how the prosecution's case might be shaping up; however, there was always plenty of room at a preliminary hearing for surprises for which there was little defense attorneys could do to prepare. Later, if the defendants were held over for trial, the defense teams would file for discovery, and the prosecution would have to turn over all relevant evidence. However, until the preliminary hearing got under way, it was a guessing game for the defense. Tables would be turned down the road, however. Discovery—the turning over of evidence— wasn't a two-way street, and when it came time for trial, it would be the prosecutors doing the guesswork as to what the defense teams had up their sleeves.

The preliminary hearing was scheduled for nine-thirty in the morning on Tuesday, October 10, in District Justice Sandra Zemgulis's small courtroom, which was located not in the county courthouse but in a shopping plaza in South Side. Though many might have expected that a large and emotional crowd would attend the hearing, adequate provisions hadn't been made to accommodate such a charged turnout. Few had truly appreciated how powerful the sentiments were that had been stirred within those involved in this case, and what explosive potential they might have.

The small district courtroom filled up quickly as all of the interested parties began to file in, including the press, Devon's family and friends, and members of the defendants' families. Tensions mounted as all of these parties began to assemble together, clustering in groups just feet from one another, in one small room.

Sheriff's deputies led Michelle Hetzel and Brandon Bloss, dressed in orange prison garb, to seats placed side by side in front of the judge's bench. If Michelle had truly been pregnant, she would have been showing it by now. Since she wasn't, people figured out that the pregnancy claim had been a lie. The newlyweds did not exchange so much as a glance. It was ten minutes to go before the hearing was set to begin, when suddenly there was an abrupt movement in the court, and the tension in the room erupted into violence.

Devon's father leaped at Brandon, frothing with rage, releasing months of stored pain since his daughter's unthinkable death.

"I got a pair of pliers and a fucking blowtorch!" he screamed. "I'm gonna kill you!"

Brandon's gaze remained riveted to the floor. Michelle visibly withered at the specter of such blistering rage. Reporters madly scribbled the ferocious quote.

Sheriff's deputies rushed in to restrain Rick, enveloping him and quickly ushering him to an interior room. Years later, Rick Guzman's recollection of that day remained vivid and dreamlike, like an out-of-body experience.

Since his daughter's death, "it was the first time I got to see them in the flesh," Rick said. "So I walked in. Such a small room, and he's just sitting right there, six feet away from me." Clasping his hands together behind his back, he imitated how Bloss was seated in the courtroom with cuffs around his wrists. "And I just went after the guy. I was gonna choke his neck, do something with his neck. Not break it, not on purpose, but something. And you know I didn't even think. I just saw him, went after him.

"Got half a step, and six deputies carried me out. Six of 'em. I was level with the ground. Two holding me here, on my legs, two on my arms, two on my belly. I remember my scarf was running along the floor. I had a scarf on. They took me into the back room. They could've arrested me. But you know I guess they realized, they understand, your little girl, just mowed down, you know."

The deputies grabbed him so fast, he hadn't even had time to get momentum, but they didn't hurt him. "They handled me with kid gloves, even though they physically removed me."

Next, "I was in the back room on my face, trying to figure out what's going on, and I look up and my mom . . ." Reflecting on what might have happened, he said, "Thank God I didn't get in trouble, you know. But they got to me before I got to him."

After that, a delay was announced so that the hearing could be moved someplace larger and with better security measures. The assemblage disbanded, crossing South Side and reconvening a half hour later in courtroom 5 of the Northampton County Courthouse.

"It was weird, riding up there," Rick said. "I had to get special permission from John Morganelli to be able to sit in at the courthouse. He's like, 'You can't be doing that. You know, I understand your frustration.'" Rick had calmed down, so he was allowed to stay, although precautions were taken. "There's a short wall between the two tables and the spectators, or whatever, and I don't think they let me sit closer than the third row. But that was fine, that was fine."

The move and the space around people discharged

some of the tension that had filled Zemgulis's courtroom earlier, and now there were some smiles, tears and awkward maneuverings, but no more outbursts as Devon's family clustered in one area and those who supported the pair accused of taking her life gathered in another. Devon's family and friends could be identified by the purple ribbons pinned to their clothing.

Moments of levity marked the waiting period before the hearing began, but once the judge took her seat and began the proceedings, the mood instantly sobered. A grueling six hours lay ahead. For some, these would be among the bitterest, most unbearable hours life would ever thrust upon them; for now they would hear, in excruciating scientific detail, the horror of Devon's final moments. It was a necessary exercise, however, and when it was over, prosecutor John Morganelli had achieved his goal. The evidence was sufficient to hold the couple over for trial. Even though the case, so far, had holes, the decision wasn't much of a surprise, given the forensic evidence alone.

27

Even as the crowd that had assembled in courtroom 5 on Tuesday, October 10, for the preliminary hearing had listened intently as the experts asserted that forensic evidence proved Devon had not been killed in her car, authorities had to admit that just where and how she had been killed remained a puzzling missing link. It seemed strange that after almost four months of investigation, these crucial details remained unknown.

The question was: would they remain so? Most investigative avenues had been exhausted, and the two principal suspects weren't talking. In the two months of incarceration in county jail since their arrest, Brandon had lawyered up, as the police put it, and Michelle wasn't talking, either. DA John Morganelli had considered offering one or the other of them a deal to come clean, possibly in exchange for some prosecutorial concessions. The problem was, no one knew who might have done what and who should be offered a deal. Morganelli was afraid to guess wrong, so he didn't push the issue. "We explored the possibility where one would acknowledge guilt, but neither of them would do that," the DA said.

The fact was, despite all the details investigators had

uncovered, the very heart of the murder eluded them. Where and how, exactly, was Devon Guzman killed? These questions remained mysteries.

But not necessarily to everyone.

Among those who had an inkling of where and how the murder may have been committed was Cara Judd, the girlfriend of Brandon's sister, who had heard from Michelle Hetzel's own lips specific details regarding this very matter. Before today, Cara had harbored doubts about whether Michelle had been telling the truth when she confessed details about the murder. It seemed absurd that any rational person would incriminate herself in such a way. But with each witness who testified, Cara became more and more convinced that what Michelle had told her might indeed be the terrible truth. The testimony of Joseph Welsh, Detective Golazeski, the forensic experts— so much of it agreed with the awful secrets Michelle had imparted. It seemed that, for whatever reason, Michelle may have unburdened herself honestly to Cara back in the summer. It was a chilling possibility, and as the court proceedings went on, she grew more and more spooked at the thought of it.

Why the details Michelle had shared with her were not being discussed by any of the eleven witnesses called to testify that day was not Cara's concern. It wasn't as if she'd kept the information entirely to herself. At first, she'd gone back and forth about whether to report Michelle's confession to authorities, with fear holding her back and a sense of moral obligation urging her forward. The issue resolved itself a week or so ago, however, when an investigator came to her home, on September 28, and recorded an interview with her. She'd told him all about her various conversations with Michelle, including the shocking revelations Michelle had made in the washroom that night in July while the two were sitting on the laundry machines at Brandon's mother's house.

But the investigator was working for Brandon's attorneys, and the information she told him did not make its way to the detectives and prosecutors in the case. And so, unbeknownst to the detectives and prosecutors, after the preliminary hearing ended that day, Cara Judd left the county government center still in possession of vital secrets they'd been pursuing for months.

Loose lips sink ships, the saying goes, but the more people talk, the better it usually is for police. After the preliminary hearing, people talked plenty around Easton, and some of that talk made its way to the halls of police headquarters. As a result, on Thursday, October 12, the phone rang for Cara Judd. She was surprised when the caller identified himself as Detective Barry Golazeski, of the Easton Police Department, and even more so when he went on to inform her that he'd heard rumors that Michelle Hetzel had told her some things about Devon Guzman's death.

Whatever Michelle had told her, Cara had passed on a couple of weeks ago to the investigator for Brandon's attorneys. But Golazeski wanted to know if Cara would be willing to come to police headquarters and tell him the same information. Cara said she would, then arranged to meet the detective at the stationhouse that evening.

When Cara arrived at the stationhouse, she was met by Detective Golazeski, along with Detective William Crouse. After some preliminary discussions about the information she had to share, Cara went on record with her story. The recorded interview began at 8:50 P.M.

"OK," Golazeski began. "We've had some information come to light and we've been talking here a little bit, and

I'd just like to have you go over what you've told us about what you found out about Michelle Hetzel, how you met her, and certain conversations that have transpired between you since then."

Cara answered that she knew Michelle through Natalie and Brandon Bloss. She said that the first time she'd ever seen Michelle was during a court proceeding involving a foster-care matter, but that the first time she actually spoke to her was several months ago, on July 17, for a celebration of Michelle's birthday.

She described for the detectives Michelle's behavior during that visit: "She was saying she was pregnant and she was eating. We were all together for her birthday. She was eating, shoveling food in her mouth with both hands, saying that she had to eat for the baby, and basically that's all she was talking about—her pregnancy."

About a month had passed since the murder. It was a Monday evening, and a handful of people were present for the celebration. When Cara arrived with Natalie, Brandon and Michelle were already there. Cara had already heard from Natalie that the two young newlyweds were suspects in a murder that had taken place in Easton in June. It was weird for her to meet them—Brandon was quiet and nice; Michelle seemed a little odd.

She remembered having seen them earlier that year in court, and the impression Michelle had made on her on that occasion was not a good one. Michelle lied about things, tried to force Brandon to lie in court, and just seemed so fake.

Cara finally concluded that maybe Michelle behaved the way she did because she was young—still a teenager, really. She decided to give Michelle the benefit of the doubt and get to know her better. That night, they had a cake and sang happy birthday to celebrate Michelle's nineteenth birthday. Everyone continued to tease her about her voracious eating, her shoveling in the food with two hands. "Well, I'm eating for two now," Michelle quipped.

Later that night, Brandon, Michelle, Cara and Natalie went out for a drive. It was a pleasant summer night, the cool night air refreshing. After the cruise the party broke up. It was still fairly early. Michelle and Brandon left to go see a movie, and Cara and Natalie departed to do their own thing, too.

With the tape recorder running and Golazeski and Crouse listening closely, Cara continued to describe getting to know Brandon Bloss and Michelle Hetzel. She proceeded to outline a second encounter with Michelle shortly after the first. It took place later that same week. The date was July 21, a Friday night. Brandon, Michelle, Natalie and Cara first went to pick up a pizza at Rocco's Pizza on Main Street in Hellertown and then went back to Natalie's house on Main Street for dinner and a movie.

They had wanted to watch the comedy *Half Baked* that night, but they couldn't find it. So instead, they settled for *The Bone Collector*, with Denzel Washington and Angelina Jolie. Its selection proved a double irony—the film featured forensic investigators seeking to catch a killer, and also cast an actor with an ironic last name, given this particular audience. The actor was Luis Guzman, a familiar face from the television crime dramas *New York Undercover, NYPD Blue, Homicide* and *Law & Order.* As the plot unfolded, the film set an appropriately ghastly mood for the revelations that were to come.

"At one point in the movie, I got up, probably about ten, and I left to go to the bathroom," Cara told Golazeski and Crouse. "I first went to get a drink in the kitchen and then I was going into the bathroom.

"I did not know Michelle was in there, and I ran into her coming out as I was going in, and she was upset and that's when she said that she was sick because of the baby and that she was so upset because she misses Devon and she loved her so much, and she said it over and over again.

"She just kept repeating, and I asked her if she was OK and if she needed to sit down, if she needed some water, if she needed to talk to somebody, and we ended up sitting on the washer and dryer. I was on the washer. She was on the dryer."

What happened after that was so surreal and unsettling that before Cara went to bed that night, she got out a sheet of paper and scribbled some quick notes so that she would not forget. Then she got out her diary and began writing furiously, trying to get it all down, even though the hour was late. It was after two o'clock in the morning.

The journey into a nightmare that was all too real had begun with plans to hang out with Natalie, Brandon and Michelle at Natalie's house. The foursome had ordered pizza at Rocco's and chatted while the pie baked. Her opinion of the newlyweds had improved a little since meeting them earlier in the week. She thought Brandon was cool; Michelle seemed nice enough.

When the pie was done, the two couples brought it back to Natalie's and sat down to watch *The Bone Collector* for the second time that week. Cara decided to show everyone some recently developed photos in which she and Natalie were dressed up for a night out at the dance club Players. She retrieved the photos from Natalie's room and brought them down to hand around. Michelle's reaction to the photos was so bizarre, it made Cara first uncomfortable, then angry.

Michelle gushed. "Oh my God, you are so hot, Natalie! Natalie, you are so hot. Cara, your girlfriend is so, so hot."

The fawning was over-the-top. Cara couldn't believe she was making these comments in front of everyone, her mother-in-law included.

After extolling her sister-in-law's sex appeal, Michelle mentioned to Cara that she wanted to talk to her later. Around ten o'clock, Cara went to the kitchen for a drink, and then went around to the bathroom, where she unexpectedly encountered Michelle. Michelle didn't look good, so Cara asked if she was OK. Michelle replied that she was sad and that the pregnancy was making her sick. Cara asked if she wanted to sit and talk, or if she wanted a drink of water. Little did she know, it was an invitation she would regret ever having extended. Reflecting on this later, she would wonder, *What was I thinking?*

As the two sat down to talk, a concerned Natalie appeared, wanting to know if everything was OK. Cara requested water. Natalie fetched some from the kitchen for Cara and Michelle and then left them alone, sitting on the laundry machines.

"Michelle started telling me how much she missed and loved Devon and how she was out with Devon the night that—the night of the fourteenth of June," Cara said. Next, Michelle told her that she and Devon were drunk and had gotten into a fight before each returned home that night. Michelle said she hadn't felt like talking to Brandon when she arrived home, and that she wanted Devon to come over.

"A little while after she was at home, they—she said 'we,' meaning Brandon and Michelle—called Devon to come over," Cara told the detectives. "She wanted to talk to Devon, and she said she was sick. She told Brandon she was sick and then Devon came over, but Keary was with her, and Michelle got very upset over this," she said.

Michelle told Cara she "just couldn't handle it" when Devon showed up with Keary. She made it clear to Brandon that Keary could not come in. "She was like, 'I told him that she was not welcome in this house, that Keary had to leave, she could not be coming to this house,' so Keary did not come in the house."

Michelle told Cara that Keary never entered the house that night, but that Devon had come back alone. When Devon did return, she and Michelle got into "an argument in the living room, and they were yelling at each other. And then at one point it got physical and they started pulling hair and they started trying to hit each other, and Brandon was on the couch and he got up and jumped in between and grabbed Devon, like, from behind.

"She said he grabbed her from behind and pulled her back because he thought that Michelle was pregnant at the time and he was protecting her," Cara said.

Here, Cara neglected to mention anything about Devon biting Brandon. This detail would come out later in the questioning.

Cara continued describing how Brandon broke up the girls' fight. "He said, 'Listen, that's enough, I can't take this. You girls need to take it outside, talk about this like human beings.' And Michelle said to Devon, 'Well, let's go talk in the garage, we'll go talk out there.' And she said, 'I persuaded her to go out there.'

"She goes, 'I went past the kitchen and I grabbed a wooden-handled knife from the kitchen. And she said, 'It's not one of our knives from the kitchen set, but another-type knife.' She goes, 'I knew Devon carried a black-handled knife, that's why I took one.'

"So they went out into the garage and they were out there arguing, and before she knew it, she said there was a lot of blood, a lot of blood, and then she was telling Devon to breathe and telling her, 'I love you, I love you,' kissing her face and [saying] 'I love you, wake up, please,' and she wasn't waking up and she was holding Devon's head in her lap kissing her face."

Cara recalled that Michelle, sitting across from her

on the dryer, "got a little teary-eyed" at this point in the telling of her story. Even so, her demeanor was "not like I thought someone in that situation would be."

Why the hell is she telling this to me? she wondered.

Cara continued her chilling story for the detectives: "Then Brandon came out a little while later, I guess to check what was going on, what they were doing, and he said, I guess, some choice words, some curse words like, 'What the hell is going on here?'"

Next, she said, Brandon put gloves on and checked to see if Devon was breathing. She wasn't.

As Michelle related these awful things, Cara said she wanted to bolt right out of there, away from Michelle and this tale of horror. "I wanted to run, but I didn't know if I should, so I just sat and listened." During the course of the creepy conversation, a worried Natalie kept coming in to check on Cara.

At one point, Natalie pulled Cara into the bathroom and said to be careful because Michelle was dangerous. Cara said she'd be OK. But when it was over, she felt confused and scared. As soon as she could, she confided what Michelle had told her to Natalie and her mother. She knew that the general consensus was that Michelle was no stickler for the truth, but even so, why would someone make up a story that she'd killed someone? It was a dilemma she'd struggle with in the days and weeks to come. "If I say something . . . will she try to do something to me, too?" she wondered. She also struggled with the moral dilemma of saying nothing.

She continued her story for the detectives. After determining that Devon wasn't breathing, "they both took Devon and put her in the back of Devon's car, in the back of her own car, and Michelle told me that she drove Devon's car and Brandon followed in Michelle's car down to the falls, and that's where they left her," Cara said.

She was a little uncertain about the part involving who drove which car. Michelle's car had an automatic transmission, but Devon's Sunfire did not—it was a standard shift, and Cara was sure that Michelle was only just learning to drive stick. It seemed strange that Michelle would have attempted to drive the car with the stick, especially under such extreme duress, and it made Cara wonder if Michelle would actually have been able to do it.

"I don't know if she could," she speculated to the detectives. "I know she was learning to drive standard, so I know she may have been able to, but I don't know. I don't know whether she did drive her car, or if it was the other way around with him driving [Devon's car]. I'm not sure."

In any case, the detail was of lesser concern for the time being. Golazeski quickly moved on, gently pressing her for more of what Michelle had told her about the night of the killing. "There came a time you said you saw her about a week later when she mentioned a few more things?"

"Yes," Cara said. "She mentioned that, she said that this was done in the garage, and the pool cover—she was laying in the pool cover, and Brandon hosed the pool cover down and then he hosed down part of the sidewalk out in the back."

Here Cara departed from what she'd been told about the murder, interjecting to the investigators that in the space of one week, Michelle had not only extended the privilege of asking her if she and Natalie would be the godparents of her twins, but also ominously threatened her.

"She asked me if I would be a godparent, if I would be a godparent and if Natalie Bloss would also be a godparent to her twins, because she said she was having twins. And she also threatened me that week and said if I ever tried to do anything wrong, she would hunt me down, she would find me and she would kill me."

"Were you scared of her?" Golazeski wanted to know.

"Yes, I'm definitely scared of her," Cara answered, describing her fear in the present tense, despite the fact that months had passed since that threat was made, and that since August, Michelle had been locked securely behind bars, where she remained.

In the conversations preceeding the recorded interview, Cara had mentioned to Golazeski that she had long been a writer of journals in which she recorded many of the significant events of her life. The detective prompted her about these now. "You said you keep a journal. Did you make entries regarding these, both these dates in that journal?" He was talking about July 17, the birthday party at which Michelle claimed to be pregnant with twins, and July 21, the night of her inexplicable washroom confession.

"Yes, I did," Cara told him. She recalled having written about at least those two encounters. The laundry room conversation she had written about at 2:00 A.M., right after it happened. She also volunteered that she had written a detailed entry about "another incident, when Michelle asked me to go to her house, and she gave me a shot of vodka, and I thought I saw her put something in it."

"Do you remember what day that was?" Golazeski asked.

"Yes, I do," Cara replied. "August second."

August 2 was a date she was unlikely to forget, for she would probably always wonder this: if indeed Michelle Hetzel was a murderer, had that been the date Cara Judd almost became her second victim?

28

August 2 was a Wednesday, and Cara Judd had been babysitting all day, from ten o'clock that morning until after ten that night. When she was done, she went to Natalie's home in Hellertown, only to be disappointed that she'd missed a cookout of burgers grilled by Natalie and Brandon, along with corn on the cob, salad and watermelon.

Michelle Hetzel was there also, and shortly after Cara arrived, Michelle received a phone call regarding her living arrangements. Sometime after the murder, Michelle had moved back to her parents' house, but now, as Cara understood it, Michelle's father was calling to tell Michelle he was kicking her out of his house. Cara's impression was that he was angry with Michelle and Brandon, and that part of the reason was that they had neglected to ask anyone from Michelle's family to be godparents of their twins. Michelle told Cara she had until 11:30 P.M. to claim anything she wanted from the house.

Cara's impression was that Brandon couldn't go with Michelle to help her get her stuff because he wasn't getting along with her father at the time. So Michelle asked Cara to accompany her. Cara was scared because, based on their past conversations, she didn't know if Michelle was dangerous or just a strange but harmless fabricator of wild stories, but she agreed to go. Michelle was in such a hurry to get going, Cara hadn't even had a chance to tell Natalie she was leaving.

Together Michelle and Cara drove the twelve miles from Hellertown to Easton. Michelle acted odd and paranoid during the drive through the dark August night. "She was so weird, making jokes about not opening the trunk or something, and she was talking to the people who, she said, bugged her car." She told Cara she liked to talk to them while she was driving.

The two arrived at Michelle's parents' home in South Side at about 11:15 P.M.

"It was so dark in there," Cara recalled. "I said to her to hurry up and get her stuff so we could get out of there. Michelle went upstairs to get some of her clothes. I was downstairs talking to her mom. This was like the first time I ever met her. She was crying and standing half in the house and half on the back porch. She kept saying, 'I don't know why my daughter is doing this. Brandon is not a murderer.' She talked about how she couldn't 'believe all this crazy stuff is happening.' She goes, 'You know, I blame this all on my daughter. Why does she try to destroy people's lives? I just don't understand.'" (Mary Hetzel denied this conversation in court. She claimed she said little to Cara Judd that night.)

"I had absolutely no idea how to reply to this woman, so I asked her if I could go to the bathroom. I went to the bathroom, and then when I came out, I said I was going to go upstairs to help Michelle carry her stuff [because] I didn't think she should be carrying anything down the steps since she was pregnant. I found her with a few small bags up on the third floor and I helped her with them. Michelle said good-bye to her mom.

"When we got outside, Michelle asked me to drive her

car and she asked if I would mind stopping at her and Brandon's house for a minute. I said that was OK, but we should be quick about [it] and get back to Natalie's."

On the way they stopped at a little beer store, and Cara picked up a six-pack for herself and Natalie for later. Then they continued on to West St. Joseph Street and parked the car in front of the little two-story house. The neighborhood was quiet. It was around midnight. Cara was going to wait in the car, but Michelle asked her to come in.

"We went into the house and to the kitchen. She said, 'We have to have a shot of Absolut to toast the babies!' I immediately told Michelle that she should not be drinking while she's pregnant. She told me that she had talked to her doctor and it was OK for her to have a glass of wine a day. So she said there was no problem with her having just one shot of vodka that day."

Cara agreed to the toast because she wanted to get out of there and back to Natalie's.

"She got shot glasses and a bottle of vodka from the cabinet. I wasn't really watching her [because] I was looking at the cool blue couch and the computer on the desk. I glanced over and I thought I saw her get a small unmarked bottle as well. I didn't really think much of it at the time [because] I had started to look at all the CDs and videos. There were so many!"

Impressed by the George Strait box set, she asked Michelle about it, and was told it belonged to Brandon.

"She called me from the kitchen and handed me a shot glass and kept one for herself. We drank the shots, toasting the babies, and then she said we should get going. I don't even think she got anything from the house to take back [with] us to Nat's."

After downing the shots, Cara explained in her interview with Golazeski and Crouse, "Michelle asked me to drive her car back to Hellertown." She headed toward Interstate 78 to return to Hellertown. But something was happening to her. By the time she reached the entrance ramp, she felt like she couldn't move and she couldn't see. She knew she couldn't drive in that state, so she pulled the car over and turned the wheel over to Michelle, who continued on toward Hellertown.

Pulling off the exit for Hellertown, Michelle didn't turn left at the light toward Natalie's as expected, but instead went straight through the intersection and parked her car in a parking lot behind a Wendy's restaurant.

The two young women sat alone in the dark. Michelle told Cara she wanted her to hear a song. "This song reminds me of Devon," she said. "I miss her so much. I want you to listen, I want you to hear this."

Cara thought it was an Usher song. She was feeling out of it, like she was about to pass out.

While the song played, Michelle suddenly leaned over to Cara. Cara abruptly turned away, avoiding the kiss, and said they should be getting back to Natalie's.

But Michelle wasn't ready to go home. She said she felt like going out somewhere.

"How are you going to go out?" Cara asked. She knew Michelle was underage. "You're too young to go out."

Michelle said it didn't matter, she could get in anywhere. She started driving. Cara felt too weak and incoherent to resist.

Michelle drove them to the Tally-Ho in Bethlehem, but they were turned away at the door because Michelle didn't have an ID. Michelle decided to try Diamondz on Broad Street in Bethlehem next, thinking she could get in there. They arrived at the club at around 1:00 A.M.

This time they were a little luckier, and managed to get into the club. But once inside, the bartender refused to serve Cara a beer, because she appeared extremely intoxicated. "I looked like I was on drugs, some kind of drugs, not like I was drunk," Cara recalled.

The bartender's refusal inflamed Michelle, sparking a fracas that escalated until the girls left.

"Michelle was yelling at the bartender and at the owner that they had to serve me because I only had one drink and they had no right to refuse service to me," Cara said, "and she was going to call the cops because I only had one drink. She kept saying that, and the bartender and the owner were upset."

Outside in the parking lot, Michelle continued to threaten to summon police.

Despite Cara's impaired state, the two attempted to leave Diamondz with Cara once again behind the wheel. She was so groggy, it took forever for her to back the car out of the parking space, and she almost struck a parked car and the side of the club building during the attempt. Finally after Cara somehow maneuvered the car out and around to the back of the club, Michelle agreed to switch seats.

Michelle said she'd take them to a place she knew would serve them. It was a bar she and Brandon had gone to, and Michelle said she got served there all the time. Everything grew hazy as they drove. Cara felt herself drifting in and out of consciousness. She didn't remember the name of the bar they arrived at, but she remembered that Michelle pulled up in front and parked along the curb.

Inside, Michelle cued up some music on the jukebox. "I attempted to play pool with her," Cara recalled. "I may have ordered a beer. I know she ordered some beer. I don't know if I drank mine or not.

"We stayed till closing time and we left, and then on the way home back to Hellertown, I think I threw up out the window of her car, the passenger window of her car, and

I know I had my head hanging out the window the whole ride home."

Arriving back at Natalie's, Michelle left Cara in the car and went inside for help.

"We got home, she went in to get Brandon to come pick me up and carry me in because I couldn't even move, and Brandon came out and got me," Cara recalled.

Brandon's mother demanded answers from Michelle as Brandon carried Cara in. "What happened?" she wanted to know. "What's going on?"

Michelle wanted to leave, but her mother-in-law wouldn't let her. She lashed out. "Michelle punched Brandon's mom in the face twice," Cara recalled.

Brandon carried Cara upstairs to Natalie's bedroom and put her on the bed. Natalie, who had fallen asleep downstairs, woke up and climbed the stairs to see what was going on.

"Both Natalie and her mom decided there was something wrong, because I kept saying, 'I don't feel right. This is wrong. I don't feel right,'" Cara said.

Natalie, being an emergency medical technician (EMT), recognized that something was very wrong. They dialed 911, and police and EMTs were dispatched to the house. "I kept telling them, 'I don't do drugs. I didn't have too much to drink. I only had one shot of vodka.'"

Everyone in the house was worried. Cara recalled that Brandon was crying when the EMTs came, and Michelle was out in her car, drunk.

Natalie told the police, the EMTs and later the staff at St. Luke's Hospital that she thought Cara had been drugged. Cara recalled that her blood alcohol level was tested that night, and she believes that the result came back off the charts. She remained in the hospital until about 8:00 A.M.

The next day, Cara was completely incapacitated. The

hospital had tested her blood for street drugs and found nothing, but Cara was still worried about what she might have ingested. Her family doctor sent her to a Hellertown lab for blood testing, but a nurse there told her their tests wouldn't show anything different from the ones done by the hospital.

Besides the drug issue, some other things were bothering her. She'd found Michelle's gold necklace around her neck and Michelle's license, credit card and gold bracelet in the back right pocket of her shorts. Michelle's mother phoned looking for Michelle, and then came by to pick up her daughter's jewelry and other things. Cara recalled lying on the couch, barely moving, while Michelle's mother stood in the doorway, commenting on her daughter's behavior.

Reflecting on this same subject, Cara wrote in her diary:

> She (Michelle) is a threat to anyone around her. Please, God, I pray for her and everyone near her that no one else is hurt. I am beginning to think what she told me is true and that she was trying to eliminate me. I don't know what to do. If I say anything she will definitely get me. There is no doubt in my mind. Or she may try to hurt Natalie or Pauline or Brandon. God please protect us all and keep us safe from harm.

Cara believed that Michelle had drugged her, possibly with crystal meth, a roofie, nail polish remover or rubbing alcohol, and that she had almost died because of her.

If indeed Michelle has put something in Cara's drink that night, and that substance showed up in a blood sample that still existed, it could provide further evidence of misdeeds by Michelle. When Cara Judd told this story to Detectives Golazeski and Crouse, Golazeski wondered if maybe the lab Cara had gone to had drawn blood, and if she might still have the sample somewhere.

"Do you know what happened to that blood that you got tested?" Golazeski asked. "Did you leave that with the lab, or did you take it with you?"

Cara said that the lab had not taken any blood; she was told that any testing the lab might do wouldn't show results that were any different from the tests done at the hospital.

"So there wasn't any blood draw done on you?" Golazeski asked.

"They may have some still at the hospital. I don't know," Cara said.

"They usually destroy that," Golazeski said. It was a dead end. If Michelle had put something in Cara's vodka shot that night with the intention of harming her, the evidence to prove it was long gone now. The detective moved on to a new avenue of inquiry: Brandon and his possible role in the events surrounding the murder.

"Did Brandon ever talk about this during the time frame? Did he ever talk about what went on or anything?"

Cara said Brandon had mentioned to her that "Michelle's jeans were full of blood" and "all the chemicals that were put in the washer would dilute the blood from her jeans so they'd never find it."

"Do you think you would have written that in your journal?" Detective Crouse wanted to know.

"I may have," Cara told him.

"Do you think we would be able to get a copy of that?" Golazeski asked. "I mean, I don't want to read your journal—"

"We're not trying to get into your private life," Crouse assured her.

Golazeski added, "But just the pertinent—"

"No, I understand," Cara said.

"Did Natalie ever discuss this with you at all?" Golazeski asked.

"The—"

"The murder?" Golazeski prompted.

"The night that Michelle told me, I was a little bit scared and a little bit confused as to why she told me," Cara said. "I also kinda thought somebody else should know this, so I told her." Natalie seemed to chalk it up to Michelle's propensity to depart from the truth. "She's like, 'You never know.' She's like, 'This girl lies so much. Why would she do something that incriminated herself?'

"That's why I never went to the police or anything, I just—and then when they got arrested, I thought maybe I should go and tell, but I didn't know if she was going to be held or not. And then Tuesday I found out she was still going to be held, so I'm figuring while she's in there, I'm safe. I mean, I even had Natalie put bars up on my windows because I was afraid she would break in because she'd said she'd hunt me down and kill me."

"Did you ever see the mark on Brandon's arm or the bandage there?" Golazeski wanted to know.

"Yeah. I saw, I saw a Band-Aid, but that was it."

"Did he ever talk about it at all?" Golazeski asked. The problem was that all the evidence they had so far—the bite mark, the forensic pathologist's interpretation of how the fatal injury had happened—pointed to Brandon as the probable killer. But now here Cara was saying that Michelle had claimed *she'd* done the killing. If so, what exactly was Brandon's role? How did he get bitten?

Detective Crouse refined the question asked by Golazeski. "Michelle said that when she was having these physical altercations in her living room, Brandon was there and Brandon was trying to protect her. That's why he grabbed Devon. But did she say anything to you about Devon possibly fighting him?"

Cara answered that Michelle had said "that's when Devon bit Brandon."

"She did say that?" Golazeski asked.

Crouse pointed out, "But you didn't mention that the first time, though." When Cara first told them about Brandon's breaking up the fight, she'd neglected to mention the bite. This was why they needed her journal. Someone listening to the tape of the interview later on could view her recollections with skepticism, arguing that Cara hadn't recalled anything about a bite mark on her own, and that it was only after prompting by the detectives that she did so. If this detail was recorded in her journal entries, however, it would be a different story. "Too bad you didn't bring your journal today, but that's fine," Crouse said. "We'll get to that."

"I'll bring it to you," Cara promised. "But she did tell me that. She said that's what made him really angry. [He said] 'Take it someplace else and act like human beings.'"

Golazeski tried to match up the details Cara provided him with the blood evidence from Brandon's clothing. He came up with some possible inconsistencies. If Michelle had done the killing, how did Devon's blood wind up where it did on Brandon's sweatshirt? "Well, one of the things with Brandon though, too, is we have blood on his right sleeve and on the right top of his sweatshirt he was wearing that night," he said. "Then he's got the bite here and he's got the blood on his wrist cuff of his right hand, which, I mean, it's OK if he gets bit when he's pulling her off, but he has to have his hand in front at some point to get blood on there."

Based on what Michelle had told her, Cara could offer no explanation for how the blood might have gotten on Brandon where it did. "I don't know. I just know what she said, the words directly from her mouth."

"Do you think Natalie would be willing to speak with us at all?" Golazeski asked.

"Yes."

"She would be?" he repeated.

"Yes, I'm pretty sure she would."

"How about Pauline?" he wondered. "I know when I spoke with her, she was very upset."

"She might. I think she might. Michelle has done an awful lot."

"Of damage to her family," Golazeski surmised.

"Yeah, an awful lot. . . ."

Not the least of which included entangling her son in the murder of a girl he would never even have known if not for his young wife.

"I think the only reason Brandon's in the position he's in is because he ran into Michelle," Golazeski said. "He's a bright young kid and he had a heck of a future in front of him until he met her."

Cara agreed. "I mean, his older brother even offered him a thousand dollars not to marry her," she added.

"That's a good brother," Golazeski said.

"And his sister Natalie dropped out of the wedding party," Cara said. "She didn't want any part of it. She knew that Michelle was still with Devon. Devon was out by the church when they were getting married. [Natalie] was like, 'I don't agree with this. Pick one or the other. I'm not going to stand up before God and be a witness for your wedding.'"

Cara went back to the story Michelle had told her. She told Golazeski that she got spooked at the preliminary hearing when the evidence all seemed to agree with what Michelle had confided, indicating that she'd probably been telling the truth.

"It all fit," Detective Crouse said.

Cara agreed. "I heard all this and I was like, *why did she tell me?*"

"And we got blood out of the water, too, that the jeans were in," Golazeski mused, remarking on the fact that what Michelle had confessed to Cara about the washing machine and the jeans appeared to square up with the evidence in the police locker. "Not enough to determine whose it was or anything—it was very diluted—but we did find blood in the water."

Then he asked Cara if Michelle had told her anything more. "Is that all she told you? Anything else you can remember? Did she say why she called nine-one-one or anything like that, reported her missing? Did she go into any of that?"

"No, she didn't. She said she just . . . 'The falls was where we used to meet and that was our place.'"

As an aside, Cara mentioned that friends of Brandon's had said Michelle used to wear Brandon's clothing, sometimes even pulling his dirty clothes out of the laundry basket and wearing them around the house. It was something to think about with regard to the blood on Brandon's clothes, but Golazeski indicated he thought it unlikely that Michelle had committed the crime wearing her husband's attire. "She'd have to put all of his clothing on, you know?" he speculated.

Cara was at a loss. "I don't know, I don't know, I wasn't there. I'm sorry."

"No, no," Golazeski assured her. "You've helped us out tremendously, believe me. Did she ever mention about anybody else being involved?"

"No, but she did say while she was sitting at the house one day on Main Street, she was like, 'Oh, we should get our nails done; oh, we should go to a spa; we should go to get a spa,' all this. She just kept asking me all these things, go to the spa, get our nails done. She did try to kiss me in the car, but I did tell you that, and I like totally turned away and she said that 'it doesn't matter anyway because we're going to pin this all on Keary and I'm going to come out smelling like a bed of roses.'"

"She's going to pin it all on Keary?" Golazeski repeated.

"Mmm-hmm."

"Well, she sure tried," Golazeski said. "She tried real hard."

"I think she did," Cara said. "I feel bad for that girl."

"But you and Michelle never had any romantic relationship?" Golazeski wanted to know.

"Oh, no, no, definitely not. Like I said, I barely knew her."

"And you never had any disagreement with her that would lead you to falsely make statements against her. Correct?" Crouse pressed.

"Oh, no. That's correct, yeah."

Golazeski asked Cara what people she'd talked to about what Michelle had told her. Cara replied that she had talked on September 28 to the investigator for Brandon's attorneys. The detective wondered how he knew to talk to her. How did he know she knew something about the murder? "Did they ever say how they came up with your name?" he asked.

"No. Actually, they didn't really come up with my name." Cara said they came to talk to Pauline and someone said, "You might want to hear what she told Cara." The investigator said, "OK, is it going to take long?" Cara said no. But once she started talking, he said, "We better tape this."

"They taped the conversation, and basically what you told us is the same thing that you told them?" Crouse asked.

"Yes."

"And that's fine," Crouse said. "There's no problem with that. You don't have to be sorry."

"You're free to tell whoever you want," Golazeski told her, "and the thing is unfortunately in this situation Brandon's kind of thrown his life away over her, and we gave him ample opportunities to talk to us and he's really kind of lawyered up after the first day. He didn't want to say anything and, you know, physical evidence just goes where it goes. It doesn't change the story, it doesn't, just is."

It was 9:18 P.M. when the detectives turned off the tape recorder. The tape contained therein answered questions that had been lingering for months. If indeed Cara had recorded in her journal entries any of the information she'd just relayed to them, it would really help solidify their case. It would cause some problems also, because some of it conflicted with the evidence against Brandon. But in police work, it's often a matter of taking the bad with the good. Cara's information would also give them the grounds they needed to go to a judge and ask for a search warrant to go back to West St. Joseph Street in search of evidence of whether the crime did indeed take place there. This time they'd have a much better idea of where to look.

On October 24, Cara Judd delivered two diary books into the hands of Easton police, in exchange for a property receipt. One had Mickey Mouse on its cover, and the other a fuzzy, textured leopard-skin pattern. They looked so girlish and innocent, it seemed as if they could contain secrets no more compelling than perhaps the object of a girlish crush. To look at them, it was almost inconceivable that they might, in fact, contain evidence pertaining to a young woman's brutal and bloody murder and the subsequent cover-up of that crime at the hands of a newlywed couple, who could easily be the young honeymooners next door to just about anyone.

The following day, Cara delivered a sheet of notebook paper upon which she had scribbled notes regarding one of the conversations with Michelle Hetzel. She'd been so unnerved by what Michelle had revealed to her that she scribbled the note as soon as she got home, so she would not forget the details amidst her shock and fear. Taken together, the two diaries and the sheet of notepaper hardly looked threatening at all. But when Michelle's day in court arrived, the words contained therein would resound with a very fatal ring.

With the information obtained from Cara Judd, Easton police investigators returned once again to West St. Joseph Street, on October 26, 2000. This time they brought in the big guns. Golazeski requested help from the FBI's Evidence Response Team, and the team of investigators sprayed fluorescein throughout the garage in search of evidence of blood. Going over the sprayed areas with an alternate light source, areas of suspected blood produced a glow. These items were collected and forwarded to the state police labs for further analysis. They included the spray nozzle of a hose, cut-out sections of drywall, sections of a wooden door and swabbing from the garage floor and a recycling can.

On December 1, a cold Friday in the Lehigh Valley, Michelle Hetzel and Brandon Bloss received an early Christmas present. They would not face the death penalty if convicted of the murder of Devon Guzman.

Actually though, coming from John Morganelli, it was anything but a gift. Their fate in the matter wasn't his to give or take, but rather something governed by the stipulations of law. In the state of Pennsylvania, prosecutors have some discretion in seeking the death penalty, but the decision must be guided by a set of factors called aggravators, such as rape or torture or the murder having taken place during the commission of another felony. None of those factors had been found in the murder of Devon Guzman.

Devon's family, caught off guard by the news the day it appeared in newspapers, did not conceal their disappointment. They'd already familiarized themselves with the state's death penalty laws, and had been hoping elements of the brutal death would have fallen under the definition of torture. They did not want to think about Devon's killers, if and when they were convicted, going to prison only to be paroled one day and walk free.

But the Pennsylvania Supreme Court defined torture not by how brutal a death a victim suffered, but by whether a murderer prolonged the killing to inflict more pain. This was not the case with Devon Guzman, who had died quickly. Still, Morganelli, perhaps the state's most committed death-penalty enforcer, more than sympathized with the family. "I would have liked to try this case as a death penalty case, but it's just not there," he told the press.

29

By the first week of January 2001, John Morganelli was eager to make headway on the homicide caseload looming ahead and ready to proceed with the trial of Brandon Bloss and Michelle Hetzel. On January 5, the first Friday of the month, he proposed scheduling the trial for February, arguing that to wait any longer could endanger the couple's right to a prompt trial. For most crimes, this right meant that the accused had to be tried within six months of arrest or released on bail to await his or her day in court. Homicide cases presented extraordinary circumstances where exceptions were often made, but Morganelli didn't want to take any chances that the couple would complain later that they hadn't received a prompt trial.

The DA's eagerness to go to trial also suggested he had a strong case, or that he wanted the defense attorneys to think he did. If, on the other hand, the evidence was weak and the defense knew it, they'd be the ones wanting to rush to trial.

But as it was, the four defense attorneys representing the accused balked at the suggestion of a February trial, complaining that they hadn't even received all of the prosecution's evidence yet, and that a trial so soon would hardly allow them enough time to prepare.

Defense strategies were still being formulated as the attorneys for the accused sifted through the evidence they had in hand and speculated about the evidence still to be received. Morganelli said that he'd already turned over 90 percent of the evidence and promised to hand over the rest by the end of January. Even so, it was a big case in terms of the number of people and relationships involved, and it was a complicated case in terms of the evidence and the science behind it. Preparations were going to take time. A February trial would mean that the defense teams had to digest the totality of the evidence, outline trial strategies, file any pretrial motions they were going to file and then prepare for their day in court.

The debate over the trial date kicked off the back-and-forth pretrial maneuvering that goes on between prosecution and defense, and here Judge Jack Panella sided with the defense, declaring that a realistic time frame would be to hold the trial in September. Michelle and Brandon, who'd come over to the court hearing from their cells in county jail attired in prison orange, waived their rights to a trial within the normal six-month window. It was a victory for the defense teams, winning them six more months of preparation time.

Morganelli, for his part, had no time to fret over the matter. Last year had set a record for murders in Northampton County, which meant this year would be a record year for murder trials. The DA's office expected to prosecute a dozen homicide cases in 2001, and a homicide case a month was more than had been handled in Northampton County in anyone's recent memory. Homicide cases were perfectly routine in larger cities, but here in Northampton, they were not. A string of murder cases that tied up courtrooms, judges and courthouse support staff for weeks on end would seriously strain the system's ability to handle the three thousand less serious criminal cases that would be filed over the course of the year. It was only January, but Morganelli was looking ahead and he was concerned.

Among his immediate concerns was the fact that the first homicide trial of the year was set to start on Monday. That was the trial of Douglas Crist, a twenty-three-year-old Allentown man. The Crist case had been a roller coaster from the start. For those anticipating the Bloss/Hetzel trial, it was a preview of Morganelli's prosecutorial style with regard to younger defendants and a look at the starring role DNA and forensic evidence play in circumstantial cases today. In December 1999, Crist was accused of killing his girlfriend's mother, Debra LaForm, with a hammer three days before Christmas. Authorities charged that Crist set fire to her house in Bethlehem after the murder to destroy the evidence.

Immediately following Crist's arrest, Morganelli said he wouldn't seek the death penalty, because the crime lacked any necessary aggravating factor. At his preliminary hearing, Crist claimed he'd acted in self-defense after the forty-two-year-old woman came at him with a hammer during an argument over her nineteen-year-old daughter, Stacy, with whom Crist had two children.

Crist told police he'd gone to LaForm's house the day after being arrested over a domestic dispute with Stacy. He wanted her to call Stacy for him, but she wouldn't. Instead, she told him to stay away from her daughter. They argued. LaForm threw things at him, slapped him in the face and then fetched a hammer from behind a TV, according to Crist's version of events.

He said she'd stuck him in the chest with the hammer once. When she went to hit him again, he snatched the hammer away and retaliated with a blow to the face. She dropped to the floor, and then he hit her several more times "to put her out of her misery." In a videotaped statement to police he said, "Something took over me—I just wasn't myself."

After that, he went upstairs to make sure no one else was in the house, and then he washed the blood off himself in the bathroom. Back downstairs, a burning candle gave him the idea of setting the fire. He scattered papers around the body, used the candle to light them on fire, flipped on three gas stove jets in the kitchen and fled the house.

Firefighters arrived at 9:43 A.M. They found the body in front of the charred living-room sofas. There was a hole in the victim's skull and a claw hammer next to the body.

In the course of their interviews during the early investigations, police noticed a maroon stain on Crist's sneakers. First he claimed it was transmission fluid, then pheasant blood from a bird he'd shot while hunting, but forensic testing proved it to be human blood.

Crist tried to change his story, blaming the killing on a large Hispanic man he claimed to have encountered coming out of LaForm's house wearing a tool belt with an empty hammer loop. He said the man put a gun to his head and told him to keep his mouth shut about what he'd seen. When police didn't buy the story, Crist abandoned it.

Despite the horrific nature of the crime, Morganelli said he could not seek the death penalty for Crist, because the murder lacked any of the specified aggravating factors required by state law to do so.

But then, in late summer 2000, forensic DNA results changed everything. A DNA test on semen found in LaForm's body during the autopsy—semen that everyone expected would be shown to be her husband's—established that it had in fact come from Crist. The forensic pathologist reviewing photographs and crime scene video concluded she had been sexually assaulted.

With this new evidence, the DA now had an aggravating factor. He announced that he would be seeking the death penalty, after all. It would be the fourth case in which he'd sought the death penalty since being elected DA.

Crist had been planning to present self-defense arguments in hopes of nothing more than a voluntary manslaughter conviction. But now, with the threat of death by lethal injection hanging over his head, he changed his mind and pleaded guilty to murder in mid-November 2000.

The only thing left were sentencing hearings to determine whether he was guilty of first-, second- or third-degree murder. The first two would mean a sentence of life behind bars. But the defense produced a surprise in the midst of the sentencing hearings. Crist's public defenders said they had just received a forensic psychologist's evaluation that concluded that Crist's low intelligence level and lack of education made him easily influenced by police and possibly incapable of making a voluntary confession.

With the possibility now that his confessions might very well be excluded from evidence that could be presented to a jury, Crist suddenly withdrew his guilty plea and decided to take his chances with a jury. Morganelli angrily called the change of heart a disgrace, accusing Crist of playing games with the justice system. The DA said that no more deals would be made with Crist, and that in addition to seeking the death penalty, he was going to add rape to the charges against him, something that had not been done to date.

At first, Crist denied having had any sexual contact with LaForm. When the DNA evidence proved otherwise, he claimed to have had consensual sex. But the forensic pathologist considered that claim to be inconsistent with the crime scene evidence. It was a brutal crime, so brutal it deserved the death sentence, Morganelli maintained on the eve of the trial. At issue would be Crist's mental capacity, and what role it might have played in the killing. How the jury viewed Crist's mental abilities could make an astonishing difference in the outcome—the difference between a sentence of as little as five years for manslaughter to a sentence of death by lethal injection for first-degree murder. With stakes so high, it was going to be a big trial, and the DA was pulling no punches. He had a dozen witnesses and twenty exhibits lined up. Crist's public defender, James Burke, cleared his entire calendar for the month so that he could devote himself to the trial.

Morganelli had no such luxury. Among other responsibilities, he was scheduled to present arguments on January 11 in federal court in Philadelphia pertaining to the 1987 conviction of death row inmate Josoph Henry.

The Henry case was a major one, for several reasons. Statewide, the appeal could have far-reaching effects in terms of Pennsylvania death penalty law. And nationwide, the case was tied to a federal law affecting all public and private institutions of higher learning that participated in federal student aid programs. Not only that, but the Henry case was one of two capital cases over which Morganelli had sued Pennsylvania governor Robert Casey in 1994 to force him to issue death warrants against Henry and another defendant, Martin Appel, who had been sitting on death row for three years since the state supreme court had upheld their death sentences.

The case itself was fairly straightforward. Henry was a Lehigh University student from Newark, New Jersey, who on April 5, 1986, entered the room of freshman coed Jeanne Ann Clery to commit burglary. He gained access to her dormitory through doors that had been propped open with pizza boxes. When she awoke to find him burglarizing her room, he savagely attacked her, biting her, committing a sexual assault and finally strangling her to death. It had been only days since her parents dropped her off at school.

The crime changed her parents' lives, and they in turn changed federal law regarding crime on campuses. After the crime Clery's parents, Howard and Connie Clery, advocated for something to be done about their discovery of gross underreporting of violent crimes on college campuses. They founded the nonprofit organization Security on Campus, Inc., and their efforts resulted in the Jeanne Clery Act. The Clery Act, first enacted by Congress and signed into law by President George Bush as the Crime Awareness and Campus Security Act of 1990, requires colleges and universities to disclose information on campus crime and security.

Obviously, the Henry case was an important one for Morganelli, and the federal court appearance was one more thing that had to be shoehorned into his schedule. (Henry's appeal was resolved after it was found that unconstitutional jury instructions had been given during trial. In light of that, Morganelli agreed to forgo seeking to have Henry put to death, in exchange for Henry giving up future appeals and agreeing to life imprisonment.)

With Northampton County judicial system in high gear, January passed in a blur. Jury selection alone in the Crist case took up six days, in part because of the difficulty of putting together a jury for a death penalty case. The trial itself didn't start until January 16. Morganelli presented the jury with a case of clear-cut premeditated murder as evidenced by Crist's own words, while the defense maintained the defendant's statements had been unduly influenced by police and that the killing was actually an instance of overzealous self-defense. The prosecution presented its evidence of rape, while Crist accounted for his semen at the crime scene by claiming that he'd had a secret nine-month affair with his girlfriend's mother, and that they'd had sex at midday the day before the murder.

Testimony lasted six days. On the seventh, the jury found Crist guilty of first-degree murder and arson, but acquitted him of rape, possibly because the act was likely committed after the victim was dead. It was a victory for the prosecution, but the rape acquittal had major implications for the defendant. Even with the first-degree murder conviction, without the rape conviction, the possibility of the death penalty could now be taken off the table. But Morganelli said he was happy with the verdict, maintaining that the rape charge had been added only because Crist had played games with the system.

In the end, the DA and James Burke, the chief public defender, struck a deal that rendered the point moot. Their agreement put an end to Crist's death penalty hearings and spared his life in exchange for Crist's agreeing to a life sentence without parole, plus forty-six years.

By the time the Crist trial concluded, the end of January had arrived. One of Northampton County's twelve murder trials was over. Now there were eleven more to go.

30

January became February, and February gave way to March in the gray and cold Northeast. For those awaiting justice for Devon Guzman, the months passed slowly. New developments trickled to a stop and the case faded from the public light.

But even though the case had vanished from the front pages of the newspapers, behind the scenes, the attorneys for Michelle and Brandon were working every angle to put together arguments for their clients' innocence.

As spring approached, Brandon began to doubt his court-appointed defense team of local attorneys. He petitioned to be allowed to be represented by a pair of young lawyers from Melbourne, Florida, who were said to be experienced in complicated homicide cases. Their names were Kepler Funk and Keith Szachacz, and although they were certified criminal trial attorneys under the Florida Bar Association, they were not licensed to practice law in Pennsylvania and had never tried a case in the state.

Even so, DA John Morganelli said he wouldn't stand in the way of Brandon's exchanging his publicly funded court-appointed attorneys for the out-of-town team, as long as the money for his defense stopped coming out of taxpayers' pockets. Morganelli also capitalized on the public relations opportunity the occasion provided, touting the strength of his case with cavalier confidence. "No matter who the lawyer is, the evidence doesn't change," he was quoted in the press.

Touting the evidence suggested a strong case for the prosecution, but in truth there were holes in the case and gaps in the evidence. Morganelli had certainly tried stronger cases.

Some observers scoffed at the insistence on bringing in out-of-state attorneys, the kind of thing that is more often done to apply special expertise in high-profile cases. Kepler and Szachacz had been practicing law for less than ten years in Florida, but they'd recently grabbed headlines for their appeal of the death penalty conviction of Lamar Brooks, a twenty-five-year-old Pennsylvania man on Florida's death row who'd been convicted of helping his cousin plan and carry out the 1996 stabbing murders of an air force senior airman named Rachel Carlson and her three-month-old daughter. In that case, as in the Bloss/Hetzel case, prosecutors alleged a conspiracy between the accused killers, but the evidence was unclear as to what role each of the accused played in the crime. In the Brooks case, a lab analyst and blood pattern expert could not testify as to whether one or two people committed the crime or whether one or two knives had been used.

In addition to the notoriety achieved in the Brooks appeal, Kepler and Szachacz sometimes served as television commentators on various legal issues.

Judge Jack Panella agreed to allow the Florida lawyers to take over Brandon's defense, provided that Brandon begin paying his own way and that the Florida lawyers consult with an attorney certified by the Pennsylvania Bar.

Robert Sletvold, one of Brandon's current attorneys, agreed to stay on as the consultant.

From as early as her first interview with Detective Golazeski right after the body of Devon Guzman was found at the canal museum, Michelle Hetzel had contrived to deflect blame in the direction of her onetime close friend Keary Renner. At the end of April 2001, with her trial date about four months away, she employed this strategy again, this time calling public attention, for the first time, to an unpublicized fact in the early investigation of the case—the fact that a polygraph had been administered to Keary.

In early July, going on three weeks after the murder, police were still trying to navigate through the maze of relationships of those closest to Devon Guzman to determine how it all fit and who may or may not have been involved in her death. Keary Renner remained a strong suspect at this time, and she was eager to clear her name by any means possible. Toward that end, it had been suggested that she take a lie detector test. Perhaps naively, Keary agreed. "I wanted people to know that I didn't do it, that I wasn't involved," Keary explained to the press.

Christopher Sullivan, a Pennsylvania State Trooper out of Bethlehem, sat with Keary to administer the test, and posed the following questions:

"Did you cut Devon's throat that night?"

"Did you plan with anyone to cause Devon's death?"

"Were you physically present when Devon was cut that night?"

"Are you the person who put the knife in Devon's hand?"

Keary answered each question in the negative. Sullivan noted in his report that the story Keary told him regarding the time surrounding Devon's death remained consistent with the story she'd told police previously. This consistency was an important indicator of Keary's truthfulness, because very often when someone tries to maintain a lie over a period of time, inconsistencies creep into the story with each retelling.

However, despite the fact that Sullivan found Keary's story consistent with her previous versions, he noted that during the polygraph exam, her physiological responses to the questions were inconsistent. He reported that he was "unable to render an opinion about Renner's truthfulness."

Although law enforcement officials like lie detector tests as investigative tools, if only for their intimidating utility as psychological weapons, polygraph results are highly dependent on the skill and experience of the operator administering the test and interpreting the results. They are far from infallible, and not always helpful. There are people out there who can "beat the box" and other people whose responses are just plain hard to interpret. Sometimes the results are inconclusive to the operator— he can't tell what they mean—and this was the case with Keary Renner.

Keary said that when she finished the test, she was told she "did a great job." But court records indicate that investigators had a few concerns after the test, and sought from her an explanation of the inconsistent physiological responses. Authorities claimed Keary told them that she had been reluctant to say anything that might incriminate Michelle Hetzel and that she wanted to keep her options open with Michelle, in case it turned out that Michelle had not been involved with the murder.

But after these details were reported in the press, Keary told the *Express-Times* that she never said those things. "I don't know where they got that from," she insisted.

The court records say that Keary also told police that

Michelle had once approached her asking if her husband, a soldier, could "blow up" Devon, and that Devon was afraid of Michelle. She said that Michelle was a very manipulative person who held Devon as a fantasy, but that Devon had wanted to get out of the contentious relationship with Michelle after the trip to the Virgin Islands.

A few days after the story about Keary's inconclusive polygraph appeared in newspapers, Keary wrote a letter to the editor disputing several aspects of the report. She claimed that she never said Devon was afraid of Michelle—only that after the island trip, Devon had told her that Michelle laughingly said that if she couldn't have Devon, neither could Keary. She also said that when she found out the polygraph results were inconclusive, she wanted to take the test over, but authorities insisted she'd done fine. She admitted that at the time she took the test, she wasn't yet convinced of Michelle's guilt. "I didn't think Michelle did it, because she was supposed to have loved Dev so much," she wrote. "I never thought she could do that. But now I can see little things that lead me to believe she is involved."

Much had changed in a year.

31

As Devon's June 9 birthday approached—the day she would've turned twenty—her mother, Melody, unpacked the items amassed from the memorial that had started growing at the canal museum in the days after Devon's death a year ago. The memorial had been a stirring testament to just how many people she'd touched in her short lifetime, and the eclectic array of mementos was worth cherishing. Construction at the canal museum last summer had caused the Guzmans to move the memorial from the riverbank location to her mother's house on Ferry Street, where it was arranged outside the house so those who missed Devon could still pay her a remembrance. When winter came, Melody packed up the memorial for safekeeping from the elements, but fair weather's return provided an occasion to rebuild the memorial anew in front of the home, in a blossoming flower bed, attended by angel figurines keeping watch over a photo of Devon and a plaque with her name.

Family and friends told a reporter doing a story on the upcoming anniversary of her death that Devon remained in their daily thoughts. They were learning that life goes on, but so does the longing.

After such a terrible loss, people have to find things to keep them going. Each person has to find his or her own reasons to get out of bed each day and to keep going on with life. For some who were mourning Devon, the upcoming trial became the thing that propelled them into each tomorrow, supplying the reason to keep going. A year after her death, the desire for justice for Devon remained as powerful as it had been in the early days of the case. One of Devon's cousins, Brian Otto Jr., had gone so far as to have the word "Justice" tattooed on his right arm. The tattoo he was planning for his left arm was going to say, "In memory of Devon," with a rainbow. "I haven't personally said good-bye," he told a reporter. "I will say good-bye the last day of that trial when the judge says the sentence."

For Melody, it was her son, now a seventeen-year-old sophomore at Easton Area High School, who kept alive her will to live. It was never going to be easy watching videos and seeing her daughter as she was in life, so vibrant and animated. It raised the slowly sinking sorrow, anger and hatred right back up to the surface. But at least she'd made some peace with her feelings of intrusion and soul-scorching self-doubt. "At first, I felt violated," she told a reporter. "What did I do wrong for them to take her life like this? But I didn't do anything wrong, and Devon didn't do anything wrong." She had learned not to put the blame in the wrong place and to see the past in a clearer light. "Michelle pursued Devon," she said. "She was always after her."

During a drawn-out hearing on pretrial motions on Tuesday, June 19, 2001, Michelle's attorney Brian Monahan brought up the fact that three bloodstains documented in the evidence turned over by prosecutors—one on a doorknob, another on a fence at the couple's home and the third in Devon's car—didn't match the defendants or the victim. He used the fact to support an assertion that "the one or two people who committed this crime are still at large."

District Attorney John Morganelli countered that the unidentified blood could've come from anyone at any time unrelated to the crime and "doesn't tell us anything." He accused Monahan of "trying to create pretrial diversions" and derided the suggestion that the "real killer" was still out there somewhere as a tactic straight out of the O. J. Simpson case.

"This is an O.J. defense—that the real killer is at large. I think we have the real killers in their cages right now," the DA told the press. Referring to Monahan's defense strategy, he said, "If that's the best he's got, he's losing."

Devon's aunt Esther Schoeneberger, too, mocked the suggestion that Devon's real killer was still at large, in an emphatic and indignant letter to the *Express-Times*.

"Here we go again! Murder suspects who swear they are innocent and defense attorneys who believe the 'real killers' are still at large," she wrote. "I hope the defense attorneys don't try to turn this into a three-ring circus." The letter cataloged the evidence and circumstances that pointed to the couple's guilt. After that, she wrote from the heart about the emotional toll the loss of her niece exacted on the family. "This criminal act took from us a beautiful, caring young woman who loved her family, friends and her life! Every time I saw Devon, she was always happy! Her warm effervescent personality was contagious! I will always remember her with a smile on my face and a tear in my eye. Her death created a tremendous void in so many lives. We can visit her grave and her memorial. We can treasure our photographs and memories. We can hold her in our hearts, though we can no longer hold her in our arms."

On Tuesday, July 3, Brian Monahan filed a memorandum seeking to be permitted to call Joseph Corpora, the attorney Brandon had consulted about divorcing his wife, as a defense witness to show that "such acrimony" existed between the newlyweds that they could not possibly have orchestrated and carried out a murder together.

It was an intriguing point, and one of the more intractable mysteries faced by those trying to unravel the knot of psychological factors behind the deadly love triangle. In the lead-up to the murder, Michelle was looking to run off with Devon, and Brandon was serious enough about divorcing Michelle that he'd compiled a list of what had to be done to disentangle his life and finances from hers. He'd also sat down with a lawyer to talk about legally ending his marriage.

How would such a complete about-face have happened so quickly that suddenly the two could have become partners in crime? The question was particularly puzzling regarding Brandon, less so for Michelle. Michelle had always gone back and forth between Brandon and Devon, so it seemed natural that if Devon had rejected her that fateful night, Michelle would turn back to her husband. But what would cause Brandon to abandon plans for divorce suddenly and embrace an alliance with Michelle? An alliance fierce enough to stay intact through the commission of a murder, the disposal of a body and the cover-up of the crime, not to mention arrest and incarceration. More than one person had characterized Michelle as a manipulator, but was she so persuasive that she could've turned her older, highly intelligent and college-educated spouse so completely around in such a

Even as a child playing in the bath, Devon Guzman's personality sparkled. *(Photo by Rick Guzman)*

A portrait photo captures young Devon's pensive side.

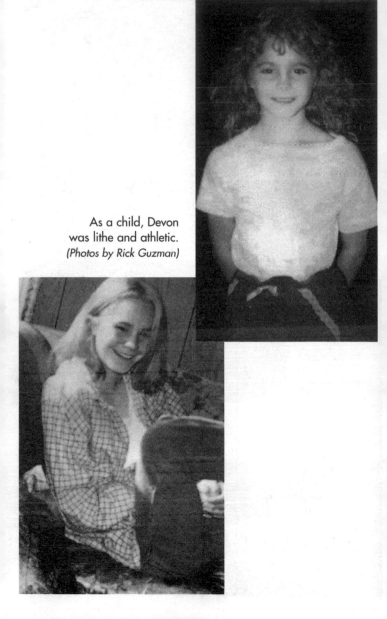

As a child, Devon was lithe and athletic. *(Photos by Rick Guzman)*

Michelle Hetzel *(above)* and Devon Guzman were classmates at Easton Area High School.
(Yearbook photos)

Keary Dehaven and
Michelle Hetzel.
(Yearbook photos)

Devon Guzman, photographed at the Forks of the Delaware. *(Photo by Rick Guzman)*

The riverside hotel and tavern where Devon and Keary became roommates after high school. *(Author's photo)*

MINERAL SPRINGS HOTEL

A scenic view at the Forks, where Devon's murder was staged to look like something else. *(Author's photo)*

Police arrived to find Devon's car parked at the scenic Forks of the Delaware.

Officials peering into the car at the crime scene did not know
if the death was a suicide or homicide.
(Photo by Bruce Winter, courtesy of the Express-Times*)*

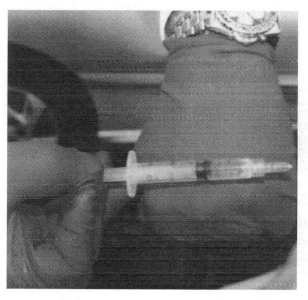

A syringe filled with an unidentifiable substance found on
the victim's body became key evidence.

Railroad bridges around which police searched for a murder weapon. *(Author's photo)*

Michelle Hetzel's Honda Accord in police impound.
A set of bloody men's clothes and four rubber gloves
were stowed in the trunk.

Police searched Michelle Hetzel and Brandon Bloss's house and yard, collecting pet hairs and other trace evidence for forensic analysis.

Bandages bearing the imprint of a bite mark turned up in the suspects' trash.

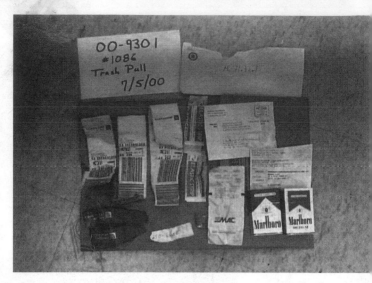

Airline luggage tags found in the trash indicated the suspects vacationed in Mexico after the crime.

The wound on Brandon Bloss's left forearm helped provide grounds for his arrest.

Michelle and Brandon awaited trial in cells behind the fortress-like façade of Northampton County Jail. *(Author's photo)*

Brandon Bloss
(Photo by Ken White, courtesy of the Express-Times)

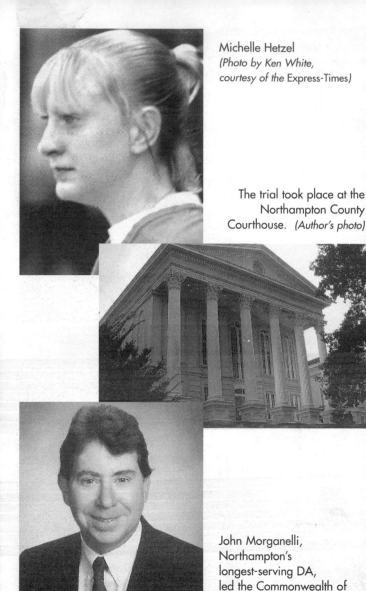

Michelle Hetzel
(Photo by Ken White, courtesy of the Express-Times*)*

The trial took place at the Northampton County Courthouse. *(Author's photo)*

John Morganelli, Northampton's longest-serving DA, led the Commonwealth of Pennsylvania's prosecution.

Much testimony focused on the incriminating bite mark.

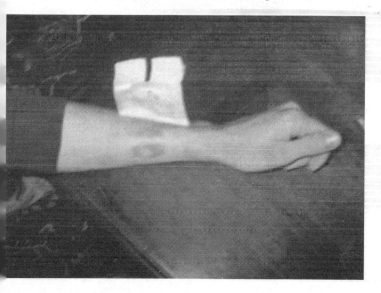

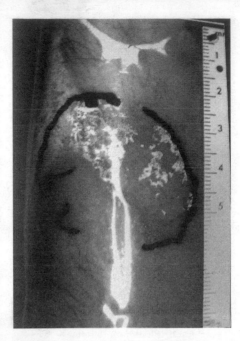

A close-up and measurement of Brandon's injury.

A forensic odontologist's tracing of the bite injury.

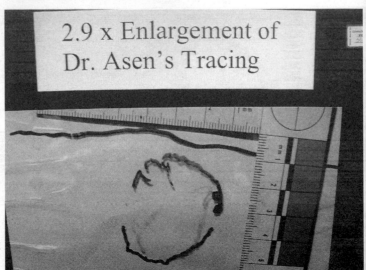

2.9 x Enlargement of Dr. Asen's Tracing

A mold of Devon's posthumously obtained bite pattern matched the injury on Brandon's arm.

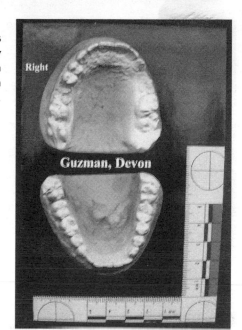

The syringe and pager found on Devon's body were among the evidence presented to the jury.
(Author's photo)

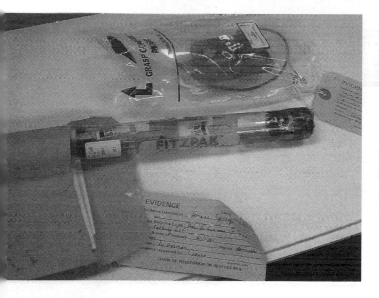

Evidence also included a water sample from Michelle and Brandon's washing machine containing traces of blood.
(Author's photo)

Express-Times reporter Rudy Miller followed up post-conviction claims by Michelle's family that she was too delicate to have committed murder. *(Author's photo)*

short time? What could she possibly have said or done to reenlist his loyalty?

Perhaps the night of the murder is when Michelle chose to play the pregnancy card to maximum effect. Perhaps this was a last-ditch ploy to keep from losing at once both the woman she loved and the man she'd married. If so, it was a claim that just might have activated his sense of responsibility and natural protective instincts. Brandon's history proved him to be a responsible young man. He took his obligations seriously. Could an appeal to this side of his personality have been the key to convincing him to abandon his plan for divorce and enlist his participation in solving the impediment that Devon presented to their having a happy marriage?

When Michelle got home from Rick Guzman's that night and slumped on the couch complaining that she felt sick, had she told Brandon that it was because of her pregnancy? Would that have been enough to ignite Brandon's sense of fidelity and responsibility sufficiently that he would agree to do something about Devon, the one he saw as sabotaging his marriage? Only Brandon and Michelle knew the answer.

Devon's family and friends watched the case closely as the defense attorneys filed their various pretrial motions in June and July. In early July, Brandon's attorney made a motion to suppress the clothes and gloves found in Michelle's car on the grounds that they were personal items protected by Brandon's right to a legitimate expectation of privacy. It was a long shot, with little chance of the evidence being excluded in court.

Devon's aunt Esther summed up the feeling of many in a letter to the *Express-Times* in which she wrote: "OK, enough is enough. As their trial date looms closer,

Brandon Bloss and Michelle Hetzel are grasping at straws to make themselves look innocent. What they are doing is making themselves and their attorneys look ridiculous!"

The final development of the summer in the Bloss/Hetzel case took place in the last days of July and first days of August, when Judge Jack Panella issued rulings on the pretrial motions that had been made by the defense and countered by the DA in filings throughout the spring and summer. He denied defense requests to move the trial out of Northampton County on the grounds that press coverage had been inflammatory, saying that he'd found the coverage factual and objective. He also denied a request for separate trials, saying that the high cost of trying the defendants separately outweighed their interests in having separate trials and that Michelle's defense team failed to support their argument that a joint trial would prejudice her. He declared that prosecutors could present the bloody clothes and rubber gloves found in the trunk of Michelle's Accord, but that Keary Renner's inconclusive polygraph would not be admissible at trial.

The rulings settled the last of the issues that had to be decided before the case could go to court. Once that bit of business was complete, the stifling weeks of August ticked away quietly in the Northampton County Courthouse. The last month of summer was a popular time for court officials to take vacations.

32

Jury selection began on Monday, September 10, 2001, in Jack Panella's courtroom. It had been a month since the newspapers reported on the case, and the *Express-Times* prepared them for the trial reporting ahead by reminding them of this "tale of love and betrayal among three women and a man."

Panella's small courtroom, in a corner of the courthouse, felt smaller than usual, jammed as it was with a large pool of potential jurors, two defendants, five defense attorneys, the DA and an ADA. The two defendants appeared that day in conservative dress and similar color schemes. Brandon Bloss was escorted into the courtroom wearing dark pants, a white shirt and a tie. One of his attorneys fixed his collar before the proceedings began. Michelle Hetzel arrived in a black skirt and white turtleneck. Typical of their previous court appearances, the pair exchanged no acknowledgements. Michelle spoke here and there with attorney Scomillio, while Brandon leafed through papers on the table before him and watched the faces of the potential jurors closely.

As jury selection took place, Melody Guzman told an *Express-Times* reporter that many family members had flown into town and were standing by to witness the trial. The road to justice for Devon had been a long one, and her family was determined to see it through to the end. But the eve of the trial evoked mixed feelings.

"I've been waiting for this so long, but now that it's here, I'm scared," Melody was quoted. The prospect of sitting through the presentation of all the agonizing details of her daughter's death was daunting.

Jury selection normally ended by 4:30 in the afternoon, but not today. Instead, Judge Panella decided to keep going into the evening in hopes of getting a jury picked today rather than going into the following day. At 6:30 P.M., the process was completed. Sixteen candidates—eleven women and five men—had been chosen to serve as jurors and alternate jurors. The painstaking selection process had narrowed a pool of seventy-five prospects to the final sixteen. Some of the prospective jurors had said that they could not be impartial given the alternative sexual orientations involved, and were excused. But overall, the selection had gone well; originally two days had been set aside to assemble a jury, since it had taken only one, the trial could start a day sooner. It would be held in the larger courtroom of another judge to accommodate the number of parties involved. Morganelli told the judge he might call as many as thirty-two witnesses. It was expected that the trial could last up to three weeks.

The District Attorney was ready, certain that Detective Golazeski had delivered the goods to convict the couple. "Barry Golazeski is a good investigator. I had a lot of confidence in his abilities," he said. "I felt we had a good case."

Still, it was a circumstantial-evidence case, with no eyewitnesses and no confessions. "It was not the strongest case I ever tried," Morganelli admitted. "It had some holes in it."

His primary concern was this: "I was not able to say to the jury who did this." The evidence pointed in conflicting directions. "The forensic evidence seemed to suggest that Bloss was holding her and cut her throat and she bit him," the DA said. "And yet we had this other witness that said that Hetzel had said that she had killed her." This presented a prosecutorial dilemma. "On the one hand, we could argue that Bloss did it; on the other hand, we had her saying to Cara Judd, 'I'm the one who cut her throat.'"

It was up to Morganelli to figure out how to argue the issue in front of the newly chosen jury. "I knew from the outset that I could not establish exactly who did it," he said. So the question going into trial was: "How do I tell the jury about this in a way that makes sense?"

At the county courthouse, the DA had just completed his opening remarks in the Bloss/Hetzel murder trial when stricken-looking court officers hastily ushered Judge Panella from his bench into chambers, along with the attorneys present. Those in the courtroom were told to stay seated and keep quiet.

Many of Devon's family members and supporters had arrived in court that morning wearing the purple ribbons that had become a symbol of their unity throughout the long road to this day. Now, however, the ribbons were no longer in evidence in the gallery, since the judge had told them they'd have to remove them due to a state law that prohibited such demonstrations in front of a jury. Devon's family and the Hetzel and Bloss families were situated on opposite sides of the courtroom, and the two sides were careful to avoid contact, both during this strange interruption and prior to it. Morganelli's opening remarks had caused tears on Devon's side of the courtroom. Now everyone sat calmly, waiting.

* * *

Lehigh Valley International Airport (LVIA) is near enough to the New York metropolitan area to be considered part of New York airspace, so when the Federal Aviation Administration shut down New York airspace on Tuesday morning, the opening day of trial, people at LVIA were among the first to know that something had gone monumentally amiss.

All outgoing flights were either outright canceled or indefinitely delayed, as the airport went into lockdown. When flights would resume was the last question on anyone's mind. The first was: *what in the world is going on?*

A pilot on one diverted flight had announced to passengers that he'd received unconfirmed reports of a terrorist attack. The flight had been headed to LaGuardia Airport in the borough of Queens, eight miles from midtown Manhattan, when it was diverted west, away from the city. Passengers scanning the New York skyline saw the World Trade Center smoldering, smoke streaming from it "like a pennant in the wind," one woman told an *Express-Times* reporter.

Meanwhile, reports came in from area commuters who were traveling by car to New York City and had turned back, and from those who were already in the city when Armageddon appeared to have struck. They called home with breathless, shell-shocked reports describing the panic, mayhem and mass confusion that were beginning to seize the city. Many of them did not yet know that they had become witnesses to what soon would be declared an act of war, on a date that would never sit peacefully in the American collective consciousness again: September 11.

In Easton, city hall closed, the mayor fled to an undisclosed location and the city's public-safety director took over as acting mayor. Hospitals cleared beds in preparation for whatever carnage had taken place or might still come. Blood centers put out a call for donations, and houses of worship issued calls for prayers. Schools were staying open, at least until parents could arrive to pick up their children, but public buildings were being evacuated and closed at the suggestion of Pennsylvania governor Tom Ridge. Police cruisers cut off an access to the city parking deck because a suspicious package had been reported at the Crayola Factory, where crayon maker Binney & Smith gave tours to multitudes of children, parents and teachers each year. The Crayola Factory closed at 11:30 A.M., and twelve hundred employees were sent home from the nearby Binney & Smith plant after a bomb scare there.

When Panella reemerged from chambers, he somberly announced that Governor Ridge had ordered an evacuation of all state buildings because of terrorist attacks in New York and Washington, D.C. "The courthouse is being closed by the order of the governor, but I want it to be clear that no threats have been made here," he said.

The words weren't very reassuring to those assembled, who had no idea of what was going on in the outside world. Panella told the jurors that an officer of the court would call each of them that night regarding when the trial would resume. As the bewildered assemblage filed out of the courtroom at 11:15 A.M., clustering outside the building as news of the terrorist strikes spread by word of mouth, Detective Golazeski packed up the prosecution's hard-won evidence and removed it from the courthouse for safekeeping.

The trial resumed the following morning, Wednesday, September 12, at 9:00 A.M., but there was one word on everyone's mind: mistrial. The day before, attorney Szachacz had tried unsuccessfully for four stressful hours to reach his father, a Long Island native who worked in

Manhattan. He understood firsthand the strain many people were feeling. Would the jurors be able to concentrate on the case? It was a fair question.

Brandon's attorneys were itching to ask for a mistrial, but Brian Monahan, Michelle's attorney, beat them to the punch, making the request as soon as the proceedings began. Panella denied it. Federal officials had been exhorting all Americans to keep going about their business so as not to let the terror strikes shut the country down, and that's just what the judge intended to do.

As the morning progressed, however, it was becoming clear that, like it or not, the national crisis reached right into that very courtroom. If the trial went forward as scheduled, one of the prosecution's key witnesses, forensic odontologist Richard Scanlon, might be unavailable to testify. He'd been summoned to use his dental expertise to help identify victims in the Flight 93 plane crash in Somerset County, Pennsylvania. (Flight 93 was the one that had been brought down by heroic passengers and crew members while en route to an attack on the nation's capital. Scanlon was a volunteer member of the Disaster Mortuary Operational Response Team, a group that helps find remains and identify bodies in federal disaster areas. The team identified twelve of the forty-four passengers on that flight, four of whom were terrorists.) Coroner Zachary Lysek was also among the experts on call, should his assistance be needed.

At noon, a second request for a mistrial was made, with defense attorneys joining together on the grounds that the jury would be unable to focus on the case. Morganelli said he'd go along with the request as long as it meant a delay of no more than a few weeks. If it was going to be months before a new trial could be held, he was afraid he'd lose witnesses.

Panella agreed to grant a mistrial. It was the first time

in three years that he'd done so, and the first time ever in a homicide case. Announcing his decision to the jury, he said he was "reluctant to grant this motion because I didn't want the terrorist acts to shut us down."

Michelle Hetzel turned back to where her family was seated, a broad smile on her face. On the other side of the courtroom, several people broke down in frustration. Devon's mother wept. It was yet another heart-wrenching delay on the seemingly interminable road to justice.

33

The September 11 terror strikes had forced a mistrial, amounting to another delay in the pursuit of justice for Devon Guzman, but this time the delay would be short. Even as the dismissed jurors made their way home, efforts were under way to assemble a new jury for a second trial. Within days, about eighty potential jurors would receive notice to appear on Monday, September 24, for jury selection. In the interim Brandon's Florida attorneys planned to return home to visit their families. They told reporters that even if air travel resumed, they'd probably play it safe and rent a car to get them home.

A new sense of tolerance and civic duty sparked by the rebirth of patriotism after 9/11 was immediately evident during jury selection on September 24. The first time around, a number of prospective jurors were dismissed because they answered they could not be impartial regarding lesbianism and bisexuality. This time no one voiced a problem with the issue. Before the day was out, a jury of seven women and five men had been seated. Three women and one man were chosen for the pool of alternates. Tomorrow the trial would begin.

* * *

Before the new trial got under way in front of the jury on Tuesday morning, September 25, counsel met in Judge Panella's chambers adjacent to the courtroom. This included DA John Morganelli and ADA Teresa Miranda; Easton attorneys Brian Monahan and Victor Scomillio, the defense lawyers for Michelle Hetzel; Keith Szachaz and Kepler Funk, who were Brandon's Florida lawyers; and Robert Sletvold, the local attorney advising Brandon's out-of-state team.

A second matter had to be addressed before the trial could begin in earnest. One of the jurors, a real estate agent, had gone home the night before and made phone calls to cancel some upcoming appointments, telling her clients she was going to be serving jury duty. One client asked if she'd been picked for the Bloss/Hetzel case. The juror said she wasn't allowed to talk about it, but asked if the client had a direct relation to the case. It turned out that her client was Michelle Hetzel's sister. It was a connection she had been unaware of throughout the jury-picking process. Now that the connection had been brought to light, Panella had little choice but to dismiss her. A woman from the pool of alternates was selected to replace her. The trial had yet to begin, and already the number of alternates had been reduced to three.

One last matter remained to be addressed. Attorney Funk asked Panella if he'd had a chance to have a "heart-to-heart" with Rick Guzman. Brandon's attorneys were fearful after the close call at the preliminary hearing.

"Is he present today?" Panella asked.

Funk answered, "He is, and he's making looks at—"

Panella cut him off, asking Morganelli to send two deputy sheriffs to bring Rick Guzman in. The attorneys exited, leaving the judge alone for the ensuing conversation.

Rick Guzman remembered this occasion well. He recalled that the two deputies approached him as he waited for the trial to start.

"Judge wants to see you," he was told.

"Well, maybe I don't want to see him, OK?" he replied, or at least that's what he remembered thinking.

"He just wants to talk to you," he was assured.

One deputy on each side, they led him out of the courtroom and into Panella's chambers. "I walked in, and I remember the door closing behind me," he said. The two deputies were still beside him, like bodyguards. It was an intimidating situation, but the judge's disarming manner proved relaxing.

"He went over this thing about when I attacked—well, went after, which I didn't get but half a step," Rick said, referring to how he charged at Brandon at the preliminary.

The conversation was a necessary precaution on the judge's part. With one mistrial having occurred already, every measure had to be taken to avoid another.

"Mr. Guzman, I need your help to get through this trial," Panella said. "I can't have any type of behavior in the courtroom. We don't want to come back and have to do this again. The district attorney's office is well-prepared and ready to try the case. Because of what happened, what was it, at the preliminary hearing—and you know I fully understand and sympathize with your emotions—if there were any type of outbursts or anything in the courtroom, the defense attorneys will jump right on that and ask for a mistrial. So I really need your cooperation. I have got to get through this trial. The commonwealth has all of its witnesses subpoenaed, doctors coming in from out of town, a mistrial would cause a major problem for them. So I really need your help."

"You got it, Your Honor," Rick said.

He kept his word. The remainder of the legal pro-

ceedings would take place without another incident like
the one at the preliminary.

Under the state's rules of criminal procedure, the attorney for the Commonwealth of Pennsylvania makes
the first opening statement, and so Judge Panella called
upon District Attorney John Morganelli to begin. Next
would come Michelle's defense team, followed by Brandon's, and this would be the turn-taking order throughout the trial.

The opening remarks not only gave the jurors a feel for
the attorneys, but also a hint at the prosecution and defense strategies, and clues as to where the weak points on
each side of the courtroom lay. As had come to be expected of Michelle and Brandon during court proceedings, the couple exchanged neither acknowledgements
nor eye contact.

Morganelli stepped forward to put forth the efforts of
his legendary courtroom preparation. Judge Panella had
warned jurors that in a complex case like the one before
them, opening arguments wouldn't be completed in a
mere ten minutes, as they are on TV dramas. He was right.
Morganelli took a good portion of the morning painstakingly laying out a detailed overview of the crime, the evidence that had been collected and the witnesses who
would testify in the days to come—a road map, as it were,
of the prosecution's case.

"In the early afternoon of Thursday, June 15, 2000,
Devon Guzman, a nineteen-year-old girl, was found dead
in the backseat of her own vehicle while it was parked in
the parking-lot area of the canal museum on Route 611 in
Easton," the DA began. "Ms. Guzman's body was discovered
with a gaping cut to the neck area, which was delivered with
such force that it not only resulted in her immediate death,
but also severed her jugular vein, her carotid artery and

her tongue, and extended far deep to the back of her neck area."

He said the evidence would show that the two defendants made numerous calls that night "in order to lure Ms. Guzman to their home" in South Side.

"When Ms. Guzman finally showed up at their home with another person with her, Brandon Bloss and Michelle Hetzel would not let her in and insisted that she come back alone," the DA said. "Shortly thereafter, when Ms. Guzman did in fact show up at the Bloss/Hetzel residence a second time, and this time alone, these two defendants, acting together as accomplices and as co-conspirators, killed her. After killing Ms. Guzman, they placed her in the rear seat of her own vehicle and drove the vehicle with the dead body of Devon Guzman in it to the canal museum parking lot, where they left it to be discovered later that day."

It was a very basic summation of a very complex case.

Before continuing, he prepared the jury for the fact that they would be hearing about lifestyles that were likely a far cry from their own, and asserted that forces arising within that lifestyle led to murder. "You're going to hear about a number of individuals whose lifestyles are far different from all of you. You're going to hear about and you're going to meet individuals who were involved in a sexual love triangle involving lesbianism and bisexual sex. You're going to hear from the evidence how the jealousies and the anger that arose from these relationships led to the murder of Devon Guzman on June 15, 2000."

The DA had prepared a poster-board depiction of the complex relationships involved, and he took pains to explain them in depth to the jury. Against a bright orange background was depicted the love triangle, with the names, Brandon Bloss and Michelle Hetzel listed at the top, Keary Renner in the lower right corner, and Devon Guzman in the lower left.

"You're going to hear from the evidence that these two girls were pulling the victim in different directions. Ms. Guzman was living with Keary Renner, but Michelle Hetzel wanted to increase her relationship with Ms. Guzman beyond the sexual relationship that it was. At the same time, ladies and gentlemen, you're going to hear that Brandon Bloss disliked Devon Guzman. You're going to hear that the lesbian relationship between his wife, Michelle Hetzel, and the victim was interfering with his marriage. And you're going to hear that there were numerous arguments at the Bloss/Hetzel residence between Michelle Hetzel and her husband, Brandon Bloss, and that these arguments were related to the fact that Michelle Hetzel was often leaving her husband and going out and running around with her girlfriend, Devon Guzman. These arguments became more frequent and more intense in the days just prior to June 15, 2000, when Devon Guzman was murdered.

"It is the contention of the commonwealth in this case that it was this love triangle between these three girls and the disruption that this was causing Brandon Bloss and his marriage to explode on June 15, 2000, leading both Michelle and her husband to the common design and common goal of getting rid of a problem, which was Devon Guzman." He had just spelled out the motive, which certainly wasn't the most clear-cut or succinctly articulated aspect of the case.

Morganelli held the attention of the courtroom as he walked through the events leading up to the murder, step by step, until the time of Devon's disappearance. He said the defendants admitted that they had summoned her to their home that night, and that when she arrived with Keary they told her to return alone. What they did not admit was that Devon had returned that night.

"Bloss and Hetzel say that she never ever came back again," Morganelli said. "That's what they told the police." But "the scientific and physical evidence that was found in this case will establish that their statements that Devon Guzman never showed up again were fabrications and lies.

"The scientific and physical evidence, ladies and gentlemen, began to develop pretty early in the case, and you're going to hear that Michelle Hetzel and Brandon Bloss killed Devon Guzman sometime when she did show up again alone. . . . You're going to hear that Michelle Hetzel and Brandon Bloss tried to act, they tried to cover up their involvement in this case by pretending that they didn't know where Devon Guzman was. And you're going to hear that they pretended to try to look for Devon Guzman."

But Morganelli suggested that Michelle made a critical miscalculation in carrying out the ruse to find Devon, when she pulled her car into the parking lot of the canal museum, right behind the victim's car. Because it was considered part of the crime scene, police had it in their custody from the time the body was found.

"Now, that establishes that the statements given to the state police that Ms. Guzman never came back after she left [at] twelve-thirty, never showed up again, cannot possibly be true, because the blood of the victim was on the clothes of Brandon Bloss in the trunk of Michelle's car when the police searched that car."

The DA outlined some of the other crime scene evidence jurors could expect, including phone records and testimony about calls from the Bloss/Hetzel home that someone had taken pains to selectively erase from Devon's pager. He pointed out that the couple's number did not appear even once in her pager's memory, although phone records indicted they'd paged her fifteen times that night. The only way to erase the calls was all at once or selectively, one by one.

Brandon and Michelle "wanted to make sure that their pages from their home didn't show up on her pager when they placed her body along with that syringe thing in the car," the DA maintained.

Even as the evidence mounted against the couple, Morganelli said the lead cop on the case thoroughly exhausted every avenue of investigation as well. Pointing out Detective Barry Golazeski to the jurors, he said, "You're going to hear that the primary investigator, that man, Barry Golazeski, was not satisfied. He continued to investigate every possible lead and checked out other individuals and ran down every lead. And the evidence continued to come back to Michelle Hetzel and Brandon Bloss."

This led to closer scrutiny for evidence, including sifting through the couple's trash, which is legally considered abandoned property and not subject to privacy protection. In that trash the bandages suggesting that Brandon had suffered a bite injury turned up, giving police the right to photograph Brandon's injuries and bring the photos to a forensic dentist, Dennis Asen, for further analysis.

"Those photographs are taken back to Dr. Asen, and Dr. Asen says, 'Yeah, those are bite marks.' He also says, 'You know, that guy looks familiar and he was here a week earlier and I think I have photographed those bite marks myself.' The fact of the matter was that by coincidence, Brandon Bloss went a week earlier to Dr. Asen's office to have him analyze these bite marks, for whatever reason, and Dr. Asen had taken photographs."

An objection from Brandon's table interrupted the flow. In a sidebar with the judge, Keith Szachacz moved for a mistrial. He argued that Morganelli had violated a pretrial ruling regarding the disclosure of when Dr. Asen became aware of Brandon and his bite mark.

Morganelli defended himself. Panella listened to the arguments and sided with the DA. The judge said his understanding of the pretrial ruling was that Morganelli could mention that fact that Brandon had been to see Asen on his own, but could not go into what his reasons were for doing so. That put the issue to rest for the moment, but the matter of Asen's involvement was a sticky one and would remain so, since Brandon had consulted him before the police did.

Morganelli picked up where he left off, detailing the bite mark and how prosecutors believed it linked back to a fatal struggle and the final moments of Devon's life. "The commonwealth will contend to you at the end of this case that that's how Devon Guzman was killed, that Brandon Bloss got that injury on his arm when Devon Guzman was attacked. She got off one last bite to defend herself, and then her throat was cut."

Morganelli began to sum up his introductory remarks, saying that the commonwealth would present its case, piece by piece. "It is a puzzle. It is a puzzle, however, that can be solved. . . .

"You're going to hear that although Devon Guzman could not speak when her neck was cut that day, her last act did speak for itself, her last bite was imprinted, the bite mark, on the forearm of Brandon Bloss.

"Ladies and gentlemen, the intense love/hate relationship that prompted Hetzel to solicit to kill this woman months earlier when they went to see George Vine and the disruption that was being caused to the marriage of Brandon Bloss by the relationship of Devon Guzman together formed the common motive in this case on this evening," Morganelli concluded.

"The commonwealth's evidence will establish, ladies and gentlemen, that these defendants acted together both before and after in luring Devon to the home, killing her, moving her body and placing it where it was and then lying to the police about that she never showed up. The commonwealth's evidence will show that they acted as accomplices and as co-conspirators, and that they committed first-degree murder."

When Morganelli had finished, the judged turned the floor over to Michelle's attorneys. Victor Scomillio elected to make the opening remarks. "Ladies and gentlemen, today you are asked to decide if this young lady killed her best friend, her only friend, and yes, ladies and gentlemen, her lover," Scomillio began, echoing Michelle's frequent claim that Devon had indeed been her only friend. "We submit that the evidence will not show that she either killed or conspired with somebody to kill her best friend, because the evidence cannot show that, ladies and gentlemen. And it's simple—the evidence cannot show that, because she didn't do it. Nothing fancy, ladies and gentlemen, she didn't do it."

Scomillio felt it appropriate to warn the jury they would hear about "a different type of lifestyle," just as the DA had done. "You will hear about different types of romantic relations. You will hear about marital infidelity."

Then he began to sow the first, tiny seeds of doubt, urging the jury to take neither the DA at his word nor the evidence at face value. "Ladies and gentlemen," Scomillio said, "you will also have to decide about what you do not hear, what the Commonwealth does not prove, what the Commonwealth does not tell you, because, ladies and gentlemen, sometimes that speaks louder than what they do tell you."

He likened the jury's duty to test-driving a new car. "You go to buy a car. The guy says that this car has great pickup.

What do you do? You get in the car and you drive it, you take it for a test-drive. That's the same process that you have to go through here today and for the remainder of this trial. Don't accept anything at face value."

Scomillio knew the prosecution's case was going to contain some connect-the-dots scenarios. Gaps remained, and the DA was not going to be able to bridge every one of them; he would count on the jury to connect the dots. The defense attorney, on the other hand, urged them to refrain from doing so.

"Do not assume any facts or evidence," he said. "Do not assume that things link up. You're not allowed to speculate as a juror. Your job is to decide from the evidence that you hear. You will hear theories of motives. I ask you to look at the actions of Michelle Hetzel. Are they the actions of a killer? Are they the actions of somebody who conspired with somebody to kill? Once, again, ladies and gentlemen, I submit you will not hear evidence to prove that theory."

To convict of first-degree murder, jurors would have to find that Michelle harbored two things. "You would have to find that Michelle Hetzel had a specific intent to kill her best friend. The law puts another element for murder, malice. We've all heard it. It's a wickedness of heart and emptiness of heart, a depravity for the actions of the person. You have to find both."

Scomillio spoke to the charge of conspiracy. "You have to find an agreement between two people to do one act. Each party to that conspiracy must have the specific intent to kill. There has to be an agreement."

Then he mentioned the knife incident between Keary and Devon after Devon and Michelle returned from the Caribbean, expressing misgivings about Keary's explanation. "They come back to Easton and there's an incident. Devon tells Keary, 'I'm going to leave you.' Keary gets a knife and Devon is cut on her hand and has to go to the hospital. Keary will tell you that Devon tried to stop Keary from killing herself and that's how the cut came about. We don't know. Keary is the only one who can testify about that."

He was hitting on a familiar theme, pointing the finger at the roommate. He next pointed to Morganelli's love triangle. "Think about the motives here and this triangle that's been depicted for you. Where do the intense passions really lie, ladies and gentlemen?"

Scomillio characterized the interactions between Michelle and Devon at Devon's father's house on June 14 as "palling around," followed by a "disagreement about Devon and Keary still living together." No physical contact was observed. He contrasted this with what took place with Keary when Devon returned home and admitted she'd been with Michelle.

"The two get into a fight. They pull hair. They throw bottles at each other. They slap each other. They hold each other's wrists. They punch each other. This fight is so loud that people in the Mineral Springs Hotel and in other rooms and in the bar below hear it."

Scomillio went on to recap the rest of the night, from when "Brandon Bloss calls and asks Devon to go to his house" to all of the steps Michelle and Keary took to find their missing friend. He completely sidestepped the issue of whether Devon ever returned to the Bloss/Hetzel house alone after being sent away with Keary. Instead, he emphasized all the searching they did for Devon, recounting how they were the ones who found her body.

"Keary will say that Michelle said, 'I could kill her' as soon as she sees the car," he maintained. "Ask yourselves, if she had killed Devon, if she had conspired to kill Devon, would she say that 'I could kill her' when she sees the car?"

Referring to the bloody clothes found in the trunk of Michelle's car, he urged the jury, "Ask yourselves, what wasn't found there? No jeans, T-shirt, underwear, socks, shoes, sweatshirt from Michelle Hetzel. It's all Mr. Bloss's items in the trunk."

He refuted other pieces of evidence in a similar vein: the syringe cap that found in Michelle's jeans, which were soaking in the washing machine two days after the murder. "There's no evidence of how those jeans got there. There's no evidence of how the cap was found in the jeans." Yes, the cap was there, he admitted. "But who placed it there?"

He continued on at some length, hinting at alternate explanations for the evidence that could not be denied and casting doubt in advance on the various witnesses expected to offer testimony detrimental to his client.

"We contend that the evidence will show that Michelle and Devon were friends and were involved in a lesbian relationship, and nothing else," he said, nearing the end of his remarks. He asserted that Michelle's marriage was breaking up, and Keary and Devon were similarly breaking up, and that Michelle therefore had no motive for murder. She could have been with Devon if she wanted to be.

At the close of his remarks, he told the jury that at the end of the trial, Judge Panella would give them two verdict slips, one for each defendant. "You will be asked two questions with Michelle Hetzel's verdict slip. Did she commit murder in the first degree? Did she conspire with Brandon Bloss to commit murder in the first degree? We submit to you, ladies and gentlemen, that there is only one answer to those questions, and the answer is no, not guilty."

The remaining opening statements were to come from Brandon's defense team. Judge Panella turned the floor over to Keith Szachacz, who kept his remarks brief. It was an indication of the approach to come from Brandon's side of the case.

"He sits here today because of an accusation that has been made against him," Szachacz began, indicating his client seated at the defense table. From the start of his remarks, Szachacz made it clear that Brandon's defense would rely heavily on the presumption of innocence.

He pointed to DA Morganelli and ADA Miranda across the aisle and said that the burden was on them to prove the accusations against Brandon. "He is presumed innocent. And I ask you not to take that lightly. Don't take the presumption of innocence lightly. Don't take it for granted, because when you take things for granted, bad things happen."

Szachacz urged the jury to be wary of accepting theories in place of facts and to be alert for the prosecution's use of the word "contention."

"Contention is another word for theory," he said. "Theories do not overcome the presumption of innocence; facts do."

He next endeavored to divorce Brandon from the love triangle, which was depicted large as life on the orange poster board for all to see.

"This trial is about the story of the lives of Michelle Hetzel, of Devon Guzman, of Keary Renner, of George Vine and another individual that you will learn. This trial will be about Michelle Hetzel. Michelle Hetzel, as you have learned, had a sexual relationship with Devon Guzman. Michelle Hetzel had a sexual relationship with Devon Guzman. Brandon Bloss was not a part of that. Brandon Bloss was not a part of this relationship with Devon. You're going to learn that Michelle Hetzel also had a sexual relationship with Keary Renner. Brandon Bloss was not a part of that, either. You're going to learn about

Devon Guzman, and you're going to learn that she had a sexual relationship with Michelle and she also had a sexual relationship with Keary Renner. Brandon wasn't a part of that. And you're going to learn about Keary Renner. Keary Renner had a sexual relationship with Michelle. In fact, something that you haven't heard yet, Michelle Hetzel and Keary Renner used to live together. They lived together before Devon and Keary did at the same hotel, at Mineral Springs, in the same room. Brandon wasn't a part of that. Brandon didn't live there. Michelle and Keary had a sexual relationship also." (This last statement was something both girls denied.)

After painting Brandon as nothing more than a peripheral figure, Szachacz added George Vine to the top of the triangle, substituting him in Brandon's place at the top of Morganelli's highly visible poster board.

"George Vine goes at the top of this triangle above Michelle Hetzel," Szachacz asserted. "George Vine was a single man in his midthirties who lived alone who knew Michelle Hetzel, knew Devon Guzman and knew Keary Renner. They would—all three of those women would go to his house and party with him. George Vine witnessed arguments between all three of them and fights and shouting matches and screaming and yelling. Brandon Bloss was not a part of that. Brandon Bloss was not a part of the screaming and yelling matches. Ladies and gentlemen, the most reliable evidence and the most powerful evidence that you will hear will be about these players. Brandon Bloss is way off to the side. He's not involved in this triangle."

He next emphasized Brandon's hardworking character, which sounded all the more impressive when juxtaposed against the wild lives of the people he just mentioned—lives he depicted as full of sex, fighting and partying.

Szachacz said that jurors would soon learn that his client was a college graduate with degrees in math and chemistry. "And you're going to learn that he worked at Ashland Chemical. Not only did he work at Ashland Chemical, but he worked a second job at Rice-Ebner. He worked two jobs. You're going to learn that he was gone from five forty-five in the morning until eight or nine at night. That was his life. And you're going to learn that he lived a life separate and apart from his wife. He was not a part of this. Brandon Bloss had no motive. He was not a part of this triangle. He had no motive to do any harm to Devon."

At the end of his remarks, Szachacz was obliged to admit some involvement on Brandon's part on the night of the murder, for that involvement could not be denied—the bite mark had been there on his arm and the bloody clothes existed, and both had to be accounted for.

After the fight at Devon's father's house, "Michelle went home and she wanted Devon to come back over because she knew Devon went to see Keary. So a phone call is made, and Devon comes back over," the attorney said.

He carefully avoided specifying who made that call. Monahan had just asserted that it was Brandon. Morganelli had said it was both Michelle and Brandon.

"And you're going to hear that Devon and Michelle got into a fight in the house, not only a verbal fight but a physical fight, and that Brandon stepped in and came in and saw what was happening. He was not a part of the fight, but he came into the room and saw what was happening. And to protect his wife, who is losing the fight, he pulls Devon off of her in the house in the living room. . . .

"They fall down and Devon bites him in the arm. And after Devon bites him, he asks them, 'Why can't you behave like normal human beings? Why do you have to fight all the time? Why can't you take it somewhere else other than this house?' And he goes into the bathroom to tend to his bite."

It was only after the murder had been committed that Brandon again became involved, according to his attorney. He went outside looking for them and saw what had happened.

"He saw what Michelle did. And he was faced with a dilemma. Devon is dead," he said. "He's faced with a dilemma. We know he doesn't call nine-one-one, because you're not going to hear a nine-one-one tape from Brandon Bloss. What they do is they put Devon in her car, that's how the blood gets on the clothing, which you will see."

Just as prosecutors are not required to supply motive for the accused, the defense need not give a motive for why a defendant did whatever it is he might have done. But the lack of an explanation for why Brandon would have helped dispose of the body of someone he had no part in murdering was a glaring omission. As Szachacz presented Brandon's version of how the murder took place, Michelle Hetzel glanced pointedly at attorney Scomillio and laughed.

In closing, Szachacz told the jurors that it was up to them to determine what the truth was. "The final outcome is not what the police or the prosecutor said, but it's what you see. And after you hear the story, the story that is true and unique, after you hear this unique story, after you hear the testimony from the stand, you will understand that Brandon Bloss did not kill Devon Guzman. You will understand that Brandon Bloss did not conspire to kill Devon Guzman, and you will understand that there was not even any motive for him to do so."

After Szachacz's statement the judge called a recess for lunch. It was about 12:45 P.M. The opening statements had taken up the morning. Panella liked to give about an hour and a half for lunch, so he announced that court would reconvene at 2:15 P.M., and dismissed the jury with a warning not to discuss the case at all. The jurors rose and stretched their legs. Some roamed about the courthouse building and surrounding areas. Smokers headed quickly outside.

As the court went into recess, juror 18 had a pressing issue on his mind. He approached a court officer with his concern. One of the upcoming witnesses was someone he knew.

The issue was the first thing to be discussed when court reconvened after lunch. "You indicated to one of my court officers that you may have now heard a name during the opening statements of someone that you may know?" Panella asked the juror out of hearing of the jury.

"Right."

"Who is that?"

"Cara Judd."

"How do you know Cara Judd?"

"Her parents are my wife's godparents and cousin." It was yet another example of the hardships of trying a big case like this in a tight-knit area like Easton. It seemed that virtually everyone was connected to everyone else somehow, it was only a matter of circumstances bringing those connections to light.

"Do you know her personally?" Panella wanted to know. It had been hard work to put together a panel of qualified jurors, and he wasn't about to dismiss one lightly.

The man said he used to see her at family picnics, but their paths hadn't crossed lately. After a series of questions from the judge and the DA, the juror was dismissed. One of the three remaining alternates would take his place. The first witness had yet to sit in the witness chair, and already the pool of alternate jurors had been reduced by half.

34

Upon returning from a recess following opening statements, Judge Panella turned the courtroom over to John Morganelli, who called the commonwealth's first witness, Easton patrolman David Beitler. After being sworn in, Beitler, the first officer to arrive at the canal museum on June 15, 2000, explained that he had been dispatched to the location just before 1:00 P.M. He described talking to city worker Richard Deemer, along with Keary Renner and Michelle Hetzel. He identified Michelle, seated almost directly in front of him with her attorneys, wearing a black dress.

Beitler stepped down from the stand to point out Devon's car as depicted on Commonwealth Exhibit No. 1, parked facing the Delaware River with the passenger door open. He noticed a female figure in a "cradle position" in the back facing the trunk. There was a green coat or jacket over her body. He noticed what appeared to be grass and mud stains on her lower back, pants and sneakers. He moved the passenger seat forward and checked for a pulse. Then he contacted his supervisor.

Morganelli walked him through a series of nine 3-by-5

photographs depicting the crime scene at the canal museum that day.

Beitler testified that Michelle told him "her friend was missing and they were out looking for her all night." The last time they saw her was at 12:15 A.M. and they'd reported her missing at 3:00 A.M. Morganelli asked the officer to describe Michelle's demeanor. "She was crying and appeared nervous," Beitler said.

Morganelli moved for admission of the nine crime scene photos, and they were passed along for viewing by the jury.

On cross-examination Michelle's attorney Brian Monahan brought out that although the officer had just testified that Michelle appeared nervous, there was nothing in the police report he wrote that day saying as much.

Keith Szachacz's cross was brief and to the point. He noted that Beitler had written in his report that Devon's car had a narrow rainbow decal on the back bumper and asked if the officer had seen something similar on Michelle's Honda. Beitler consulted his report. "Yes, sir, I did," he said.

With that, Beitler was excused. Morganelli had established that a green coat lay over Devon, which was going to be an integral factor later in his case against Michelle, who had given a statement claiming to have seen lots of blood when she first looked in the car. (No blood was visible until after the garment was removed. The prosecution's argument was that she had a preconceived notion of what Devon's body looked like.) He also managed to get in Beitler's opinion that Michelle seemed nervous, though Monahan had scored a point in noting that the opinion was never stated in the officer's report. And Szachacz, in pointing out the matching rainbow stickers—recognized "gay pride" symbols—had begun laying the groundwork for his case that it was Michelle, not Brandon, who had the relationship with Devon and therefore the motive to harm her.

Easton police officer Dominick Marraccini took the stand next. Assigned to the patrol division and working the midnight shift the night of the murder, he had passed through the canal museum twice on routine "business checks" that night. The second time was at 12:45 A.M., and no vehicles were parked there at the time.

His testimony provided half of the information needed to establish the window of time during which Devon's car had to have been left at the Forks. The next witness, Thomas Reinbold, provided the other half. Reinbold, who worked at Easton Plating and Metal Finishing, across Route 611 from the canal museum, testified that when he arrived for work at 3 A.M. on June 15, the car later identified as Devon's gray Sunfire was parked in the lot.

The next two witnesses corroborated the previous testimony. Michael Yudisky, another Easton Plating worker, testified that the Sunfire was there when he arrived for work between 4:30 and 5:00 A.M. Donald Bachman, who worked for the city of Easton's highway department, said that he noticed the car between 8:00 and 8:30 A.M. when he and his crew went to the Forks to prepare a launch area for "Heritage Day" fireworks.

Coroner Zachary Lysek was sworn next. He read off his credentials from his curriculum vitae and was offered by the prosecution as an expert witness, meaning he would not be limited to stating observations, as factual witnesses are, but could also offer professional opinions as well. Before accepting him as an expert witness, Monahan cross-examined Lysek on his credentials, pointing out that he was a lay coroner without a medical degree and telling the judge he would object to any opinion beyond the statutory scope of the coroner's duties. It was just a precautionary move that might allow him to exclude damaging testimony later. Lysek was accepted as an expert witness.

The coroner testified that he had been called to the canal museum on July 15 by Detective Parkansky at about 1:15 P.M. Morganelli went over the nine crime scene photos he'd introduced with his first witness. He emphasized two photos in particular, one in which the green coat covered the body concealing any obvious blood, and another in which the coat had been removed, revealing blood-soaked clothing underneath. Again this was something that would become significant later, when Michelle's reaction to finding Devon's body was examined closely. Lysek testified that he was the one who removed the green coat. He said that no specific injuries were visible until the body was removed from the car. "Once she was removed from the vehicle, I could clearly see that there was a massive gaping laceration or cut wound to her neck," he said.

Morganelli questioned Lysek about his time-of-death determination, which is one of the duties of the corner. He asked Lysek to tell the jury how he would usually go about determining time of death. It wasn't the clear-cut science TV crime dramas often make it out to be.

"We're going to look at rigidity, which is stiffening of the body," Lysek said. "When the person dies, muscles become stiff. It starts with the small muscles of the face, the jaw area and fingers; moves to the larger muscles, wrists, elbows, shoulders, hips, knees and ankle areas. And you could check both left and right side to see if it's equal and also to what extent rigidity is present. The other thing that we look at is lividity. We will look at any type of blood presence or drying of it or lack of blood. We'll look at several other factors, which include the investigative information that was obtained. The investigation is very, very important in determining time of death, because when a person may last have been seen may really narrow down the window of time that we may have in determining the time of death."

All elements considered, Lysek said he narrowed down the time of death to a window that was consistent with Devon's having last been seen alive between midnight and 12:30 A.M. and her car being seen at the canal museum at 3:00 A.M.

Morganelli asked Lysek how he came to his conclusion that Devon wasn't murdered in her vehicle. He answered that the wound she'd suffered would have caused extensive bleeding, yet he found a veritable lack of blood in the car. "That, in itself, was not consistent with the type of injury that she received, so it was common sense that she did not die within that vehicle. It was my opinion that the scene was a staged scene and it was a secondary crime scene, where the death would have had to have occurred at another location."

Other evidence indicated the same thing. "The other piece of evidence that was really grossly obvious was the blood on her back and the clots," the coroner said. "The clots are in an upward pattern, which defies gravity. . . . The body was on the left side, so the blood would run down onto the shirt. The body had to have been laying in another location in that blood for a period of time for the clot to form, for the blood to be absorbed on the clothing in the fashion at which it was."

One of Morganelli's crime scene photos showed a wooden-handled knife in the victim's hand. The DA asked about the knife. Lysek said he removed it before moving the body and examined it closely. It had no obvious blood on it, and appeared to have been placed in the hand in an "unnatural position."

The answers to the next line of inquiry were obvious, but Morganelli was obliged to pursue it. Had Lysek considered the possibility that Devon could have cut her own throat in the car using that knife?

"Yes. That's certainly something that we had to look at and establish whether or not that could have been the case. And in this case here, it certainly was not the case. This wound did not occur to Ms. Guzman in that vehicle, nor could she have done that to herself and put herself in that vehicle without the transfer of a considerable amount of blood."

Morganelli asked if there was any evidence in the car of the kind of blood spatter pattern that would be seen when a person's carotid artery is cut.

"There was no evidence of any blood spatter in the vehicle which would be consistent with arterial spurting if a person's carotid artery is lacerated. There's a lot of pressure there and you would have blood squirting out with great pressure, and you can essentially count how many times a person's heart beats before their heart stops for lack of blood by that pattern, and there just wasn't any pattern of blood in this vehicle."

So how did Lysek explain the presence of the knife?

"I personally feel that the knife was staged. I think it was just placed there by someone else."

"What do you mean by staging?" the DA asked.

"When we're looking at a crime scene, we're looking at whether or not it's a primary scene, where the death occurred, or if it's a secondary scene or if somebody moved the body and put the body in a place other than where the death occurred. And, in this case here, there was no evidence that would support that the death occurred here, so it's a staged scene. Somebody would have moved the body, put it in that position to make it look like something it was not."

In addition to the position of the knife and the lack of blood in the car, a third piece of evidence supported that conclusion.

"There was a Motorola pager, which was also in a kind of unnatural position. Most people wear their pager clipped on the belt or pants in some fashion. And this was essentially pushed under the waistband and it was pushing the underwear down. The pager did not go on top of the underwear or beneath it. It just kind of pushed it, which certainly was not how somebody would wear it. The clip was not fastened to anything."

Adjacent to the pager, Lysek said, he'd found a Terumo brand syringe missing its cap and containing a "yellowish orange" substance that looked like the soft drink Crystal Light. The coroner conceded that "after an extensive, extensive amount of testing, we have not been able to identify what substance is within that syringe." He concluded it had no role in causing her death.

Morganelli asked about what other conclusions Lysek had drawn from the crime scene evidence. Lysek said that linear dirt patterns on the victim's pants led him to believe "there had to be more than one person involved in the events that caused her death and the ultimate moving of her body." There were drag marks on the legs, buttocks and lower back, but not on the backs of the sneakers or upper back, he said. This seemed to indicate these parts were raised while more than one person moved the body across the ground.

With that, Morganelli concluded his direct examination. Monahan rushed his cross-examination, as the end of the day was approaching. At times he spoke too fast, and had to force himself to slow down. First he attacked the coroner's time of death estimation, taking issue with that fact that he found no mention in Lysek's report of degree of the victim's rigidity at the crime scene. Lysek apologized if it wasn't noted in his report, but said it was something he checked in every death he investigated, and that a degree of rigidity was present. Some information about the degree of rigidity could be gleaned from the crime scene photos. "If the rigidity was not present, her body would lay flat, and in photographs her body is not laying flat, so that then shows that the rigidity is, in fact, present," the coroner said.

Monahan also took issue with the fact that Lysek had not taken a core body temperature to help determine time of death. Under known conditions a victim's body loses heat at a predictable rate, and this can be used to narrow time of death. Lysek explained he'd chosen not to take a core body temperature because the investigative methods used by police had already provided a narrower window than any forensic means could.

Monahan next took aim at Lysek's testimony that more than one person must have moved the body. "You offered an opinion, Mr. Lysek, just basically that two people moved this body at some point, would that be a fair statement?"

"One or more," Lysek corrected.

Could it be more than two? Monahan wanted to know.

"It could be. I think there was at least two people involved. I think that was my exact wording."

Monahan tried again. "Could be one person?"

"No, I think it was at least two people involved."

Monahan tried a different avenue. He asked whether Lysek's opinion would change if the autopsy report indicated "there was dirt in the shoulder area."

The coroner remained resolute. "No, it would not, because I had the opportunity to examine the body at the scene with the clothing in place and undisturbed."

The end of the day was at hand when Monahan finished his questions. Funk's cross-examination remained, and again he kept it brief and to the point. He brought up the linear drag patterns Lysek had noted. "That linear pattern that you saw does not suggest in any way that more than one person actually *caused* the death, correct?"

"No, sir, that was not my conclusion."

He had successfully challenged the portion of Lysek's earlier testimony that was most damaging to Brandon.

Judge Panella adjourned at 4:51 P.M., dismissing the jury with instructions not to read or listen to any media accounts of the case.

Reporters from the *Express-Times* and *Morning Call* newspapers hastened upstairs to their respective news bureau offices, a pair of utilitarian offices tucked away in an upper corner of the courthouse, to compose the first in a series of daily reports on the complex and confusing trial. *Express-Times* reporter Elizabeth Warmka led off her coverage stating that husband and wife "wasted no time Tuesday pointing the finger at each other during the first day of their trial."

The *Morning Call*'s Tyra Braden began her story: "Brandon Bloss says Michelle Hetzel killed Devon Guzman. Hetzel says she loved Guzman and did nothing wrong. Prosecutors say the two from Easton are equally guilty of first-degree murder."

There may be two sides to every story, but there were going to be at least three to this particular one. Warmka summed it up as follows: "None of the attorneys denies that a confusing and infuriating lesbian love triangle between Hetzel, Guzman, Renner and Bloss led to Guzman's death. But each presented a different story about who is guilty."

If it was a perplexing array of perspectives for reporters to outline and newspaper readers to try to follow, the people who really had something to worry about were the jurors, who bore the charge of making sense of it all.

35

Wednesday, September 26, 2001, began with a conference in chambers around a familiar theme. Yet another juror had discovered a heretofore hidden connection to one of the principals in the case. Juror number 2 had nervously approached a court officer saying that during a phone conversation with his sister, he'd learned that his brother-in-law worked with Brandon Bloss's father. After some back-and-forth among the attorneys, Panella dismissed the juror, replacing him with one of the two remaining alternates. There was still a long way to go, but the case could afford to lose just one more juror—any more than that and a second mistrial would have to be declared.

Once the jury issue was settled, the commonwealth called Rick Guzman to the stand. Morganelli began with the direct questioning, establishing that the witness was forty years old and employed as a truck driver with Johnson Motorlines in Easton. Then he delved into the substance of the case. "Now, Mr. Guzman, do you know the defendant Michelle Hetzel?"

"Yes, I do," Rick answered.

The DA asked him to point her out.

"Sitting in the middle table in the tan suit," he said. It could not have been easy to see her there. His own daughter had been gone more than a year now, and here was the very friend accused of cutting short her life. This was a friend who at one time used to enter his home without knocking, and sit down with the family on any given night to share a pizza. This was someone he'd once liked a lot and trusted without question.

Rick explained that Devon and Michelle had met as girls, were classmates in school, lost contact when Devon moved with him to Phoenix and then rekindled their friendship when she returned at age sixteen.

"Now, were you aware, Mr. Guzman, of what kind of friendship or relationship your daughter had with Michelle Hetzel?" Morganelli asked.

"Not at first, but Devon was pretty forthright. She told us pretty early on, but not right away. The first year I was ignorant of it, but after that, I knew, a couple years down the road."

Moving ahead, Morganelli asked about the trip to the tropics.

Rick said she went to the Virgin Islands and Puerto Rico for a week with Michelle. "Michelle financed the whole trip." He said he spoke with both Devon and Michelle while they were away. "They called me—I believe it was either a cell phone or on the plane phone—and told me that they got married and wanted to know if they could stay with me until they got their own place."

"Speaking about what Michelle told you, what did Michelle tell you?" the DA asked.

"She was excited that they just got married and wanted to know if it was OK if she stayed with us."

"With you and Holly?"

"Right, because they evidently didn't have a place of their own yet."

"OK. Now, what was your reaction to the fact that Michelle told you that her and Devon got married over there?"

"Well, it didn't surprise me, but I just was glad to see that Devon was happy. They were both happy. They came back from that trip, and everything seemed OK."

"All right. Now, when they actually got physically back, did you have the occasion to be with Michelle Hetzel in person?"

"Yes."

"What did she tell you about the trip, anything beyond the fact that they got married, when you actually were with her physically?"

"Well, you know, just filling me in on the fun times of the trip, you know. She would be sitting there waiting at my house for Devon a lot and she—"

"Go ahead."

"Asking me to call her at Keary's house to get her over there. She would wait sometimes for hours and sometimes Devon wouldn't even show up."

Rick explained that Devon and Michelle never moved in with him because upon returning from the trip, Devon went back to Keary's.

"Now, did Michelle ever indicate to you, when she asked you if she could move in with you or until they got a place, did Michelle ever tell you what was going to happen to Brandon, her husband?"

"No, there's very little talk of a man from them."

Moving on to the night of the murder, Rick said Devon arrived at his house around 7:00 P.M. His girlfriend, Holly, and his sister, Candy, were there also. So was Michelle. She had been waiting an hour to an hour and a half for Devon.

"So Michelle Hetzel was at your home, to your recollection, before your daughter got there?"

"Yeah, that was the case most of the time because she

couldn't call Devon at Keary's house, so she would just come over and have me call."

"OK. Now, could you tell the jury, please, what happened when Devon got to your home, and what did you do?"

"We were hanging out for a little bit and those—those two were always, you know, in their own little world, and we just hung out, like, for a little bit. And then we went to the store."

"OK. Now, when you say we went to the store, Mr. Guzman, who went?"

"Devon, myself and Michelle. Michelle drove us."

"OK. And what vehicle did Michelle drive you in?"

"Her red Honda."

"OK. Where did you—do you know what time, approximately, you went out to go?"

"It was around eight, eight-thirty.

"All right. And where did you go, sir?"

"We stopped at the Fifteenth Street Shopping Center, so I could buy myself a fifth of vodka. And then we went to the mall to purchase some CDs."

"When you got back to your house, what did you observe or hear at that time, what did you do?"

"Well, I was checking out the new CDs, and Devon and Michelle were talking in the corner. Candy and Holly were doing something on the computer. You know, the typical, you know, Thursday-night stuff."

"Was anyone drinking alcohol?"

"Yeah, we all were."

Morganelli asked if Rick saw any disagreements between Devon and Michelle that night.

"Well, they would be, like, talking normal one minute and then flare up into an argument the next, which happened quite often," Rick said.

"How about on this particular night, what did you hear?"

"Well, Michelle was annoyed about Devon not leaving Keary's house, [that] was her main beef."

Morganelli asked what time the girls left that night.

"They bolted out of there about nine-thirty, ten o'clock."

"When you say bolted out of there, what do you mean by that?"

"Well, they took off and then Devon took off and Michelle was chasing her, driving like a nut."

"What did you observe about how they left?" the DA asked.

"Well, they were arguing and they got in the cars. And Devon took off and Michelle was just like chasing after her, [across a] series of one-way streets around the house. I heard them leaving all the way to Freemansburg Avenue. Nuts."

"And by the way, when your daughter left on June fourteenth, Wednesday evening, from your home, did you ever see her again alive after that, your daughter?"

"No. When she bolted away, my last vision was of those taillights."

"You never saw her again?"

Rick Guzman shook his head. Though he fought back the tears, among the dozens of Guzman family supporters, there were many who cried for him as he recounted his daughter's final day.

Morganelli was done. "I have no further questions, Your Honor."

Panella turned to Michelle's defense team. "Mr. Monahan, Mr. Scomillio."

Victor Scomillio went straight to pointing the finger at the roommate. "Let me start off with Keary Renner," he said. "Your daughter was having a relationship with Keary Renner and living at Keary's apartment, correct?"

"That's right."

"There was some concern that you had about Keary Renner, isn't that also correct?"

"Yes."

"In fact, there were previous altercations that you and Keary had gotten into about how Keary was treating Devon, correct?"

"That's correct."

"And if I'm—if my memory serves me correct, there was some actual physical altercations between the two of you?"

"Yeah. Yes, there was," Rick admitted.

The attorney did not ask for details, though he was likely referring to the time Michelle and Keary chased Devon home, Keary gestured at him from inside the car and he lashed out and punched the window. Instead, the attorney moved to the night of the murder, pointing out that for the most part, Devon and Michelle had gotten along in their usual manner. "When the girls were over, they were constantly talking?" Scomillio asked.

"Yeah, they always were face-to-face, within inches, that's the way they were."

"And, in fact, you had trouble even trying to get into the conversation?"

"Right, yes."

"That's probably not too odd for girls being the age of nineteen years old, correct?"

"Devon was always like that with all her friends, that's the way they were, that age, I guess. I don't know, giddy, I suppose."

"And that's the way they were that night, correct?"

"Yes."

Then Scomillio targeted Brandon. "I want to talk to you a little bit about Brandon Bloss. You were aware that Mr. Bloss was making threats?"

The question brought Keith Szachacz to his feet at Brandon's table. "Objection, Judge, we need to approach then."

He objected that Scomillio was attempting to elicit heresay. Guzman hadn't heard Brandon making threats himself. He only knew what his daughter had told him. Panella sustained the objection for now, but the issue would come up again shortly.

Scomillio began again. "When Michelle and Devon came back from Puerto Rico, you described them as being happy?"

"Yes."

"They were pleased with their relationship and the way that the things were going, correct?"

"At that time—at that present moment, yeah."

Scomillio moved to attack Rick's memory of the night of the murder. "When the girls left that night, you weren't outside, were you?"

"No, when they were getting in their cars and taking off, yeah. It's a small house, so it's not uncommon to be hanging out on the porch."

"OK. But, if I'm correct, in your earlier statements to the police, you said you weren't outside?"

"I have a vivid recollection in my mind of those taillights taking off down the street for the last time. What I said then and what I'm saying now, I saw them taking off down the street is what I'm telling you."

For impeachment purposes Scomillio brought out a transcript of the earlier statement to which he was referring. "Mr. Guzman, I'm showing you page nine of this transcript, lines fourteen through twenty. If you could read this question from Mr. Crouse and your answer, does that refresh your recollection as to the statement that you made?"

Rick remained unshaken. "Yeah, that's not how it was. That statement was inaccurate."

"Can you read it out loud to the jury," the attorney pressed, "Mr. Crouse's question and your answer?"

He read the question: "How about when they left, was

there any reaction or attitude between the two girls, between Devon and Michelle?'" And then his answer: "Um, I can't, on that I can't recall because I didn't—I wasn't outside.'"

"And you're saying that that statement is incorrect?" Scomillio charged.

"Well, I saw them drive away, that's the last thing that I saw was those taillights. I'm telling you and I'm looking in my mind's eye, and this is what I see. That statement, at that time, I was so shook up, I was prescribed drugs to calm myself down. I wasn't—that is inaccurate. I'm telling you right now, I was on the porch when I saw them leave."

Scomillio let it go, backtracking to how the girls were getting along that night. He asked if Rick initially had told a Lieutenant David Hess that when the girls left, "neither Michelle nor Devon appeared to have been upset and both seemed to be their normal giddy selves."

Rick answered, "Well, the way they thought, one minute they would be giddy and the next minute they would fight. That was them, that's the way they were."

"But my question, sir, when you gave this statement to the police about your recollection of what happened two days before, your statement was: neither Michelle nor Devon appeared to be upset and they seemed to be their normal giddy selves?"

"What's the question?"

"Is that a correct statement of what you told Lieutenant Hess?"

"That would sound like something that I would say, yeah."

"You had talked about how Michelle and Devon would get into some type of disagreements. They never turned physical, did they?"

"No. Michelle—Michelle could barely walk on her own two feet, and Devon was very athletic. There was no way that they would even get physical."

"OK. Even though Devon was, what we described as petite, she was—she could handle her own?"

"Very much so. There's no way that Michelle could have—Devon would have slapped her—"

"OK."

"—and laughed at the same time. That's just the way they were."

Scomillio concluded his cross-examination by circling back to where he began: Keary Renner. He asked whether shortly after the Memorial Day trip, there had been an altercation in which Keary was threatening suicide with a knife and Devon had been cut. Rick had little first-hand knowledge of the incident, but agreed that something like that had happened.

After Scomillio concluded his questioning, Brandon's side had no questions for the witness. Morganelli took his turn for redirect examination, seeking to rebuild the witness's credibility as to the contradictory recollections by addressing his state of mind at the time of his earlier statements.

"Mr. Guzman, you were interviewed, I believe, by Police Officer Hess—Lieutenant David Hess—about a couple of hours after you learned that your daughter has been murdered, isn't that right?"

"I followed him to the police station right from where they found her, like right after—they wouldn't let me see her or anything. So they took me—I followed them to the police station and gave them my recollection of the night before."

"What was your emotional state at that time when you were trying to give the police information about the night before?"

"It—it was kind of strange. I was kind of scared, I guess, having seen Zachary Lysek's face telling me that Devon was dead and that there was nothing behind there. There

was just this blank screen of just this face saying, 'Devon
is dead.' I just went into this, you know, shock."

Rick Guzman's girlfriend, a soft-spoken nursing aide
in her early twenties named Holly Ronco, nervously took
the stand next. Morganelli reminded her to speak up and
use the microphone while she testified.

Holly said that she was living with Devon's father and
had known Devon about a year before the murder. The
night of June 14, 2000, she recalled that Michelle had
arrived at the house and then Devon showed up shortly
after. She wasn't sure about the times.

"What do you recall when they got there? Did they do
anything in particular, Michelle and Devon?" Morganelli
wanted to know.

"No," Holly said. Other than a trip to the mall with Rick,
it had been a fairly uneventful evening at the home.

"Now, during the time frame that you were at your
home with Rick and Michelle and Devon, after they got
back from the mall, were you able to observe any type of
arguments or disagreements between Michelle Hetzel and
Devon that evening?" the DA asked.

"Yes."

"Could you tell the jury what you observed?"

"They were outside and they were arguing. Michelle
wanted Devon to move out of Keary's house."

The argument over Devon moving out of Keary's was
a key component in the DA's love triangle theory and jealousy motive for the crime. The reason for the argument
between Michelle and Devon was an important point, and
Morganelli stopped to dwell on it. "And what was Michelle
saying to Devon about moving out of Keary's apartment?"
he pressed.

"I don't remember the exact words, but . . . I don't

know," Holly said. It was understandable, since well over a year had passed since the night in question, but Morganelli wanted her to try harder.

"Well, to the best of your ability, what did you hear?" he encouraged.

"I don't remember, the exact words."

"Not the exact words, but just the nature of what the conversation was about?"

"I don't know."

He took a step back to try another tack for eliciting the recollections he was searching for. "Are you a little nervous?" he solicited.

Holly nodded.

"What I want to know is during the course of the evening, other than that, was that argument just inside the house or outside?"

"Outside."

"Was that shortly before they left or, like, earlier in the evening?"

"It was shortly before they left. They left right after that."

"And do you know approximately what time it was when they left your home, Ms. Ronco?"

"It was around ten."

"OK. Other than the conversation regarding the issue of Devon moving out of Keary's apartment, were they talking about anything else that you can recollect?"

"No, not that I can remember."

"Now, after they left your residence at around ten o'clock that evening, did you hear from Michelle at all later that evening?"

"Yes."

"How did you hear from Michelle Hetzel?"

"She called the house, my house."

"And what did she say?"

"She said that she's worried about Devon being at Keary's house."

"Michelle said that she was worried about Devon being at Keary's house?"

"Yes."

"Did she say anything else?"

"No."

"What did you say, if anything, in response to that?"

"I said, 'I'm sure that she'll be allright.'"

"Did she say why she was worried about Devon going home to her own apartment with Keary?"

"No."

"Did you ever talk to Devon after she left your home that night?" he asked. "Did you ever see Devon Guzman alive after she left your home at ten P.M.?"

The witness answered no to both questions.

"I have no further questions," Morganelli told the judge.

It was Victor Scomillio's turn next. He confirmed that everyone had been drinking that night, but pointed out that no physical violence took place. "When you saw what you've called an argument, there were no physical confrontations between Devon and Michelle, were there?" he asked.

"No," Holly said.

He asked if she'd known about the island vacation the girls had taken, and Holly said she had.

"And you knew that they were happy about their trip?"

"Yes."

"You knew that there were even future plans with these young ladies?"

"Yes."

"There was even a thought about moving back down to Puerto Rico together, correct?"

"Yes."

"And during your entire time, and I don't mean just that night, but anytime that you have observed Michelle and Devon, there were never any physical altercations between the two, were there?"

"No."

Scomillio addressed the phone call Michelle had made to Holly at around 11:30 P.M. He pointed out that Holly had testified to a very limited conversation. Michelle had "just expressed some concern about Devon being with Keary." Then he showed her an exhibit displaying phone records for that night, showing that the call had lasted seven minutes.

"Would that refresh your recollection that this conversation between you and Michelle was longer than just Michelle expressing some concern, just making one statement and then hanging up the phone?" Scomillio prompted.

"No, that's all we talked about on the phone."

"But it must have gone into a little bit more detail than just the statement, 'I'm concerned about Michelle,—excuse me, 'I'm concerned about Devon being with Keary'?"

"No, that's what I recall."

"I have no further questions, Your Honor," Scomillio concluded.

Once again Brandon's defense team had no questions for the witness.

Next up was Michelle and Brandon's neighbor, Joseph Welsh. He was an important witness, because he was one of the last people to see Devon Guzman alive, and he could testify about the timing of events leading up to her death.

Welsh informed the jury that he lived with his wife and two sons across the street from Michelle and Brandon's South Side home, in a house he'd occupied since 1992.

Since January, he'd been working as the city of Easton's assistant business administrator, and before that, he'd been a self-employed political and computer consultant. For the benefit of the court, he identified the defendants, pointing out Brandon Bloss, the jacketless man seated at the table to the left, and Michelle Hetzel, wearing a brown suit and sitting at the table in the middle. He said they'd moved in across the street from him in late August or early September 1999.

Then the DA showed Welsh a series of ten photographs, which the witness identified as the house, grassy lot, the backyard and the workshop building of the property across the street from his home, as they appeared in June 2000.

Morganelli asked Welsh how well he'd known his neighbors.

"They were people who we may say hello to as we were getting in the car or walking past their house or something, but nothing beyond that," he said. They were people he saw coming and going, and occasionally he witnessed disputes and disagreements outside the home.

Morganelli asked him about the arguments.

"There were arguments that would happen sometimes outside of the home or sometimes inside the home. With the windows open, you know, we would just hear the argument going on."

"Now, with respect to the disagreements or disputes that you began to become aware of because you heard them overspilling outside, were you ever able to determine what the nature of those arguments were between Ms. Hetzel and Mr. Bloss?"

"Not in the beginning, but as we progressed further into the spring of 2000, a lot of the arguments seemed to revolve around Michelle going out with her friends."

The DA asked him to elaborate.

"Brandon did not want her going out with them, and she wanted to go with them," Welsh said. "Leading into June, the arguments had become more intense and also more frequent."

Then the murder happened.

"I found it out from my wife, who had, on the Friday of that week, read the *Express* before I came downstairs and had noticed the picture of a car that we recognized as similar to the car that we had seen across the street," Welsh said.

"Did you contact the police?"

"Yes, I did."

Welsh said he used to see the Sunfire parked across the street once or twice a week. He'd seen the driver many times, though he didn't know her name. When he saw the picture of Devon Guzman in the newspaper, he recognized her as the girl who visited his neighbors.

"All right. Now, Mr. Welsh, you stated that the disagreements or disputes between Brandon Bloss and Michelle Hetzel increased as you were getting into the springtime area. I would like to refer you specifically to the day of June 10, 2000, can you recall a specific incident regarding Michelle and Brandon that occurred that you observed?"

"Yes. In the middle of the afternoon, I was—I was working in the front room of my house. We have a computer there and I heard a voice, which was Brandon's, scream and—"

Kepler Funk quickly objected on Brandon's behalf, asking to approach the bench for a sidebar out of hearing of the jury. "It appears that he's about to elicit a statement attributed to my client that has not been disclosed," he complained.

John Morganelli countered in his defense. This was important testimony for him to get in. "It's in police reports describing the incident that occurred between Michelle, whereby laundry was thrown out the window, and he was calling her a 'fucking bitch,' or whatever. It's in one of the police reports. It's in the interview of Mr. Welsh."

Judge Panella seemed inclined to exclude the testimony, saying it wasn't relevant evidence of a homicide. Morganelli vehemently disagreed. "Well, Your Honor, it is relevant because the issue here is to show the increasing arguments that were occurring between Brandon Bloss and his wife over the issue of her running around."

Michelle's attorney had no objection to the testimony, since it hurt Brandon more so than Michelle. Swayed by Morganelli's argument, Panella decided to allow the testimony. The DA had to have breathed a sigh of relief, as this was one of a very few concrete instances he could cite as evidence for his contention that marital discord had driven Brandon to the edge.

The issue settled, Morganelli continued from where he'd left off. "Mr. Welsh, I was asking you about a specific incident that occurred on June 10, 2000, and you were beginning, I think, to tell the jury how you came about to observe an incident between Michelle Hetzel and Brandon Bloss. And you can tell us, how did this come to your attention and what did you hear?"

"As I said, I was working on a computer in the front room of my house and I heard what sounded like Brandon's voice, to me, scream, and these are the words that he used, pardon the language, 'You're nothing but a fucking bitch,' which did get my attention."

"OK. What else did you hear or observe then?"

"Michelle was in her car in a vacant lot next to [her house], and then Brandon then appeared at a side window, kind of next to that lot, and said to her, was yelling at her, and said at one point, 'Are you—aren't you going to fold your laundry before you leave?' And Michelle yelled, 'Fuck you!' back to him. He then told her that she had ten seconds to get back in the house and started a countdown from ten to one. When he reached one, Michelle put the car very pointedly in reverse and backed it out and then pulled out of the lot."

"All right. Did you observe any other conduct or actions of Brandon or Michelle at that point?"

"Not at that point."

"What happened next?"

"Michelle returned, maybe a little more than a half an hour later and—oh, I'm sorry, Mr. Morganelli, when they got down to zero in Brandon's count, he took the laundry that he had and threw it out into the lot and it ended up landing on his car. When Michelle got home, she went into the house, and a few seconds later, Brandon came out and picked up all the laundry and took it into the house."

"Now, when you observed this argument between Michelle Hetzel and Brandon Bloss, you were able to physically see Michelle at some point?"

"Yes, when she came back and she was in the car."

"And Brandon, you were able to see him as well?"

"Yes."

"And what was their demeanor at the time when they were arguing?"

"Angry, to say the least."

"OK. Now, Mr. Welsh, I would like to refer you to the date of June 14, 2000, which is the night before the body of Devon Guzman is discovered. And I would like to ask you whether you can tell the jury whether or not you saw another incident between Michelle Hetzel and Brandon Bloss on June 14, 2000?"

"Yes, I did."

"OK. Could you tell the jury how you came to overhear this and what you observed, and what time?"

"It was approximately ten-thirty, maybe a little bit after

ten-thirty, we had just put our kids to bed, and my wife and I were in the downstairs of our house. It was a warm night. We had the windows open. We suddenly heard some screaming across the street. And I looked out and saw Michelle laying down on the sidewalk in front of the vacant lot and just screaming this phrase repeatedly, 'What the fuck do you want from me?' And Brandon was standing on the walk just outside of their front door. I believe he was saying something back to her, but I didn't hear that."

"OK. Now, when Ms. Hetzel said, and please excuse my language—I'm—we have to say what you heard—when Michelle was saying, 'What the fuck do you want from me?' How many times did she say this?"

"At least three or four times."

"And who was she saying this to?"

"To Brandon."

"You didn't hear his response?"

"No, I did not."

"Did you observe then what happened? What did they do?"

"They ended up going in the house, and then Brandon came out, you know, within a minute of both of them going in the house and picked up some things that were on the sidewalk."

After that, Welsh went to bed. Morganelli asked him what happened next.

"I was awoke, and by some commotion from that residence about twelve thirty-five." He had seen the time on a digital clock by his bed.

"When you got up, what did you do?"

"Well, I looked at the clock and then I looked out the window. And I saw the car that we've discussed earlier in front of [the house], and the woman that I now know as Devon just outside of the residence and—"

"OK. Now, the car, when you looked out the window at twelve thirty-five, you saw the silver Pontiac?"

"That's correct."

Morganelli had Welsh step down from the stand and point out on photo exhibits of the house on West St. Joseph Street exactly what he saw and where. In addition to seeing that Devon's car was parked at the defendants' house, Welsh said he noticed that Michelle's red Accord and Brandon's smaller Honda were also parked at the house.

"OK. You woke up and you looked out the window?" Morganelli asked.

"That's correct."

"And you saw the silver Pontiac. What else did you see?"

"There were two people in the doorway." Welsh used a pointer to indicate where they were standing. "In the doorway depicted on photo one, and the person I now know as Devon was standing on this step."

"What did you observe or hear at that time?"

"There was arguing, back and forth. I—after observing that, I went to my bathroom, which also faces the front of the house. And I recall—I recall a voice which sounded like Brandon's, to me, something along the lines of, 'You're not going.'"

"And then what happened, what did you overhear?"

"I left the bathroom and came back to the bedroom. I was looking out the window to see what was going on, the latest argument and that argument I saw concluded. I saw the woman that I now know as Devon come around in front of her vehicle, and she pounded her fist on the hood of the vehicle and said to someone who was sitting in the passenger side in the front, and once again, pardon the language, her words, 'Fuck this, I'm taking you home.'"

Welsh testified that he knew there was a passenger in Devon's car because he saw movement on the passenger side, but he couldn't see who it was. A streetlight beyond the grassy lot next door illuminated the house and street, but he couldn't see inside the car.

When Morganelli finished his questioning, it was a minute after noon. Judge Panella announced lunch recess.

While the jurors and the people in the gallery got up and stretched their legs, the attorneys filed into Judge Panella's chambers to pick up the discussion of whether Rick Guzman would be allowed to testify to threats that Brandon allegedly had made to Devon and that she in turn had relayed to her father.

Victor Scomillio was eager for the jury to hear of such threats, which would support Michelle's contention that Brandon had a motive to kill Devon. The legal problem was that Rick himself had not heard Brandon directly threaten his daughter. Consequently Brandon's defense team held that such statements were hearsay, and therefore inadmissible.

To familiarize the judge with the statements he was looking to have admitted, Scomillio read the following from a transcript of Detective Crouse's interview of Rick Guzman:

Mr. Guzman: *From what I understood, Brandon wasn't a very nice guy. I never met the guy. Brandon has bias opinions.*

Mr. Crouse: *Did Devon ever tell you Brandon threatened her?*

Mr. Guzman: *Yeah, yeah, about, you know, wanting to kick her ass and dyke them out, girl them out, shit like that, and that—and that he was still supposed to be—at least twice, you know, within the past year or so.*

Mr. Crouse: *That's what I was going to ask you, if you could put a time frame as far as that.*

Mr. Guzman: *One of the reasons there was—there was— it's like at the end of last year, maybe the beginning of the year, but I wouldn't have heard that like last week.*

Mr. Crouse: *OK.*

Mr. Guzman: *It was ongoing, it was an ongoing thing.*

Mr. Crouse: *Did Devon ever tell you if anybody else threatened her? Was there—was there anybody she confided in you that she was scared of somebody harassing her?*

Mr. Guzman: *No, no, she would tell me.*

Panella asked for Scomillio's arguments as to why he should be able to have Rick testify about the threats. Scomillio pointed out that it represented "an ongoing threat against Devon." It showed intent and motive on Brandon's part and established the state of mind of the victim. "She was scared of him. There were physical threats made against her life," Scomillio said.

Panella contended that Devon's state of mind was irrelevant, and that the statements in question constituted both hearsay and evidence of prior bad acts, neither of which would be admissible testimony. Scomillio said that because they established intent and motive, they should be allowable exceptions to the prior bad-acts rule. Panella noted that the problem of hearsay remained.

An argument was put forth that there have been known exceptions to the hearsay rule, especially in cases where a deceased victim expressed an intent to go somewhere or do something leading up to the murder. The state supreme court recently had upheld a conviction that was being appealed on that very issue, but the threats attributed to Brandon didn't seem to fall under that exception.

Still, Monahan pressed his case. He noted that it was no secret Michelle's defense was going to constitute an emphasis on evidence that Brandon committed the murder, and so any evidence that he had threatened Devon was going to be vitally important. "Our defense is fairly well emasculated if we don't get this evidence in," he complained.

But Panella was leaning the other way. "It's hearsay," he said. "It's hearsay of prior bad acts." He suggested that the attorneys research prior cases that may have dealt with the issue, but for the time being, he sustained Brandon's attorney's objection. Unless new arguments turned up to change his mind, Rick Guzman would not be allowed to testify that Devon said Brandon threatened her. It was a victory for Brandon, and a blow for Michelle. In the end no legal exceptions turned up that would allow the testimony, and the jury never got to hear about those threats.

After lunch Joseph Welsh, still under oath, asked for water as he resumed his place on the witness stand. Monahan began his cross-examination. He tried to chip away at Welsh's knowledge of the Bloss/Hetzel property, but the attempt was unsuccessful. Welsh had lived across the street from the property in question for almost a decade, and for years a relative of his had occupied the house Michelle and Brandon lived in.

Monahan switched tactics, taking loose aim at Welsh's recollections of the night of the murder when sounds awakened him. "Do you remember what woke you up?" he asked.

"The noise of the commotion across the street."

"OK. Could you tell us about what you saw across the street?"

"Well, initially what I heard, I just heard people shouting."

"I'm more concerned with what you heard," Monahan said. He seemed to forget he'd just asked about what Welsh had *seen*. It was going to become something of a pattern with Monahan, these little slips. Whether they were honest mistakes or intentional slipups to trip up witnesses was hard to judge.

"I heard people shouting, you know," Welsh said. "This was over an air conditioner. I didn't hear discrete words, except when I had walked over to the bathroom."

Monahan switched gears again. He asked if Welsh had seen Devon's car leave the house that night.

"Yes, I did."

"Do you remember what time that would have been?"

"It was approximately ten minutes after I awoke at twelve thirty-five, so approximately twelve forty-five."

"And I think you testified on direct that you saw Devon get into the car?"

"That's correct."

"You never saw Devon come back, did you?"

"No. I went back to sleep after the twelve thirty-five to forty-five episode."

"And you never heard any kind of a commotion or anything across the street?"

"No, I didn't."

Monahan had no further questions. His cross-examination had done nothing to shake Welsh's precise memory of the details of that night, but he had managed to establish that the witness last had seen Devon leaving the Bloss/Hetzel home with an unknown person next to her in her car.

Now it was Brandon's defense team's turn. Kepler Funk took the floor. He had Welsh step down from the stand and painstakingly go over the photo exhibits of West St. Joseph Street, identifying the gray two-story house, the small side-building that previous owners had used as a woodworking shop, and the detached multicar garage along the back of the property. Welsh confirmed that an alley ran behind the house.

Proving no more successful than Monahan had been in shaking Welsh's credibility regarding his knowledge of the property, Funk allowed him to return to the seat in the witness-box. "You testified that you saw Brandon picking up some objects off the sidewalk?" he queried.

"Correct."

"OK. Did you notice that that was Michelle's keys and her purse?"

"I didn't know what it was. It appeared to be small objects; I thought it could have been change. I didn't know specifically what it was."

"Is that because of your distance away that you couldn't tell what they were? Is that why?" It was an attempt to cast doubt on what Welsh could or could not see, but it was a minor point.

"Right," Welsh agreed. "And it appeared to be something he was picking up from the flat pavement."

Funk had won the point, but it was a small one, since those objects did not appear to be relevant evidence in the case. (Unless, perhaps, they were the rings Devon was believed to have thrown back at Michelle at Rick Guzman's house. It was a question people would speculate about, but one to which they'd get no satisfactory answer.) He concluded his questioning by having the witness emphasize that the only thing Welsh had really understood of Brandon's words to Devon was that she could not come in.

When Welsh's testimony concluded, the photos of the St. Joseph Street property were passed to the jury before the prosecution called its next witness, George Vine.

A number of the people involved in the case were rather unusual characters, and this certainly applied to Vine. The story he was about to tell was a big piece of the prosecution's argument for premeditation by Michelle, but would the jury buy it? Morganelli and Miranda had to be sweating it a little when Vine took the stand.

The middle-aged machinery assembler informed the jury that he had known the victim for about three years before the murder. He met her while working at Pino's Pizzeria in South Side. He said he considered Devon a friend, and saw her often, every other day or so.

"How did you meet Michelle Hetzel?" Morganelli asked.

"Through Devon at Pino's, and then they came to my house and stuff."

"All right. And did you ever meet Brandon Bloss?"

"Only on two or three occasions. He was looking for Michelle."

Vine said he also met Keary Renner through Devon, and that they had all become acquainted at Pino's.

"Now, were you familiar with the relationship between Devon Guzman and Michelle Hetzel? What kind of relationship did they have?" Morganelli asked.

Like so many people who knew them, Vine seemed to find the true nature of Devon and Michelle's relationship elusive. He struggled to define it, using the same type of contradictory sentiments others had used so often.

"Up and down, you know. They were in love, fought a lot and stuff, a lot of jealousy, I guess."

Morganelli next asked about the relationship between Devon and Keary.

"They also had a love for each other, and in the same manner. But, you know, there was [a] little fighting sometimes."

The DA moved on to the day Devon's body was found, asking Vine why he'd contacted police at that time.

"Because I found out about Devon's death and I found out some other things—who she was with that night, and all," he said. "I heard some bits and pieces and I added two and two together in my head and I remember[ed] what Michelle had said to me once." Vine said the conversation with Michelle had taken place two or three months before the murder.

"Where did this conversation take place with Ms. Hetzel?" Morganelli asked.

"In my kitchen."

"Who was present for this conversation?"

"No one."

"Just you and Michelle Hetzel?"

Vine nodded.

"Could you tell the jury what Michelle Hetzel said to you in that conversation?"

"Well, she said that she wanted to get rid of her and dispose of the body and she wanted me to help her. I didn't take her serious, but that's what she said. She offered maybe money or sex, or anything. Like I said, I didn't take her serious at the time at all. . . ."

Vine paused ruefully, voicing the inevitable regret. "I should have said something to Devon or maybe all of this wouldn't have even happened."

Morganelli pressed on. "What I want to know is when she said that she wanted to get rid of somebody, who was she talking about?"

"Devon."

"And what exactly did she say? What did she say—did she use those words 'get rid of' or use other words?"

"Get rid of Devon, her problem, and dispose of the body."

"And dispose of the body. And what did she ask of you, if anything?"

"Just to help her do it, that's all. That's all I took it as."

"OK. And what did you say in response to that?"

"I can't exactly remember the exact words, but I didn't acknowledge it," Vine said. He thought he might've said something like, "No, we can't do that." And that was that. After that night, Michelle didn't bring the subject up again.

Before turning his witness over for cross, Morganelli had to get to the bottom of why Vine had thought to contact police only after Devon was found murdered. If Morganelli didn't bring this out in a light that was favorable to the prosecution, Michelle's attorney surely would attack this point viciously on cross. Morganelli pointed out that Vine had said he didn't take the proposition seriously at first.

"No, I didn't," Vine agreed.

"But on June sixteenth, you called the police to tell them about that, right?"

"Yes, I did."

"Now, did Ms. Hetzel indicate to you why she wanted to get rid of Ms. Guzman and dispose of her body?"

Here again Vine seemed to struggle, as others had done before him, to come up with an adequate explanation of what may have moved Michelle to murder.

"The only thing that I can get out of it is that she was just fed up with the arguments and stuff, and maybe she wanted to make [a] life with Brandon and she couldn't do it without Devon being gone. I don't know."

The answer was speculation on Vine's part, and Michelle's attorney Victor Scomillio rightly raised an objection. The speculation was stricken from the record.

Morganelli regrouped. "Mr. Vine, without speculating at all, what I want to know is whether Michelle stated to you specifically why she wanted to get rid of Devon Guzman and dispose of her body?"

"She didn't give a good concrete reason—only that she wanted to get rid of her problems."

Yet again, the lack of a clear, explicit answer to *why* this crime happened eluded explanation. It was one of the most enduring and frustrating mysteries of the case.

Having failed to elicit a clear motive, the DA reemphasized the request itself, asking if Michelle had specified exactly what she wanted Vine to do.

"No, she did not. She just told me that she wanted me to help get rid of her, to kill her, to knock her off and get rid of the body. That's it."

Vine concluded his testimony on direct examination recounting that the night of the murder he'd received a call from Keary looking for Devon. "I was sound asleep and it woke me up and I didn't pay much [attention] to it and put the phone back down and went to sleep, because I figured it was just another fight."

Now came Michelle's defense team's opportunity to cross-examine Vine. Victor Scomillio quickly moved to discredit Vine by alleging that his story had changed over time. Scomillio challenged Vine's assertion that Michelle had mentioned disposing of a body, asserting that Vine had not mentioned this during his preliminary-hearing testimony almost a year before. "You never said anything about disposing of the body, correct?"

"I'm sure I said it in some words, but I can't remember exact words. I didn't write it down or anything. I'm sure you guys know more than I do."

Scomillio handed Vine the statement he gave to Detective Gibiser the day after Devon's body was found. The less-than-explicit nature of Michelle's alleged proposal made the statement an easy target for attack.

"There's nothing in there about sex, correct?" Scomillio asked.

"No, sir," Vine agreed.

"Nothing in there about money, correct?"

"No, sir."

"Nothing in there about disposing of the body, correct?"

"No, sir," Vine admitted.

Scomillio asked Vine to think back to earlier that night.

Vine said he'd had a beer or two, as he usually did after work. He wasn't sure whether Devon or Michelle had been drinking, but thought that Keary had probably not been drinking because she wasn't much of a drinker.

The defense attorney asked Vine to confirm that Devon and Keary had gotten into a physical fight that night and that Devon had given Keary a bloody lip.

"I can't recollect if she had a bloody lip or not, sir," Vine said.

"But they were in a fistfight, weren't they?"

"I believe so, sir, yes."

"And then Devon leaves with Keary, and Michelle says, 'I could kill her.' Isn't that correct?" Scomillio asked. His words hung in the air as he waited for Vine to confirm this subtle but significant difference, from Michelle asking, "Will you help me kill her?" to "I could kill her."

Vine held steadfast to his earlier testimony. "She said that she wanted me to help her kill her, something like that, in those words, and then dispose of the body. Those are the words."

Scomillio's next tactic was to present Vine with a section of the transcript of his testimony during the preliminary hearing, where ADA Teresa Miranda asked Vine why he hadn't notified police immediately after the conversation with Michelle in his kitchen.

"Your answer," Scomillio read: "'Cause I never really took it for serious. I never imagined someone as nice as I pictured her would even . . . I mean, some people always say, "I'm going to kill her or kill him," and that's what I took it as. I never . . . if I even would have thought   I would have told Devon, at the very least. But I didn't want to cause any problems, so I didn't say anything. You know, I just didn't and kept it to myself until after Devon was killed and then I just couldn't. I had to tell, you know?'"

Scomillio pressed on, noting that when Vine talked with Easton police on July 2, he'd described Devon as "a pretty tough little girl."

"Certainly," Vine agreed.

"She could handle her own. And actually, at one time there was some type of disagreement going on and you tried to hold back Devon. She spun around and put you on your ass, correct?"

"She kicked off the wall and made me fall backwards overtop of a little box."

Scomillio asked Vine if he ever saw Brandon Bloss after Michelle's proposal.

"Yeah, he was looking for Michelle, I believe, on one occasion at my house," Vine said. "His mother and the whole crew was there."

Scomillio had finished his questioning. Approaching the bench for a discussion with the judge and other attorneys, he said he thought he smelled alcohol on Vine's breath.

"So what? There's no law that says you can't have a drink," Morganelli chimed in, though adding that he'd smelled no alcohol, saw no evidence of intoxication and that he believed Vine was answering the questions in a satisfactory manner.

"We would ask that he publish his breath to the jury," attorney Monahan interjected.

"That request is denied," Panella said. "If I sense in any way the witness is under the influence, I'll order the prison to run a Breathalyzer on him. Personally, I don't see the necessity yet, but your request is on the record."

When the sidebar ended, Brandon's attorneys had their chance to cross-examine Vine. Kepler Funk kept it brief. He confirmed that Vine had told Detective Golazeski that "Ms. Hetzel had offered you money and sex." He also elicited testimony that Devon had possessed a key to his house and that sometimes she and Michelle would spend evenings there, but that Michelle had never brought Brandon along. It was testimony to support his opening argument that Brandon did not belong in the love triangle depicted by the prosecution.

With the cross-examinations finished, Morganelli had the opportunity to redirect. The DA brought out the preliminary hearing transcript and had Vine read a portion in which he *did* speak of Michelle referring to disposing of the body, rebutting Scomillio's assertion that the disposing claim was a new one. Finally he returned to the physical fights between the girls. "Now, lastly, you indicated that Devon was, I think you used the term 'a tough little girl'?"

"Yes, sir."

"Was she pretty feisty?"

"Yes, sir."

"You observed her in fights with Keary Renner?"

"One or two, yes, sir."

"You observed her in fights with Michelle Hetzel?"

"Only little spats, not like sometimes—Keary and her, you know, got in better fights."

Vine continued. "See, one time Devon punched Keary right in the nose or mouth or something, and then Keary hauled off and nailed her back, you know." The fights between Devon and Michelle were rarer and milder, he said. "Only once Devon and Michelle slap maybe, or something."

Morganelli's second round of questioning gave Scomillio the opportunity to recross-examine the witness. He zeroed in on the fact that Vine said most of the fights he witnessed had been between Devon and Keary.

"You never saw anything physical between Michelle and Devon, correct?" the attorney asked.

"Like I said, only a little bit of spats, maybe a little bit of slapping or something. That's about it."

The questioning of Vine concluded. Making his way down from the stand, he mouthed an apology to Michelle. This did not escape the notice of Brandon's attorneys, who made note of it.

Next on the prosecution's list was Keary Renner. So much had been said already about the love triangle that led to murder, but none of it had come from anyone with any real firsthand knowledge. Now one of the participants would speak. And unless either of the defendants decided to testify, which most observers thought unlikely, this was as close as anyone was going to get to gaining a first-hand understanding of the mysteries at the heart of this troubling threesome.

36

John Morganelli got a breather while Assistant District Attorney Teresa Miranda took the floor to question Keary Renner. Keary said she was currently living at Fort Drum, New York, with her husband, a serviceman. In June of the previous year, she was living in Forks Township with Devon Guzman, whom she'd known for about five years. She said they'd met through Michelle Hetzel.

"What was your relationship with Ms. Guzman?" Miranda asked.

"In the beginning it just started out as friends, and then we had a romantic relationship, off and on, until about October of '99, and then we started getting more serious."

Keary explained that Devon had proposed a pact. "Devon had said that if I would leave my husband, she would leave Michelle, and we would move in and be happy together. So we were planning on taking our relationship to the next level at that time."

"When were you planning to do that?" Miranda asked.

As soon as existing relationship issues were resolved, Keary said. "She was with Michelle at that time, so she was going to break it off with Michelle, and I was going to break it off totally with my husband."

Even though Keary and Devon had made a commitment, Michelle was never really out of the picture. Keary said that as far as she and Devon went, "we always had a serious relationship, but it always went back between me, Michelle and Devon. OK, what I meant by going to the next level was that we were planning on moving in together and starting our own life then and having a baby. Only plans didn't go out that way because she kept still seeing Michelle. So it was still us all going back and forth to each other."

Miranda backtracked to the start of the relationships. "How did you know Ms. Hetzel?" she asked.

Keary replied that they became friends when she moved into South Side, Easton, Pennsylvania, when she was in around sixth grade.

"And did you remain friends from sixth grade on?" Miranda asked.

"Not as close friends as we were," Keary said. When Devon came back from Arizona, she and Devon "started a romantic relationship, which took away from mine and Michelle's friendship. And then she started having a romantic relationship with her also, which drained our friendship. So we still remained friends—if like she needed something, she could call me, or if I needed something—but we weren't hanging out like we used to."

"So Ms. Hetzel started having a relationship with Ms. Guzman after you did, correct?"

"Yes."

"OK. Was there ever a time when you were involved with Ms. Hetzel?"

"No. The farthest that me and Michelle had went was kissing. We never had—we never went all the way. We never had a relationship."

"Was there ever a time when you were roommates?"

"Yes."

"When was that?"

"The apartment that we got in Forks Township that Devon and I stayed in, Michelle and I got in April when she said that Brandon wouldn't let her in the house no more."

"And did Ms. Hetzel actually live with you?"

"Well, she started moving some of her stuff in, just mainly like her clothes and everything. And then one day, about three days after the fact of us moving in, and I came home and her stuff was gone, she had moved out."

"So that roommate period only lasted three days?"

"Yeah, three or four."

"Where was Ms. Guzman during those three days that you were living with Ms. Hetzel?"

"At that time neither one of me or Michelle was talking to Devon."

"Was that common?"

Keary said it was. At any given time, it was common for two of the girls to be close, while the third was excluded.

"How would you characterize your relationship with Michelle and Devon Guzman? Can you describe it?"

"They had like a love and hate relationship."

"What do you mean by that?"

"It was stormy. They fought often and then Michelle would make up, like, things to take her to the Ramada Inn to show that she's sincere this time and she wants to be with her, or the trip that they took to the islands was the way to try to get Devon to come back to her to see that Devon would have a better life with Michelle."

Miranda asked Keary if she and Devon were still together when Devon took the trip with Michelle. Keary said they were. She asked if they had any plans for Keary's birthday, June 17.

"Yes. The weekend before was Devon's birthday. We went camping with her and she was going to surprise me with something on the weekend following, which was my birthday."

She next asked about the significance of the June 11 anniversary.

"On June 11 '97 is when we were going out, when people more so knew. That was significant to us, like an anniversary."

"Were you planning on remaining in Forks Township with Ms. Guzman?" Miranda asked.

"No, we were not. We were planning on leaving in the beginning of June to go to Arizona."

Miranda asked her about Brandon. Keary said she'd spoken to him a few times, but she didn't know him well. Miranda asked about the relationship between Brandon and Devon.

"They pretty much didn't like each other because, for one, he was married to Michelle and Devon kept interfering. And then Devon and Michelle were together before Brandon was, so Devon felt like Michelle was hers. So Brandon didn't like her because of that."

Moving on to the day of the murder, Keary's voice broke occasionally as she testified, but she maintained her composure. The details tumbled forth rapidly, as if she'd waited a long time to tell the story. Sometimes Miranda had to interrupt to keep her from jumping around in the sequence of events.

Keary said Devon went to work at Servpro, as usual, that day, June 14, 2000. She got home around four-thirty or five o'clock, and the two of them sat on the couch and watched TV for twenty minutes to a half hour. Then Devon said that she wanted to go to her father's house. She was supposed to have gone the night before, but she'd spent the night at home with Keary instead.

Devon "didn't want me to go because she said it was just going to be something with her and her dad, and she swore that Michelle wasn't going to be there." Keary was concerned, but Devon went anyway. While she was gone, Keary paged her several times, but the pages weren't returned. When Devon came home at 10:00 or 10:30 P.M., she said she'd left her pager in her car.

"Let me stop you there," Miranda said. "She came home and she was drunk. Did you talk at all about the party?"

"We did. We fought when she got home," Keary said. The argument began because Devon was drunk.

"OK. So tell me what happened."

"The bottle of vodka was sitting on top of the refrigerator and I took it and I went to pour it, like, in her mouth. And I told her to drink some more, and she took the bottle and threw it at the back of my head. We started fighting, and I slapped her and she slapped me back, and we were yelling. And in the meantime, she was getting pages from Michelle's house."

"Let me stop you there," Miranda said. "Was the only thing you fought about was the fact that she was drunk?"

"No. We had fought because Michelle was there also."

"How did you find out that Michelle was at the party?"

"Because she told me. She always ended up telling me when she was with her."

"Did she tell you anything else about Michelle at the party?"

"Yeah, she did. She said that I had nothing to worry about, because she wasn't going to be with her. She found out all she needed to know, meaning about how Michelle treats her and how their relationship was," Keary said. She added that Devon told her Michelle asked her to marry her, outside of her father's house, that Devon had said no, and one of them got mad and threw a ring in a tree.

Keary said that she and Devon stopped fighting that

night because Devon kept receiving pages from Michelle and Brandon's house. Devon thought something had to be wrong, and wanted to call back. She wanted to use the pay phone outside by the bar below, but Keary wouldn't let her leave. "So then she decided to use the phone in the house. When she used the phone in the house, I heard Brandon on the other line. Brandon was the one that was paging Devon."

"So you heard Mr. Bloss's voice on the telephone?"

"Yes, I did. I was sitting right next to Devon."

"Could you tell what he was saying?"

"No, I could just hear his voice."

"Could you hear anything else?"

"I could hear Michelle screaming in the background."

"OK. What else happened?"

"Well, after they hung up, Devon had said that she was all panicked and said that Michelle had said that she was in cardiac arrest and she needed Devon to come take her to get care. And I didn't want her to go, and I told her that if Michelle was really sick, there was plenty of ways for her to get medical attention without Devon having to go down there.

"And I even told Devon she could go see her in the morning in case she was really sick. I had a feeling that she wasn't. I had a feeling—she had said stuff like that before, like her leg was broke or she was sick, so Devon would come to her. And so—"

"Was it true when she said it in the past?"

"No, it was not."

"OK."

"And so Devon wanted to go and she wanted to go alone, and I kind of argued with her and I wanted to go, so she said that she didn't care. Michelle needed her and she would do the same for me. So I went with her down to the Bloss/Hetzel home."

Keary was supposed to be going to work, but she wanted to go with Devon instead, to make sure what she was saying was the truth, that things were really over with Michelle. Devon, who usually did the driving when she and Keary were together, drove to South Side, parking at Michelle and Brandon's house. Devon went to the door, and after a minute or two, Brandon came to the door and said to get Keary out of there.

"You heard him say that?" Miranda asked. It was a key point, part of the prosecution's evidence of premeditation, that Brandon and Michelle cooperated to get Devon to their house alone.

"He might not have said in those words he did not want me there, he did say take me anywhere, just take me to my mom's."

"And then what happened?"

"Then Devon came to the car and was mad at me for having to come along and said now she got to take me home, and she slammed the hood of her car."

"What happened next?"

"On the ride home, she said that she—because I was advising her that Michelle is just playing these games, that she really isn't sick and she just wants another chance to win you over. And she said she knew, but she needed to know for herself, so she was going back. And we got home and she left the car running with the headlights on. She walked me up the steps and she said that she loved me and she promised she would be back home and I had nothing to worry about. And she gave me a kiss and she left."

The time was about midnight or a little after, Keary said.

"Did you ever see her again?" Miranda asked.

"No, I did not, alive."

While Devon was gone, Keary sat down on her couch to continue a letter she had been writing, on and off for three weeks to a month, in a journal book. The letter was to her husband and expressed her confusion and frustration over being torn between two relationships. Although the letter had little, if anything, to do with the prosecution's case, it was something the prosecution had to address to defuse its impact before the defense brought the information out.

Miranda asked why she worked on the letter that night.

"'Cause I was aggravated. I didn't know if Devon was serious, if she was going to move forward with our relationship or not, and so I was writing to my husband, and he had a girlfriend at the time, to go back with him, because several times before we were going to go back. I was going to go back up there and either he stopped the plans or I did, and so that's why I was writing to him."

"OK. So you were still kind of keeping your options open with him, is that a fair statement?"

"Yeah."

Miranda handed Keary a notebook. "Could you please read to the jury the portion that's in that notebook that you wrote that night after Ms. Guzman left?"

The entry began with the time: 12:32 A.M. Keary began reading. "It says, 'Help me please, Devon just came home drunk and threw a vodka bottle at my head, trashed my house and she kept hitting me. . . . I'm all full of blood and I have no one to talk to. She pulled hair out of my head. Why does she have to do this? All I want is you, is that too much to ask. Why won't she leave me alone? I want to die. . . . Please, our marriage deserves a chance.'"

Miranda asked about the injuries mentioned in the letter. Keary said that she had been writing for her husband's sympathy, but that she had not really been injured by Devon. "The only thing was that she threw the vodka bottle at my head, and she came home drunk," Keary said.

"That was true?"

"Yeah. And my neck, I don't believe it was sprained, but it was hurt from the bottle of vodka."

While she was writing the letter, Michelle called and said that Devon never showed up. "Then she insisted that Devon was there [at the Mineral Springs] and I was not telling her."

The time, Keary recalled, was about 12:45 A.M., a half hour after Devon left the Mineral Springs. If correct, it was an interesting point. Easton police officer Dominick Marraccini had testified earlier that the night of the murder, he had passed through the canal museum at 12:45 A.M., and there were no vehicles parked there. If the times were accurate, Devon's body had not yet been moved to the canal museum when Michelle made that call.

Keary continued, saying that Michelle called back several times, insisting that Devon had to be with Keary. "I told her, if she didn't believe me, she could come and see herself," Keary said.

The calls from Michelle continued, until she said she was coming over, and wanted to know if Brandon could come with her because she was still drunk and didn't want to drive by herself. She arrived at the Mineral Springs around 2:30 A.M.

By now, the body had been moved to the canal museum; Devon's Sunfire was seen there at 3:00 A.M.

"Brandon stayed in the car and Michelle came in and she was real worried. She was upset about Devon," Keary said. "Me and Michelle talked for a while. She realized that Devon wasn't there and she was upset and worried and she wanted me to call and report her as a missing person to the police."

"Did you?" Miranda asked.

"No, I did not."

"Why not?"

"Because I wasn't concerned for her, because she had

left before, but she's always come home. And the fact that she was drunk and she had just lost her license, so I didn't want to have another fight about something that I could have prevented."

Miranda asked her to explain what she meant about Devon having left before.

"Like, if she would go out, no matter how bad our fight was, she would always come home that evening," Keary replied.

"OK."

"And we never went to bed still angry at each other."

"So what happened next?"

"Then she—Michelle decided that she was going to phone her in as a missing person," Keary said. She placed a call to the Forks Township PD.

Two officers came and took a statement, promising to put patrol on alert.

"After we reported her missing to the police, we took Brandon to his house. He had to go to sleep because he had to go to work at six o'clock that morning. After we dropped him off, we went downtown to Wawa and we got coffee and Michelle had talked to the lady that was ringing us up and asked if she had seen a short girl with spiky hair, and if she did, to tell her that she was in trouble," Keary recalled. "When we went outside, there was a car that was similar to Devon's and we went to approach it and she said that it wasn't her."

Then they returned to the Mineral Springs and called around to some of Devon's friends and then waited. "We sat up all night and watched TV and waited to hear something from the Forks Township police."

Around 6:00 A.M., Michelle said she was going to go home and get some sleep.

"Did she go?" Miranda asked.

"Yes, she did. And then I thought that was a little

strange, because she waited all night for Devon and she would be expected home within the hour, hour and a half, to get ready for work."

"What time did Ms. Guzman normally leave for work?"

"At around eight o'clock."

Michelle called from home asking Keary to call her if she heard from Devon. Then she called back later, to see if Keary wanted something to eat. "So she brought me lunch from McDonald's and brought it to my apartment. And then we got ready and we were going to look for Devon."

With Michelle driving, they went past Servpro on Seventh and Ferry because by that time Devon should have been at work. Next they went by Devon's mother's house, which was nearby on Ferry Street. "So Michelle suggested that she was certain that she should be at Rick's house," Keary said. The two drove there, and after that, they headed over to South Side to go by George Vine's place.

"So then we were out of places to go, and I told her that we should go to the bridge, which is the place that me and Devon went to." It was a place on Industrial Drive in South Side, where they could go to be alone.

"Did you go to the bridge?" Miranda asked.

"Yes, we did. She said that she wouldn't be there, but I tried explaining to Michelle, she didn't understand that she could have been—if she was really that mad at me, she might have went there to get some time to her—time to herself."

"Was that a place that she went?"

"Yeah, Devon did. And Michelle insisted that she would be at the falls, because that was her and Devon's spot to go."

"Her, meaning Michelle and Devon's?"

"Yeah, that's where they went, like me and Devon went to the bridge. I suggested that we would go to the bridge first, because then that leads right down to six-eleven, which would then go up to the falls."

Devon wasn't at the bridge, so they proceeded to the falls at the old canal museum. "Michelle had had her blinker on, about maybe fifteen feet, I'm not sure if that's exact, but a little bit before we got to the entrance of the falls, so we turned in and we saw her car and we were both mad," Keary said. "And she said, 'I could kill her. I mean, she didn't come home. This is the last time that she's going to do this to me.' Things like that, and we were both pretty upset, and she told me to go over and talk to her. And I was going to go over and talk to her because I was angry with her."

Michelle went over to talk with the city worker locking up a gate while Keary went to Devon's car.

"What did you see?" Miranda asked.

Keary saw no one in the car at first, and told Michelle that Devon wasn't there and must've gone to a friend's place. "She said, 'What do you mean that she's not there?' And I looked again. I said, 'Wait, it looks like she's sleeping in the backseat.'

"And so she stepped back and kind of put her hand on her mouth and told me to go talk to her. So I did. I went to go open the door and it was locked. And it was a car that we shared together, so I had my own keys. So I unlocked the door and I saw her and I shook her and I said, 'Baby, are you OK?' because I saw the knife in her hand. And I saw that her eyebrows and her lips were purple. And so I yelled to Michelle and she didn't come over. So I yelled to her again and I told her that we had to take her to the hospital."

"And then what happened?" the prosecutor asked.

"She came over to the car and we were about to get in and the city worker guy stopped us and said that the police would be here soon. He advised us that it wasn't a good thing to do, to leave her to get care."

Prosecutors believed that Michelle carefully orchestrated the finding of Devon's body that morning. It was important Miranda emphasize whose idea it was to check the canal museum. "Are you certain that you didn't suggest to go to the canal park to look for Ms. Guzman?" she asked.

"No, I did not." Keary said she may have suggested the canal museum to Forks police the night before, but that Michelle was the one who insisted on going there rather than to the bridge.

The last thing Miranda brought up was the car mat from Devon's car discovered suspiciously in the shower at the Mineral Springs. Like Keary's letter to her husband, it was something the prosecution had to bring out and explain first, rather than leave it to the defense to do so. She asked Keary why the mat was inside the apartment.

"Because the weekend before that, we were camping with my brother and we had pickled eggs," Keary said. "And the pickled egg juice spilled inside the car, so it was in the shower being cleaned off. And it was still in the shower because Devon liked to watch the suds come out of the carpet."

"How long had the car mat been in the shower?"

"Approximately four days, maybe."

"I have no further questions," Miranda announced.

Scomillio handled the cross-examination for Michelle's side. He brought up the island vacation, subtly suggesting a jealousy motive on Keary's part. "You weren't asked to go on the trip?" he prodded.

"No, I was not."

"OK. While they were away, you spoke with Brandon Bloss, didn't you?"

"Yes, I did."

"And he said to you—I guess you expressed some concern over Michelle and Devon being together?"

"Yes. Well, I called him originally telling him that they were in the islands because Devon had called me from down there. He did not believe me."

"OK. After maybe in that conversation or a subsequent conversation, he said, 'Stay loose, I'm filing for a divorce.'"

"Yeah, he did say that."

"And he said, 'Michelle can have Devon.'"

"Yes."

"Did you see any of the pictures from the trip to Puerto Rico?"

"Yes, I did."

"They look like they had a good time down there, didn't they?"

"Yes, I would assume so."

Having established that Michelle and Devon had been getting along shortly before the murder, he pressed on, suggesting that Keary and Devon were not. Scomillio showed her a note found in the trash during the police search at the Mineral Springs. "Can you read that to the jury, please?"

"It says, 'I'm sorry about this, I didn't know any other way, we need time apart, I'm sorry, I love you, Devon.'"

Referring to the evening of the murder, he pressed, "Did you give Devon a bloody lip?"

"No, I did not. That was at a different time."

"Did you grab her arms?"

"I may have."

"Did you hold her there?"

"I blocked her from leaving the apartment to go down to the pay phone."

"You kind of restrained her in the apartment, right?"

"Yes."

Then he handed her the journal entry to her husband that she'd read from, for Miranda, and asked her to read the beginning portion, which came before what she'd already read.

Keary did so. "It says, 'Please don't rip this up. I'm not one to admit that I was wrong, so please read what I have to say. I'm so very sorry for everything that has happened. It was all my fault and I'm just now realizing it.'"

The letter continued to say that she never should have started a relationship with him while still in love with Devon, but that he'd come along and swept her off her feet.

"'You treated me like a princess and I was scared. I never had a guy who treated me the way you did. I thought it was too good to be true, and then when you proposed in the backyard, I felt I was the happiest person in the world, and that you really did love me.'"

But Devon had come around asking, "Don't you love me?" and promising to treat Keary well. Keary said she was weak. She'd always wanted that from Devon, but recently she'd changed her mind. "'I realize I think I only wanted her because she made me live a fantasy and it was cool at the time, but what we had and still could is real.'"

When Keary finished reading the letter, Scomillio continued to batter her relationship with Devon. Keary had testified earlier that she hadn't given Devon a bloody lip the night of the murder, but Scomillio found something with which to impeach the claim, showing her a statement to Detective Golazeski. "You told the police, 'No, no, her lip was bleeding. I mean, it wasn't bleeding bad, because we drove to Michelle's.' So she did have a bloody lip?"

"But I did not intentionally give it to her," Keary protested. "How she—we only slapped each other. How she got the bloody lip, I cannot recall."

* * *

Kepler Funk took on the cross-examination for Brandon's side. "It's fair to use the word 'competed'—that you and Michelle had competed for Devon. That's fair to say, right?" he asked.

"Correct," Keary replied.

Funk showed her a sheet of paper found on a shelf in the Mineral Springs apartment, colorfully adorned with balloons and hearts. He asked Keary to read it.

"It says, 'Devon loves Keary, June eleventh, nine forty-nine P.M.,' and 'Getting married June 13 of 2000,'" Keary read.

"You and Devon also had another kind of plan," Funk said. "The two of you discussed having a baby?"

"Yes, we did."

"Devon had got preapproved for a ten-thousand-dollar credit card?"

"Yes."

"And to that end, the two of you were going to move to Arizona?"

"Correct."

But Michelle had a plan also, Funk pointed out. "And Michelle, Ms. Hetzel, she had discussed about buying tickets to go back to the Virgin Islands?"

"Yes."

"Tell the jury about that."

"Well, she was going to get the tickets to take Devon back and stay down there, because that's what she wanted. She wanted to get Devon away from me so that they could live down there, because it was so great when they were there."

"And the point and purpose was to leave prior to your birthday?"

"Yes. They were going to leave that Friday, which was the sixteenth, because she didn't want Devon to be here for my birthday."

"In fact, Devon rejected going, isn't that true?"

"She did."

Funk had just aided the case against Michelle greatly by delineating a clear link between the jealousy motive and the timing of the murder.

Funk touched briefly on the pager codes various people used to contact Devon. Keary's code was 617, which was the date of her birth. Devon's father's code was 7425, which were the last four digits of his phone number and also spelled out "RICK" on the phone pad. Michelle's code was 36, which stood for "DM," or Devon and Michelle. In keeping with his strategy of divorcing his client from the relationships surrounding Devon, he asked, "Brandon didn't have a code, did he?"

"No, he did not," Keary agreed.

"You have said before and used the phrase that Michelle would 'cry wolf.' Do you remember that?" Funk asked her to tell the jury what she meant.

"Meaning that she had always—when she felt that she wasn't going to have Devon, she would always call, saying that her leg was broke or she was sick and she needed Devon to come to her. So that is why I used the example of crying wolf."

"OK. Michelle would feign some type of illness so that Devon—"

"Yes, it was either that or she would show up with a night at the Ramada Inn or tickets to go somewhere or like someplace nice to get her to go with her to show her that her life would be better with Michelle."

"Better than what you had to offer her?"

"Yes."

"And would there be some times when she would feign an illness so that Devon would come to her?"

"Yes, she did that also."

"And when that would happen, you wouldn't go with Devon to Michelle's, would you?"

"No. A lot of times I didn't know about it, and the times that I did know about it, I didn't know until afterward."

"This is kind of a triangle?" A triangle that did not include Brandon was the implication.

Scomillio was getting annoyed, and raised an objection. "Your Honor, first of all, this line of questioning is really irrelevant. I assume that it was going to be a couple questions and move on, and now we're also finding out that the witness didn't know about some of these occurrences and found out about them later, so I—I would object to the continuation of this line of questioning."

Panella overruled the objection, but Funk didn't push it, quickly moving on to another line of inquiry. He asked Keary the significance of the rainbow sticker on Devon's car. Keary said it was "a symbol for gay pride, which is why she had them on her car, because she didn't care who knew."

When Funk was done, Scomillio had the opportunity to recross-examine. Now it was his chance to tear down the rosy picture Funk had painted of the relationship between Keary and Devon. He brought up the unfulfilled promises between Keary and Devon. "Now, she said about going to Arizona. That never happened with you?"

"No."

"She said about getting married to you on June thirteenth. That never happened, did it?"

"No, it didn't. I was already married."

"But Michelle and Devon did go to Puerto Rico together, didn't they?"

"Correct."

"No further questions, Your Honor," Scomillio said.

Keary stepped down from the stand. Funk, who had her

under subpoena, agreed that now she could be released. Her testimony had brought to light much of the angst and confusion involved in the love triangle among the girls, but done little to clarify how things had really stood among them at the end. It also hadn't really touched the heart of the mystery of how and why three years of competition and brimming tensions had finally culminated in murder. Despite this shortcoming, however, Keary's testimony had been credible, because her answers seemed frank and honest. She didn't try to minimize her role in the physical altercations with Devon or gloss over other unpleasant aspects of the relationship. Keary's testimony would have to play a major role in the jury's understanding of the relationship dynamics the various attorneys had tried so hard to explain. But exactly what it all would boil down to in the deliberation room was anyone's guess.

The end of the afternoon was nearing. Judge Panella decided to call it a day a little early, adjourning at 4:29 P.M.

37

Thursday, September 27, 2001 was a hard day for Devon's family and supporters. It included the testimony of Richard Scanlon, who had performed the bite mark analysis, and Sara Funke, who had conducted the autopsy and now described in clinical detail just how the murder had been committed, in terms of the story told to her by the various injuries, large and small, on Devon's body.

Easton detective William Crouse led off the day's parade of witnesses, becoming the twelfth to testify for the commonwealth so far. Crouse was a veteran officer who'd been with Easton PD about thirty years. He was working the day shift back on June 15, 2000, and had been called to the canal museum with a report of a body in a car. Other officers had begun stringing crime scene tape when he arrived.

Crouse said his lieutenant put him in charge of the case (the responsibility later passed to Barry Golazeski when Crouse went on vacation in early July). Crouse testified that he coordinated the duties of the other detectives as they arrived, photographed the crime scene and collected some of the evidence, including the green Servpro coat, the victim's clothing, her pager and the syringe that was found.

Later that day, he applied for a warrant and searched Keary and Devon's Mineral Springs apartment, collecting some items of evidence there also.

"Were you able to make any determination as to whether there was any evidence that the murder occurred at that location?" Morganelli asked.

"From what we were able to gather, it didn't appear that it had taken place there," Crouse said. The staged crime scene really hadn't fooled anyone for very long.

Later in the investigation, on August 4, Crouse had looked into Michelle's employment at the office of Dr. Rajen Oza on North Sixteenth Street in Wilson. "The doctor turned over to me a Terumo brand syringe," Crouse said. Morganelli produced an unopened package containing a syringe, which Crouse confirmed was the one he'd obtained from Oza. The implication was plain. The syringe found with Devon's body could have been obtained by Michelle at her workplace. It was the same size and brand as the ones Oza stocked.

Pursuing the connection further, Morganelli asked if Michelle had been employed by Oza in August when the detective went to the office.

"He had her employed, but said that she hadn't picked up her last paycheck or returned her office key."

Monahan struggled to compose himself for the cross-examination. He apologized for the delay, saying he was having a difficult morning. When he did begin his cross, the direction of his questions hinted at a familiar theme—casting suspicion on the roommate.

Monahan asked Crouse if the police had looked into whether Devon's car could be locked without a key.

"Not that I'm aware of, no, sir."

The significance of this may have escaped the jurors unless they recalled Keary Renner's having said that Devon's car was locked at the canal museum and that

Keary herself, who had her own key, had been the one to unlock it. Devon's key had been left in the ignition. The thrust of Monahan's question was that if a key was needed to lock up the car from the outside, Keary was the one who had the means to do so. He was suggesting that the onus had been on the police to investigate this issue, and that they had neglected to do it.

This type of attack was something he would use time and time again, suggesting that investigators could have done a more thorough job. Would it win points with the jury? It was hard to say. The tactic could cut both ways. Raising speculative questions about the prosecution's evidence could raise some doubts; however, questions were just questions. The absence of any hard fact to contradict the evidence could lead to the conclusion that such facts did not exist. In the example of the locked doors, whether it was possible for the accused to have locked the car behind them was an answerable question. If the answer was favorable to the accused, why not supply it?

Later in the cross-examination, Monahan moved on to the syringe, asking Crouse how the one collected from the doctor's office compared to the one found at the crime scene. "It appeared to you to be similar, is that right?"

"Yes, sir."

"It had a needle on it, though, didn't it? Right?"

"No, it did not."

"The one from Dr. Oza's office does not have a needle?"

"I don't believe it does, sir."

Whether an honest mistake or a gimmick to trip up the witness, it was another example of Monahan's little gaffs.

Setting off on another line of inquiry similar to the door-lock issue, Monahan asked if Crouse had looked into whether Oza's office was equipped with an alarm system. If Crouse said no, Monahan could suggest that the office may have had alarms and could have been tripped had Michelle tried to slip in and steal a syringe.

This time the detective had his bases covered. "When he took me to the room where the syringes were, I noticed that there was no lock on that drawer. At least it wasn't locked at the time. And I asked him if he had a security system. I believe he said no."

Monahan's last question was a final attempt to sever the tie between his client and the syringe found at the crime scene. "Detective Crouse, from your own knowledge, were there any fingerprints found on the syringe that was recovered at the crime scene?"

Crouse admitted that the item had come back negative for prints.

Szachacz's cross-examination was again brief. Little if anything in the preceding testimony had been damaging to his client, so he took the opportunity to emphasize what would be damaging to Michelle—the fact that no blood could be seen before the green jacket covering the body was removed. He showed Crouse one of the initial crime scene photos. "As we are looking at that photograph, do you see any blood on the back of Ms. Guzman? You can't, because of the green jacket, right?"

Crouse agreed.

Next to take the stand was Detective Michael Gibiser, who had eleven years behind him with Easton PD. Gibiser became involved in the case the day after the body was found. He was charged with going to the office of Magistrate Nancy Matos-Gonzales to apply for two search warrants—one for Michelle and Brandon's house and the other for Michelle's car. He detailed how those searches were conducted, and what items were taken into possession by the police department. The search of the house had produced an assortment of items, including the size-five Hilfiger jeans from the washing machine, water samples, hair and fiber, sixteen knives, and dirt and grass samples from the yard. The search of the car produced thirteen items, including the full set of men's clothing, four rubber gloves, hair and fiber picked up in evidence vacuum filters, and an envelope containing Michelle's résumé and a cover letter.

Morganelli held up the items of clothing, one by one, and had the detective identify each piece—large black sweatshirt, black Lee jeans (size thirty-two by thirty-two), white medium T-shirt; red-white-and-blue underwear, white Nike sneakers (size eleven), and white-and-gray socks.

Gibiser testified that he'd searched Devon's car and also examined the list of calls stored in the memory of Devon's pager. He noted that nine pages were saved in the device, and he read off the strings of numbers to the jury. The first call had come in at 9:00 P.M. and the last at 10:07 P.M. Phone records indicated calls had been made the night of the murder from Michelle and Brandon's home phone to Devon's pager. Morganelli asked if the couple's phone number appeared in the device's memory. Gibiser answered that it did not. A later police witness, who examined the matter in more depth, would testify that pages from the Bloss/Hetzel home had been selectively erased.

Monahan began his cross by apologizing for his manner of speech, admitting that he sometimes asked "unartful questions" and had a habit of mumbling. But then he proceeded to score some points. He stressed that Michelle's fingerprints were not found on the pager. He established that the pager only saved the time pages were received, not the dates, and that the strings of numbers saved did not necessarily correspond to the callers' phone numbers, but could be numbers the callers chose to punch in.

He got in that when police searched the couple's

house, they entered using keys readily given to them by Michelle's father, and that when they searched Michelle's car, they had keys voluntarily handed over by Michelle herself. Finally he emphasized the fact that the bloody evidence found in the trunk of her car included only men's clothing, not women's.

He did commit one of his typical blunders, however. Prompting the detective about the evidence found in Michelle's car, he said: "There were photographs which you recovered from the glove box which were from Michelle and Devon's trip, right, to Puerto Rico?"

"Those photographs were found in the victim's vehicle, sir."

It was a complex case, with many minute details to remember. Anyone could lose track of a few of them here and there. Monahan's consistent slips, though, had to cause some to wonder if there was not some strategic intent behind them.

The cross-examination by Kepler Funk on Brandon's behalf lasted longer this time than with previous witnesses. Initially he skipped briefly over the damaging find in the trunk of Michelle's car. As incriminating as the clothing appeared, the defense's position was that they were the result of Brandon's involvement in moving the body, and nothing in the detective's testimony compromised that position. Also, Funk may have wanted to avoid making too much of the issue, lest the added attention lead jurors to give it additional weight. Instead, Funk focused on supporting his opening argument that it was Michelle, rather than Brandon, who had the close ties to the victim. He pointed to a photograph of Michelle's car in the police impound garage, singling out the rainbow sticker on the back that matched the one on Devon's car.

But then he circled around to the items in the trunk. "Mr. Monahan asked you if you found any items of clothing that belonged to Michelle Hetzel, and you answered no. Let me bring that up again," Funk said. Noting that two pairs of rubber gloves were found, he asked if the detective knew who wore them.

"No, sir."

"They may have been worn by Michelle Hetzel?"

"It's a possibility."

The admission didn't do anything for Brandon's case, one way or the other, but it did keep Michelle from walking away with clean hands, so to speak.

The last thing Funk cross-examined the witness about was the pager. Back when Monahan had his turn, he'd walked the witness through the series of nine calls, winning an admission after each one that he didn't know where it came from or what it meant. But Funk pointed out that Monahan had skipped one. Was it another of his innocent blunders?

"Mr. Monahan forgot to ask you about one of them," Funk asserted. "He went from number seven to number nine. But there's a number eight, isn't there?"

The detective agreed there was.

"Let's go over the numbers slowly: 4-5683-968. Do you see that?"

"Yes."

"Number four, the first number, that corresponds with the letter *I* on the phone pad; number five corresponds with *L*; number six, *O*; number eight, *V*; number three, *E*. And then there's a hyphen and number nine, *Y*; number six, *O*; and number eight, *U*. Those eight letters spell out 'I love you,' don't they?"

"Yes, sir."

"Judge, I have nothing further," Funk said.

It was a cute stunt, managing to make Michelle's defense look like it might have been trying to hide something. Who'd sent that 10:07 P.M. page? No one could miss the point that it probably wasn't Brandon.

The next witness was Richard Scanlon, the dentist from Lewiston, Pennsylvania, who'd conducted the bite pattern analysis. He defined his area of expertise as forensic odontology, "the application of the science of dentistry to areas of criminal and legal proceedings, mostly pertaining to the identification of individuals' teeth when they cannot be identified in any other means, bite mark analysis, child abuse analysis and disaster identification of victims." He said he had twenty-seven years of continuing education in the field and had served as chief deputy coroner in Mifflin County, Pennsylvania, for nine years.

Scanlon said he got involved in the Guzman case when Detective Golazeski came to his office with photographs and some bandages that he thought could be evidence of a bite mark. District Attorney John Morganelli asked if he'd formed any opinion about the materials at the time.

"Not any strong opinions," Scanlon answered. "I said that the wound he showed me in the photograph and what I saw on the bandages resembled what could be a human bite mark, but the injury was too indistinct and too healed to make a strong opinion as to its actually being a bite mark."

He'd needed better materials to work with, so Golazeski brought him the photographs obtained from Dr. Asen, the Allentown odontologist. Morganelli had to skirt carefully around the issue of where these photos came from, however, to avoid being stopped in his tracks by objections from Brandon's defense. The fact that Brandon had consulted Asen before the police did made this issue a minefield of legal technicalities throughout the trial, and even afterward.

Establishing that Scanlon had received photos adequate for analysis, Morganelli had him step down from the stand to explain what could be seen on a blowup of one of those photos, showing the injury to Brandon's left forearm, now before the jury.

"This is what we refer to as a classic pattern of a human bite mark, in which you see both indications of the upper arch and the lower arch, with the area in between being the tissue that has been compressed . . . where the upper and lower teeth come together and squeeze very hard."

Morganelli asked about the severity of the bite mark.

"I categorized it as moderate to severe bite mark, because crushing of the tissue, the well-defined pattern of the teeth in the tissue. Oftentimes, with moderate bite marks, we'll see the tissue fade rapidly and the tissue will not have these individual markings on them, and also the crushing and removal of the tissue. There's tissue here that was actually abraded away."

How much pain would the recipient of the mark have suffered, the DA wanted to know. Scanlon said "rather severe," a six or a seven on a ten-point scale.

To match the bite mark to a particular person, Scanlon explained that dental casts were taken from the three suspects—Brandon, Michelle and Keary—and the victim. From these casts, computer-generated overlays were created, and these overlays were compared to enlarged photographs of the bite injury in search of a match. In Keary's overlay, a number of teeth on the maxillary arch did not fit the bite pattern. On Michelle's, a number of teeth did not align with the mark. With Brandon's, the arch was too wide and a number of teeth fell outside the injury pattern. That left Devon. Scanlon said her overlay matched Brandon's injury.

Illustrating the support for his conclusion on the blowup, he said, "You can see that there's minimal, minimal biting pattern in this side here, and this refers to the area where Devon has been missing some teeth on this side also. This tooth was rather sharp and I believe this showed that this was an area where the upper jaw, when biting, usually drags, and this is the sharp area, the upper eyetooth is causing this. The lower jaw is usually fixed during a bite, and the outline of this is facially consistent with her tooth pattern."

The last thing Morganelli wanted to cover with Scanlon is how Brandon and Devon had been positioned for the bite to occur they way it did.

"Let me ask you, if I was Mr. Bloss and I was coming toward you in this fashion"—he came at Scanlon head-on, his left arm out—would it be possible for this bite to be inflicted from this direction?"

Scanlon demonstrated the unlikelihood that it happened that way. "I would have to grab your arm and reach in and bite in that manner."

Morganelli circled around, coming in from the rear. "If I came from behind you in this fashion, how would that fit?"

Scanlon agreed that was the more likely scenario, that Devon had been grabbed from behind, that she'd bitten the arm in front of her face.

Monahan kept his cross-examination brief, since the bite mark had no real implications regarding Michelle's guilt. But since it looked so bad for Brandon, especially after the graphic demonstration Morganelli had just conducted, Monahan capitalized on the moment, dwelling on the image of the victim biting her attacker. He asked if it would take "substantial time, as well as pressure, in order for that type of bite wound to form."

"Yes, I would assume it would be a bite of a duration of maybe six or seven seconds."

"Substantial?"

"Substantial, yes."

"And presumably the person who received that bite would scream—would that be a fair statement?"

Funk objected that the question called for speculation, but Monahan had made his point.

Funk took over next. His cross-examination was no longer than Monahan's. Brandon wasn't claiming that Devon hadn't bitten him, so there was no need to challenge Scanlon's analysis, only to curtail the conclusions that could be drawn.

"You concluded that Devon bit Mr. Bloss?" Funk asked.

"That's correct."

"Right. You're not aware of any of the circumstances surrounding that bite, are you?"

"No, I'm not."

Sara Funke replaced Scanlon on the stand, describing at length the various injuries she observed during the autopsy of the victim, which included the cut across her neck, bruises on her arms and hands, the red petechia on her face, indicating asphyxia, and the postmortem abrasions on her back.

Morganelli asked her to explain, using evidence photographs, the cut to the neck.

"It's a deep wound," Funke said. "It goes almost to the spine, but not quite to the spine. It severs or completely cuts off the tongue and separates it from the rest of the throat structures and also cuts in half the right carotid artery and the right jugular vein."

Funke explained what the cutting of the carotid and jugular told her about how the injury had been inflicted. "Both of those were cut on the right side. They were not cut on the left side, and that indicates that her head had to have been turned to the left, because the left side was protected that way, and the right vessels would be popping out and would be easily cut."

Morganelli asked what else she could tell about how the injury was inflicted.

Funke replied that a "constellation of injuries" to Devon's face—including fingernail marks—pointed to "a left hand being placed over her face, with the web space between the thumb and forefinger by her nose and the fingers by her right cheek." If the attacker's left hand was placed in such a way, turning her face to the left, "then the assailant's right hand can draw the knife across her throat and get the right side of the vessels," Funke concluded. She agreed with Richard Scanlon's testimony that the assailant had to have been standing behind her.

"So I don't want to get too personal here," Morganelli said, moving into position for a demonstration similar to the one he'd conducted with Scanlon. "If I was behind you in this fashion, and this is kind of what you are describing, the person would have cut from the left to the right side, and the wounds on the side of her face as indicated on the second photograph may be fingernails or scratch marks?"

"Yes."

He asked if the victim would have been able to speak after the injury occurred. Funke said no. This detail would be picked up long after the trial, when Court TV's *Forensic Files* profiled the case, titling the segment "Cries Unheard."

Monahan's cross-examination focused on two issues. One was time of death. He asked Funke if she'd taken a core body temperature. She said her job had been to conduct the autopsy, which was the wrong time to take a core body temperature. Monahan pressed the issue, asking if that was something that should have been done at the crime scene. It was an issue he'd attacked Coroner Lysek on when he was on the stand.

"I cannot second-guess that call," Funke said. As Lysek had done, she stressed that determining time of death was far from an exact science. "It's never possible to determine time of death, despite what the media may try to tell you and portray to us on TV. Time of death is an estimation."

The other issue Monahan focused on was the constellation of injuries, including a scrape on the earlobe, indicating a hand having been placed over Devon's face. He brought out a transcript of Funke's testimony at the preliminary hearing, which had taken place about a year before, and read from her testimony: "'If the hand is big enough and the face is small enough, the fingers can even reach far enough to scrape the earlobe.'"

Funke agreed that's what she'd said.

"That's your opinion in this case, that there was a very large hand on her face, right?" Monahan queried.

Whether Funke knew it or not, it was a tricky question. At the time of the preliminary hearing, the only evidence prosecutors had as to who had used the knife was the forensic evidence, which, through the bite mark particularly, pointed to Brandon. But right after the preliminary, Cara Judd came forward with her journals spelling out a confession by Michelle that she had used the knife. Although the two points of evidence were contradictory, Morganelli had made the decision to present both of them in court and let the jury try to figure it out. It was a gamble, because the jurors could throw up their hands and say they couldn't figure it out, resulting in a mistrial, or they could reject the contradictory evidence and return a verdict of not guilty.

The question was, if Funke's expert testimony pointed definitively to Brandon, and Brandon alone, as the one who used the knife, how would the jury receive Cara Judd's testimony when her turn came to take the stand?

It turned out to be a moot point. Like so many other questions in this case, a definitive answer proved elusive. Funke could not commit to saying the hand on Devon's face had been a "very large one," that is to say, Brandon's.

"There was a hand on her face, yes, that's my opinion," she said.

But Monahan kept trying. "And the hand was big enough for the fingers to scrape the earlobe, right?"

"Yes."

He let it go at that.

Kepler Funk, during his cross-examination of the pathologist, treaded lightly. The forensic evidence was fairly damaging to Brandon, but he found a few openings through which to attack Dr. Funke. He pressed her on why she had not examined the many knives collected by police during the investigation and compared them to the fatal wound.

She answered that such an examination would not have helped "narrow down the field of knives" that could have been the murder weapon. Any knife with a cutting edge on it could have been the one used, she said. Unlike the bite mark, which told a detailed story about its source, this wound could not "pick out which knife did it."

Two more witnesses remained for the day. Angie O'Neill, an employee in the office of District Justice Sandra Zemgulis, testified briefly about the criminal harassment complaint Michelle had filed against Devon in January 2000, just before her wedding. She was followed by Detective David Ryan, who had interviewed Brandon Bloss the night Devon's body was found.

One of the important things his testimony established for the commonwealth was that Brandon had been involved in summoning Devon to his house that night. Ryan related that Michelle had come home that night appearing exhausted and intoxicated, but wouldn't explain why. So he "chose to call Devon Guzman and ask her to come over to see if she would help to ascertain why Michelle Hetzel was in the condition that she was in."

Another thing he established was that Brandon admitted being instrumental in bringing Devon back to his house alone, after she'd arrived with Keary, saying that he was the one who told her she'd have to take Keary home and come back.

Morganelli asked what Brandon had been wearing when Ryan interviewed him. The detective answered that it was a dark, long-sleeved sweatshirt. He asked if Brandon had mentioned a struggle between his wife and Devon, or the fact that he'd been bitten on the arm. Ryan said he had not.

On cross-examination Scomillio emphasized another of Brandon's omissions of fact that night. "He did not say anything about moving a body?" he asked the detective.

"No, he did not."

It was a major point, because the whole of Brandon's defense was that he'd *only* helped move the body. If that's all he did, and all he was guilty of, why did he go to such extremes to cover it up?

The cross-examination for Brandon's side was the briefest one yet. There was little to be done, given the fact that Brandon obviously had not told the truth back then. Szachacz asked only one question, referring to a point made about Brandon and Michelle having given virtually identical statements to police the day the body was found. "Are you aware that Michelle Hetzel gave her statement to Mr. Golazeski at two-fifteen in the afternoon, seven hours before Brandon gave you his statement?"

"Yes," the detective replied.

If the point was that Brandon was only following Michelle's lead, covering for her by sticking to the same story she'd told, it was a weak one. In the absence of an explanation for why he might have done such a thing, it did little to earn sympathy. Also, the idea of Brandon's covering for Michelle didn't jibe with his defense that he was far removed from the love triangle and emotionally detached from its jealousies.

Court adjourned for the day at 3:58 P.M. The commonwealth was nearly finished putting on its case as the end of the week approached. The following day, Friday, Detective Golazeski would take center stage. It was a good night for him to go home and get some sleep, because a long day on the stand awaited.

38

Judge Panella began on Friday, September 28, 2001, the same way he'd begun each of the preceding days, with a roll call of the witnesses who'd testified previously, to keep the progression fresh in jurors' minds. He tallied off seventeen names. Today's witness, the eighteenth, would be Easton detective Barry Golazeski, the case's lead investigator. Golazeski told the jury that he'd been with the Easton police since 1992, that he'd held the rank of inspector in the criminal investigation division at the time of the murder, and that the criminal complaints charging the defendants with homicide and conspiracy to commit homicide bore his signature.

Morganelli led off his direct examination by asking Golazeski about his interview of Michelle after Devon's body was found. The DA produced a cassette tape of the interview, marked as commonwealth Exhibit No. 40. "Your Honor, with the court's permission, I would like to play the tape."

"That's fine," Panella said.

Monahan, who was on his own representing Michelle today while co-counsel Scomillio attended a funeral, noted that the tape player contained a cassette he planned to play later, adding distrustfully, "so don't erase it when you take it out."

"We won't do that, Mr. Monahan," Morganelli assured him.

It had to be a tense time for Monahan. He was lacking Scomillio, on whom he relied heavily, and now his client's own words were about to come back to haunt her. It would be very powerful evidence for the jury to consider. Knowing what they now knew, they would be able to compare the facts in evidence with the things Michelle had told police, then judge for themselves. Her story had changed from then to now. As the tape played, the jury could plainly hear what could be construed as efforts to steer suspicion toward Keary Renner.

"She has a temper," Michelle said on the tape. "Keary is very jealous of a lot of people." Michelle also evaded the truth, denying a romantic relationship with Devon. "We never slept together," she claimed. And she disparaged the victim. "Devon's the kind of person where she can't be alone. And when she is, she gets very angry," she said. And later, "Devon gets angry when she drinks. . . ."

Immediately after someone dies, there's often a tendency to idealize that person briefly, forgetting faults and recalling only the good qualities. There's a sacredness in the death of a close friend or loved one that can make disparagement of the deceased feel like a sacrilegious betrayal. This might have been expected of someone who called Devon her best friend, her only friend. It was not evident in Michelle's conversation with Golazeski, as it played to rapt attention in the courtroom.

Michelle's words painted a frank picture in which Devon—intoxicated, emotional, confused—may have collided violently and fatally with Keary—jealous, abusive, easily antagonized by Devon's drinking. Michelle also opened the door for suicide to be considered, introducing the idea more or less off-handedly in the negative, saying, "I never heard Devon talk about suicide."

Brandon had gotten off easier the day before. Detective Ryan had testified about his interview of Brandon, but no tape existed from that interview. His own words could not come back to haunt him. It was one thing to have a witness take the stand and say a defendant had not told the truth; it's quite another for the jury to hear it for themselves.

And that was what Michelle was facing.

When the tape concluded, Morganelli zeroed in on Michelle's statement to Golazeski that Devon's back was "all bloody" when she looked in the car. The DA produced the gray Champion sweatshirt in question, along with the Basic Equipment T-shirt the victim had worn underneath, so that the detective could identify them. The shirts were walked before the jurors, so they could see them, front and back. The backs of both were red with blood. Some of the jurors could not suppress gasps. On the Guzman side of the courtroom, some people covered their eyes, crying softly. Morganelli asked the detective's opinion of the "credibility of Michelle Hetzel's statement that when she looked in and saw the back of Devon Guzman, it was 'all bloody.'"

"There was a coat covering her back; you couldn't tell that there was any blood there," Golazeski replied.

The DA believed Michelle knew Devon's body was in the car and was aware of the bloody sweatshirt under the green jacket. Her preconceived notion that blood would be visible, when in reality it wasn't, indicated prior knowledge of what was under the green coat, he maintained.

Moving on to the ensuing investigation, the detective said he'd subpoenaed Brandon and Michelle's telephone records, and that the night of the murder from 11:28 P.M. to 6:47 A.M.—the hours Michelle was looking for her missing friend—fifteen calls had been made to Devon's pager. Notably, the last call from the house to the pager was at 1:32 A.M. Michelle and Brandon did not arrive at Keary's Mineral Springs apartment until about 2:30 A.M. That meant a full hour passed in which Michelle, who'd paged her friend fifteen times over two hours, had suddenly stopped bothering to dial the pager, which was the one direct line of communication Devon carried on her person. The connect-the-dots scenario the DA alluded to was that Michelle and Brandon had paged Devon obsessively to get her to their home, then stopped once they'd achieved their goal. If Devon truly had never returned to their house, wouldn't they have continued to page her?

Golazeski further testified that any evidence of the pages from the Bloss/Hetzel home had been selectively erased from the device. Someone had to have gone one by one, deleting those pages but leaving others. Unfortunately, no fingerprints were found on the pager.

The DA continued to plot his connect-the-dots scenario of the cover-up. "Now, in the trunk of the Hetzel car, we've had testimony that—from Detective Gibiser—that there were found two pairs of latex gloves in the bag with the clothes of Brandon Bloss, correct?"

"Yes."

"If you have latex gloves on, would you leave prints on pagers or syringes or anything that you touched?"

"Most of the time, no."

Morganelli asked Golazeski how he'd come to find the three rings symbolizing the vows Michelle and Devon exchanged in the islands. These were important, because they constituted tangible evidence of Michelle's romantic attachment to Devon, something she had denied in her recorded statement. The detective said that one of his trash pulls had produced a charge card receipt in the amount of $1,044.60 for a jewelry purchase at Zally Jewelers in Christiansted,

St. Croix. He contacted the store, and the owners mailed him photographs of the rings and faxed him diagrams. They matched the rings he later found in Michelle's parents' house.

Morganelli next moved on to how the detective happened on the trail of the bite mark on Brandon's arm. This was crucial evidence because it established that there had been physical contact between Devon and Brandon prior to her death, something both Brandon and Michelle had neglected to mention in their statements to police. If Golazeski had not discovered evidence of that bite mark and correctly deduced what it was early on in his investigation, the injury might have healed without anyone but Brandon and Michelle ever having been the wiser. That connection between Brandon and Devon would have been gone for good, instead of documented, diagrammed and photographed for a jury to see. Advanced forensic technologies had played a big part in the case, but it was good old-fashioned detective work that had produced the bandages in the trash, and plain old cop intuition that suggested to Golazeski that the impression on the bandages resembled a human bite. Morganelli asked him to explain this fortuitous bit of detective work.

Golazeski said the trash pulls had produced Zee bandage wrappers, Mycitracin antibiotic tubes and used bandages with discolored stains on them.

"When you examined them and looked at them, did you come to an opinion as to perhaps what they represented?" the DA queried.

"Well, as the investigation went on, I kept looking at the shape of the injury pattern that was left on this pad," Golazeski said, illustrating on mounted photos exhibited for the jury. "On the plain gauze pad, the shape of the wound isn't clear, because it just kind of absorbs into it and it doesn't do anything. But this pad has a nonstick surface on it and has a distinct pattern-type injury to it. And as I—I continued to look at it and from—I decided that I believe it may have been a bite mark wound."

His answer was decidedly unscientific, something not easy to explain in a court of law. It more or less came down to a hunch.

This is why in crime fighting there's no substitute for the human mind. Forensics have done much to advance the field in recent years, but there's still no substitute for the mind of an experienced detective. Forensic tools are powerful weapons, but they require people who know how to apply them. Forensics can detect things never before visible to the human eye, but it takes human experience to know where to look. Without that human element, the bandages may have turned out just like the cigarette packs in the trash pulls—just more pieces of non-meaningful evidence.

Once Golazeski had validated his hunch scientifically that Brandon had been bitten, then and only then did he have the legal grounds to bring him in to examine and photograph the bite wound. He brought Brandon in for this purpose on June 29, 2000, which was more than a month before arresting him. At the time he also took a set of major case prints, which included a fingerprint card of ten rolled and static prints, along with an impression of the entire palm surface. When he was done, he had Brandon sign the fingerprint card, noting that he signed with his right hand. Similarly, he'd had occasion to observe that Michelle was right-handed also. These small observations mattered, because the forensic pathologist's testimony suggested that Devon's injuries were consistent with a right-handed killer. If either or both of them had been left-handed, the distinction could have been significant.

Continuing to examine how the detective tied various pieces of evidence to the defendants, Morganelli asked how the crime scene syringe compared to the sample collected from Michelle's employer. Golazeski said they were both 3cc Terumos.

"Now, during the course of your investigation, were you ever able to determine whether or not Ms. Hetzel had access to that office?" the DA asked.

"Yes. After Detective Crouse had been up there, I stopped back up there to talk with the staff myself and it had been determined that she hadn't turned in her key for that office."

Taking it one final step, he obtained a key to the doctor's office, which he later matched up to a duplicate key found at Michelle's parents' house.

Morganelli's last line of inquiry had to do with the Cancun trip taken by Brandon and Michelle after the murder. One of Golazeski's trash pulls had turned up an airline ticket envelope and baggage tags.

"Did you follow up on that?" the DA asked.

Szachacz interrupted. "Judge, I'm going to object and ask that we approach on this topic."

An important battle lay ahead. The attorneys gathered for a sidebar.

"Is it your intention to get into the trip to Mexico?" Szachacz wanted to know.

Morganelli addressed Judge Panella. "The issue that we'll get into is that Mr. Golazeski revealed information, Your Honor, that Bloss and Hetzel took a trip to Cancun."

Szachacz wasn't happy. "Pretrial, I had asked you about that. You had told me, off the record, that you were not going to get into that, and obviously you changed your mind."

"Only the fact that they went together to Mexico," Morganelli countered. "One of the issues that's been raised in the trial is that the Bloss/Hetzel marriage was on the rocks. And yet, shortly after the murder, they take a trip to Cancun, Mexico. Of course we are arguing that this was conspiracy that they acted together."

Morganelli argued that the defense had forced him to bring up the issue by claiming that the couple had such antipathy for each other that they couldn't have cooperated in a murder. The antipathy was a valid point. Brandon really had consulted a divorce lawyer, and Michelle really had asked to live with Devon at Rick Guzman's house. But obviously that wasn't the whole story. Again and again Brandon's attorneys had argued that Brandon wasn't part of the three girls' triangle, and that he wasn't like them. Yet his relationship with Michelle seemed to share in the same strange and troubling love/hate phenomenon, this ability to bounce between the two extremes of passion. How could Brandon have been about to divorce his wife one week, and then helped her dispose of a body and vacationed in Mexico just a short few weeks later? How could they have had too much antipathy to commit murder together, but not to join together in a cover-up? To get to the bottom of this, the Cancun trip was a part of the story the jury had to know.

"When was the trip?" Panella asked.

"It was the beginning of July is my understanding," Szachacz said, quickly adding, "I would object on behalf of Mr. Bloss that it is not relevant, and any probative value is outweighed by the prejudice."

"What's the prejudice?" Panella queried.

"The only reason that Mr. Morganelli is going to introduce this is that he's going to argue that there's some flight going on. That they, you know, were fleeing," Szachacz complained.

The judge asked Monahan for his position regarding Michelle's side of the case. Monahan agreed with Szachacz, joining in the objection.

Panella was disinclined to see it their way. "In all honesty,

I'm the person hearing this, if not for the first time, almost the first time. I don't believe the flight is a factor. Although I can't tell you that it's not evidence of a relationship which would support a conspiracy, but that's again what the commonwealth is trying to prove, so the objection is overruled."

"Judge, one more point," Szachacz said, not giving up this important fight. "Any conspiracy would have ended with the murder, so any information two weeks to three weeks later will not be relevant."

But Panella had decided. "You're covered," he said.

The sidebar concluded, Morganelli queried Detective Golazeski briefly about the finding of Continental Airlines ticket stubs in the names of Michelle Hetzel and Brandon Bloss, for a flight from Philadelphia to Houston to Cancun on July 1, 2000, just two weeks after the murder.

With that, Morganelli concluded his direct examination, and Panella called a break for lunch. At 1:30 P.M., the jurors filed back in. The trial resumed, with Detective Golazeski facing cross-examination by the defense teams.

Before launching into his questioning, Monahan asked the detective's indulgence if he mispronounced words or mumbled. "If you don't hear anything, please let me know. I'm not doing it intentionally. It's Friday, it's been a long week."

It was a sentiment everyone there could second.

The first issue Monahan addressed was whether Michelle could have seen blood on the victim's back, as she claimed. He won an admission that people had "attempted to arouse and check on the victim," and didn't push the question any further.

He questioned the thoroughness of the investigation by pointing out that police hadn't done an analysis on Keary Renner's phone records, as they had done on Michelle's. The reason, Golazeski said, was that the two were served by different phone companies, and Keary's company didn't keep a record of local calls.

The specter of the "O.J. defense," raised once before the trial started, came up again when Monahan asked, "And with regard to blood, at one point, and even now maybe, you believed there was at least another blood source, maybe another suspect in this case that was unknown, right?"

Morganelli objected that the detective had said no such thing.

Monahan rephrased the question, bringing up a statement Golazeski had made while interviewing Jerry Ronco after Michelle and Brandon had been arrested. He brought out a transcript and asked Golazeski to read what he had said to Ronco.

Golazeski read the statement: "'Well, there's something that I'm going to do; it's a little better than a lie detector test, actually. I think there's still somebody else involved that I haven't arrested yet, OK, and the only people who know that are right here, OK, and a few people on the DA's staff."

Monahan pointed out that Golazeski had made the statement on September 12, a full month after Michelle and Brandon's August 13 arrest. It may have been merely an investigative technique the detective was using to get his subject talking, but Monahan was making headway and kept at it. He pressed Golazeski about "a third DNA source on the collar of the bloody sweatshirt that you showed the jury before."

Golazeski corrected him, saying that unidentified blood had been found on a Servpro shirt located on the floor of the car.

"It was on the collar of the Servpro shirt, right?" Monahan asked.

"Right," the detective said.

"And that shirt was worn underneath the sweatshirt, right?"

"No, sir."

Morganelli had heard enough, objecting that the questions were mischaracterizing the evidence. It was the first time he'd called Monahan on one of his persistent slipups. "Your Honor, Mr. Monahan knows that was not the clothing worn by the victim. It was on the floor of the vehicle."

Moving on to the investigations behind Brandon and Michelle's house, Monahan asked, "You disassembled the garage, right?"

"I didn't take the garage apart, sir," Golazeski replied.

Monahan proceeded to talk about the syringe, asking the detective how he went about comparing the evidence collected with the new syringe obtained for comparison purposes. "So you took the cap from the pocket in the jeans in the washing machine?"

"Yes."

"And you put that on a brand-new syringe?"

"Incorrect!" It was Morganelli interrupting. "The question, again, is mischaracterizing the fact." The DA went on to explain that the cap in the jeans was placed on the syringe found on the body.

Monahan pressed on, undeterred. "So the needle wasn't broken off the syringe that was found in the victim's body?"

By now, Golazeski had caught on. "You can examine the photo on the exhibit," he said.

"So if there's testimony here to the effect that the needle was broken and that's the way that had come from the crime scene—"

"There's a photo from the crime scene on the exhibit, sir. You can examine it."

With that, Monahan dropped the issue.

A later line of questioning produced better results. Regarding Michelle's appearance when Golazeski interviewed her after finding the body, he asked, "Did you see any cuts or bruises or abrasions on her, or anything like that?"

"No, I didn't notice any at any time. Her face was fine. Her nails were fine. They were long. Her hands seemed fine. I didn't see any scratches or anything like that."

"OK. She didn't complain or walk with a limp, or anything like that?"

"No, other than appearing that she hadn't slept."

Given the number of bruises and abrasions observed on Devon's body, and the severity of the bite mark suffered by Brandon, the fact that Michelle bore not the slightest visible injury may have given jurors something to think about.

At the end of his cross-examination, Monahan played the series of five 911 calls, the first of which was placed at around 3:00 A.M., asking the detective to confirm that in fact both Michelle's and Keary's voices could be heard on the calls. Michelle was making the calls and Keary was speaking up occasionally in the background. Golazeski agreed that was the case. The calls were played in the courtroom. One of the curious things about them was that with each call, Michelle seemed to grow calmer, rather than more anxious as one might expect her to as the night wore on.

It was haunting to think about that fact that at the time these calls were being made, Devon was already dead, and the whole thing could have been a farce put on by a cold-blooded killer covering up her tracks. As the voices of Michelle and the dispatcher went back and forth, Devon's mother ran from the courtroom.

The time was nearing four o'clock when Monahan concluded cross-examining Golazeski. After a short recess, Szachacz got his turn.

In keeping with his strategy of divorcing Brandon from the love triangle, he asked Golazeski if Brandon's fingerprints had been found on the torn-up photos of the Caribbean trip found in the Bloss/Hetzel garage. They had not.

There was a lighthearted moment when Szachacz asked Golazeski about his investigations into how long it took to drive from the Mineral Spring to the home of Brandon and Michelle. Keary Renner testified that Devon typically drove fast. As dedicated as he was to the case, Golazeski said he was willing to go only so far replicating in his own car what kind of time she made. "I didn't fly. I believe Keary had said about driving ninety, ninety-five miles an hour. I'm not up to handling that."

Further on, Szachacz asked about Brandon's fingernails. The question was relevant because the forensic pathologist had observed fingernail scratches on Devon's face. Monahan had made the point that Michelle's hands were unblemished the day after the murder. Golazeski said that he'd observed Brandon sometime after the murder with short fingernails.

"They're lower than the skin, right?" the attorney asked.

"Yes."

He contrasted this with Michelle's fingernails, asking, "And your testimony was that her nails were fine, they were long?"

"Yes, they were manicured, polished."

"OK. She had long fingernails?"

"Yes."

With that, Szachacz completed his cross-examination.

On recross Monahan battled back on the fingernail issue. "It's certainly possible that Brandon's nails may have been in [a] different state on the day of the murder than many days later?"

"Possible," the detective agreed.

It was a draw. Had Michelle produced the scratches with

her long fingernails? Had Brandon done it, but cut his nails afterward? It was another of those questions without a satisfactory answer; soon enough, the burden of trying to answer these various questions would fall upon the shoulders of the jurors.

39

After the weekend break, the trial resumed on Monday, October 1, 2001, with the commonwealth ready to finish up its case with three remaining witnesses: Carol Ritter, the serologist from the state police crime lab, Kenneth Mayberry, a forensics supervisor in the DNA lab, and Cara Judd, who was going to be a blockbuster.

Ritter was called in from the hallway to take the stand and was admitted as an expert witness regarding the analysis of blood, hair and bodily fluids. In response to questioning by ADA Miranda, she said she'd matched a hair in Devon's car to Brandon, a hair on the green Servpro jacket to Michelle and the blood on the clothes in Michelle's trunk to Devon's blood type. She'd found weak signs of blood on the sneakers and socks in the trunk, as well as in the water sample taken from Brandon and Michelle's washing machine. No blood was detected on Michelle's jeans found soaking in the washer, but Ritter explained how she'd found the syringe cap in the back pocket and turned it over to police.

After Ritter left the stand, Miranda called Kenneth Mayberry. Mayberry explained that from one person to another,

DNA is 99.9 percent the same, and that it is the 0.1 percent that differs that is of interest in the DNA lab. Ironically, that 0.1 percent is referred to as "junk DNA" because it does not appear to do anything useful, other than help scientists like Mayberry tell one person from another with reliability and precision that would have been unimaginable to crime fighters just a generation or so ago.

Miranda held up the graph Mayberry had produced months before, showing the DNA profiles for Devon, Michelle and Brandon. She placed it on an easel for all to see, and Mayberry stepped down from the stand to point out how he'd matched various bloodstains and hairs to the profiles on the graph.

When Cara Judd was called as the commonwealth's next and final witness, most of the people in the courtroom had no idea who she was. Her name had been picked up from an affidavit almost a year before and appeared in the press once almost a year ago, but other than that no one outside of the investigators and attorneys knew what her connection was to the case, or what her testimony would consist of. Little did the spectators in the gallery know as she made her way to the stand, her spellbinding testimony would supply answers to many long-unanswered questions.

The soft-spoken twenty-five-year-old appeared uneasy on the stand, fidgeting as she testified and occasionally glancing up and smiling in the direction of the jury. Cara Judd told the jury she'd earned a bachelor's of science degree in biology from Moravian College in 1998, and that she was a graduate student in physician assistant studies at St. Francis de Sales University (which also happened to be where Brandon had gone to school). She currently worked as a babysitter.

Morganelli asked her to identify the defendants, and she obliged, pointing to Michelle Hetzel, who wore blue that day, and Brandon Bloss, in white.

Cara said she met the defendants through Brandon's sister, Natalie, whom she met in a bar in March 2000. They became good friends, and Cara moved in with Natalie, her mother and a foster child in Hellertown. She said she never met Devon Guzman or Keary Renner. She first met Brandon and Michelle in late July 2000, at the home of a friend of Natalie's mother's, to celebrate Michelle's birthday.

Since Cara's testimony would rely on the writing she had done in her journals, the DA laid a foundation for admitting them as commonwealth exhibits. "Now, I understand that you keep journals?" he asked.

"Yes."

"How long have you been keeping journals?"

"Oh, since elementary school."

"OK. And how often would you write in your journal?"

"It varies."

"Was this something that you did as a routine for a number of years?"

"Yes."

Morganelli submitted two diaries to be marked as a Commonwealth Exhibit No. 51-A, a diary with a leopard-skin pattern on the cover, and No. 51-B, a diary book with Mickey Mouse on the front.

The DA turned to an entry in one of the books, dated July 20, 2000. "I'll read this, and you tell me if it is accurate, what you wrote. 'When we got there, Pauline, Ken, Brandon and Michelle were already there. I had heard about Michelle and Brandon, and Natalie told me that they were suspects in this murder that happened in June in Easton. It was weird to meet them finally.' Is that what you wrote?"

"Yes."

The DA departed from the journal, asking Cara to recall a second encounter with the newlyweds two days later, on July 22 at Natalie's house.

"I was on the dryer and she was sitting on the washing machine."

"Were other people around, or was it just you two?"

"No, it was back in the laundry room."

"OK. And what subject did Michelle Hetzel start to talk to you about?"

"She started to talk about Devon and how she missed her."

He moved to admit a sheet of notepaper, marked DB Exhibit No. 9. He held out the note page for her to see. "Do you recognize what this is?"

"These are my notes from the night I talked to Michelle," Cara said.

"Why did you make notes of this conversation?"

"I was shocked by the details of the conversation, and I didn't—I didn't want to forget what was told to me."

The DA asked Cara what she did after scribbling the notes on the paper before her now.

"I wrote in my Mickey Mouse journal."

Morganelli showed her an entry dated August 22, 2000, at 2:08 A.M. It came right after the July 20 entry and right before an entry marked July 24. Cara said that she had written the wrong date; it should have been July 22. It was an understandable slipup, but Morganelli had to hammer the point home. It was the kind of thing that a defense attorney could use to discredit her on cross-examination.

"So what you're saying now is the August twenty-second is mistaken, it should be July twenty-second?" the DA concluded.

"Yes."

"All right. I would like for you to take your time and I'm going to point out to you, if you can read this into the microphone and speak loudly so everyone can hear you, what you wrote starting right here." He handed her the journal, pointing to the spot.

Cara took it and began reading. "'I guess it was around 10 P.M. and I went into the kitchen to get a drink. And then walked around into the bathroom where I ran into Michelle. I didn't know she had gone back there. She didn't look so well. So I asked if she was OK. She said she was sad and that she also didn't feel well because of being pregnant and all. I asked if she wanted to sit and talk and if she needed some water.'"

Morganelli stopped her to make sure the jury hadn't missed the pregnancy point. "Now, you wrote here that Michelle Hetzel told you that she was pregnant, is that correct?"

"That's correct."

"Did she ever tell you anything more about her pregnancy?"

"She said that it was going *too* well—too, too well and that she was having twins, and she wanted to know if Natalie and I would be godparents."

"All right. Continue with your entries here. Could you pick up right here?" he asked, showing her where to resume reading.

"'Well, Michelle and I were sitting on the dryer and the washing machine. Then she started telling me about the night that girl Devon died. She was telling me how much she loved Devon and missed her. She told me everything. She told me she was out with Devon and Keary that night and she and Devon were drunk. She said that she got into a fight or something with Devon before she went home. Then she said that a little while later they called Devon to come over. She said that she wasn't feeling well and didn't feel like talking to Brandon, so she wanted Devon to come over. She said Devon showed up at the house with Keary and she "just couldn't handle it.'"

Again Morganelli stopped her, to drive home a second point. "Now you wrote here in quotation marks that Michelle said that she 'just couldn't handle it.' Why did you put that in quotation marks?"

"Because those were her words."

"Those were Michelle's exact words?"

"That she couldn't handle it because Keary was there."

"Could you continue?"

"'She got so mad because Devon was with Keary. She didn't want Keary in the house and was telling Brandon to tell her that. When Devon got back, she came in the house and she was arguing with Michelle in the living room.'"

"Let me stop you there," the DA said. "So did Michelle Hetzel tell you that after Keary Renner and Devon showed up together that Devon, in fact, did come back to her house?"

"Yes."

"OK. When Devon got back."

"Oh," Cara said. She resumed reading. "'When Devon got back, she came in the house and she was arguing with Michelle in the living room. Keary never was in the house that night. Well, anyway, they were arguing and somebody started pushing and pulling hair. I'm not sure who did what. Michelle said Brandon stepped in the middle and grabbed Devon to protect her. She was like, "He held her back to protect me, his pregnant wife." Then she said Devon bit Brandon and he got hurt and mad and asked why they couldn't talk like human beings. He said that he didn't want to deal with this or see them fight. Michelle told me that they persuaded Devon to take the argument outside. Then she said that she grabbed a wooden-handled knife from the kitchen.'"

"Who grabbed the wooden-handled knife from the kitchen?" Morganelli asked.

"Michelle."

"Michelle said that?"

"Yes."

"That she did that?"

"Yes. Because she knew that Devon carried a black-handled knife. She said that it was not a knife from her kitchen set, another one. The way she was talking, it sounded like she had two knives, but I don't know. Devon and Michelle were in the garage and Michelle said all she remembers that there was blood everywhere. She was holding Devon's head in [her] lap and kissing her face. 'I was telling her to breathe and I loved her so much.'"

"Is that what Michelle said that she was saying to Devon?"

"Yes."

"Go ahead."

Cara read: "'She got a little teary-eyed, but not like I thought someone in that situation would be. I didn't know what to say.'"

"OK. Then what else did she say?"

"'But later then Brandon came out to the garage, she didn't know why he was there and checked to see if Devon was breathing or had a pulse, but she wasn't. I wanted to—'"

"Hold on." The DA stopped her, directing her to begin at a new spot. "Right there."

"'She said that she and Brandon both put Devon in her own car in the garage and Michelle drove it to the falls while Brandon followed in Michelle's car.'"

"OK. Now, did you know anything at all about the murder of Devon Guzman before Ms. Hetzel spoke to you and you wrote this down in this book?"

"No."

"Did you have any details or knowledge about what happened or what didn't happen?"

"No."

"And you recorded this within hours of when Ms. Hetzel told you about it on July 22, 2000, at two oh-eight A.M., is that right?"

"Yes."

The DA asked if she told anyone about the conversation.

"I told Natalie and her mother," Cara said.

Morganelli picked up the other journal, the leopard-print book marked Exhibit No. 51-A. He referred the witness to an entry dated July 29, 2000. It detailed a second conversation that took place with Michelle, this time upstairs at Natalie's house, in her mother's bedroom.

"I would like for you to read what you wrote regarding your conversations with Ms. Hetzel on July 29, of 2000, and we'll read it slowly and we'll start right there," the DA directed.

"'I think it was around 10 P.M. when Michelle said that she didn't feel well because of the pregnancy. She went upstairs to go to bed. I walked past the room a little while later to go to the bathroom. I saw Michelle sitting on the bed crying. I asked if she was OK, and she said that she missed Devon so much and she loved her so much. I went into the room and sat down with her to talk. I was a little—'"

She looked to Morganelli.

"Go ahead," he encouraged.

"'I was a little apprehensive, but she looked so upset.'"

"All right." He pointed out a new place to start reading. "How about this?"

"'She showed me a gold and diamond ring and told me that it was from Devon. She was like holding it and playing with it. She said that she loved Devon so much. She said, "I mean, I love Brandon, but it's not the same as I love Devon."'"

"All right."

"She kept going on and on about how much she loved Devon and missed her. She was referring to Devon in both the past and present tense. She even said that she wished that she had married Devon."

"All right. Right here: 'And then Michelle . . .'"

"'Then Michelle started saying things I didn't really comprehend. She said, "These people think that they're so smart and just keep checking my house. Well, go ahead, what do I care."'"

Morganelli asked why she'd put quotes around certain portions.

"Those were in her words."

"Her exact words were that 'these people think that they're so smart and they keep—just keep checking my house. Well, go ahead, what do I care,' end of quote, correct?"

"Correct."

"What else?"

"She said, 'Anyway, my jeans were soaking for so long that they'll never find any blood from them.'"

"I also notice, 'Anyway, my jeans were soaking so long that they'll never find any blood from them.' Why did you put that in quotes?"

"That is also what she said."

"Now, you prefaced your remarks that you didn't know what she was talking about. Did you know about jeans or what that meant or anything?"

"No."

"All right. After she said that, they'll never find any blood from the jeans, what did you write?"

"Then she mumbled something about the garage, she said the garage has a leak anyway."

"And you have that in quotes?"

"Um-hum, yes."

"Did she talk to you about wearing Tommy Hilfiger clothes?"

"Yes."

"What did she say about Tommy Hilfiger clothes in general?"

"She said she liked my Tommy Hilfiger outfit that I had on, and she said that she wished that they made Tommy Hilfiger maternity clothing."

"Now, you also have a notation here of her telling you something about the garage, and I'd like to pick up where she—you said here, she was—"

"She was talking about Brandon hosing down the garage and a leak in the garage and then the next minute she was talking about shopping."

"Now, did this make any sense to you, anything about jeans soaking in water or about the garage, or did you have any knowledge of what this was about?"

"No, I—she had mentioned the garage, when I spoke to her before, but that was all I knew."

Morganelli had her read a phrase from another entry, this one marked July 27, 2000.

"'I'm gonna come out of this smelling like a bed of roses,'" Cara read.

"And you put that in quotes?"

"Yes."

"And when she's made that statement, do you know what she was referring to, what the context of your conversation was about, do you remember that?"

"She was referring to the situation with the murder."

Morganelli did not let the impact of the moment go to waste. "'I'm gonna come out of this smelling like a bed of roses.' That's what she said?"

"Yes."

"I have no further questions."

It was 2:45 P.M. The judge called an afternoon recess.

When court reconvened, Cara Judd reclaimed her seat on the witness stand. Her testimony, bolstered by the journals, had been big for the commonwealth's case, eliciting gasps of shock from the jury and the gallery. Michelle's attorney Brian Monahan rose to see if he could undo some of the damage. He quickly moved to qualify her relationship with Natalie Bloss, emphasizing that what some might consider a crucial detail had been omitted.

"Now, in this particular case, I think you testified that you were friends with Natalie and you moved in, right?"

"Yes."

"OK." Monahan moved in for the score. "Now, would it be a fair statement that you were more than friends with Natalie?"

"Yes."

"It is a fair statement, right?"

Cara agreed it was.

"At one point you were lovers, right?"

"Yes."

The defense lawyer's next tactic may have been to try to trip her up by mischaracterizing her earlier testimony. "You testified earlier that the first time that you heard about the murder was Michelle told you about it July twenty-first, right?"

"No."

"I'm sorry, July 22, 2000?"

"No."

"That's not true, you heard about it well before then, right?"

"I knew that they were suspects in a murder."

"And you knew about it because Brandon had to make statements to the police, right?" Brandon had been largely absent from Cara Judd's previous testimony, and Monahan brought him into the mix, raising the possibility that Cara

might have heard details about the murder from a source
other than Michelle.

"I don't know."

"You don't know about that?"

"No."

"You never heard Pauline, his mother, or his sister
talking about that?"

"I don't recall."

"You don't recall?"

Cara shook her head. Failing to budge the resolute witness, Monahan abandoned the line of questioning and
moved on. He called her attention to a journal entry that
read: "What a complete surprise for me, I got a phone call
from Investigator Golazeski and the Easton Police Department. They wanted to talk to me. . . . I thought that they
would have known the whole thing, since I have already
been recorded and interviewed."

Monahan challenged that statement. "You were never
recorded or interviewed by the Easton Police Department
or anyone else prior to October twelfth, were you?"

"Yes, I was," came the answer.

"You were?"

"Yes."

"And who did that?"

Cara mentioned the investigator who'd come to her
house and recorded an interview with her.

Attorney Szachacz requested a sidebar. He explained
to Judge Panella that the investigator had been hired by
Brandon's previous legal team, the court-appointed attorneys he'd replaced in favor of the Florida pair. Szachacz
argued that whatever took place between the investigator
and Cara Judd was privileged work product, about which
Cara could not testify in open court.

Monahan still wanted it known who this mysterious

investigator was. "Bring it out, then, who this guy was," he demanded.

Panella disagreed with Szachacz's argument that work product privilege should keep Monahan from questioning Cara about the subject. "If he asks any questions as to what this investigator said, then maybe you would have an objection, but he can cross-examine her and ask everything she told the investigator. There's nothing privileged about that."

The sidebar ended and Monahan resumed his cross. He could no longer make the point that Cara hadn't told anyone about her conversations with Michelle until Detective Golazeski called her in. But he could still make a point about her not going to the police on her own with what she knew.

"And you never went to the Easton police until October 12, 2000, when they called, right?" he charged.

"When they asked me to come into the station."

"Is that right? Officer Golazeski called you, right?"

"Yes."

"You didn't volunteer, right?" Monahan asked a little aggressively.

"No."

"You went to the preliminary hearing, you saw all the witnesses?" he charged.

Keith Szachacz objected to the argumentative tone. Cara's testimony was supporting his case that Michelle, rather than Brandon committed the murder, and he didn't want to see her get roughed up. Judge Panella allowed Monahan to continue.

"You saw all the witnesses and you didn't volunteer any statement, right?" Monahan resumed.

"Correct."

He showed Cara the note page on which she'd scrawled details of Michelle's first admissions. "Now, you have down at the bottom, the very bottom of the note says, 'Brandon later checked Devon's pulse,' right? And then you have, 'blood everywhere, jeans, head in lap, cry, kiss, breathe, on garage floor,' right?"

"Yes."

Pointing out that Cara had relied on this note page to later write her journal entry, Monahan tried to chip away at the reliability of her memory by posing questions about the dates the various conversations took place.

Morganelli objected. He pointed out that the events she was being asked to recall took place more than a year ago and that her testimony consisted of what was written in the journal, not what she now recalled.

But Panella permitted the line of questioning to go on. Monahan continued to attack her memory of dates, and pointed out that her journaling had been sporadic, not something she did every day. The writings went back several years; some years had a dozen or more entries, while the year 1998, for instance, had none.

Monahan next raised the issue of whether Michelle could drive stick shift, which was a problematic question that came up during Cara's recorded police interview. Cara's recollection was that Michelle claimed to have driven Devon's car, a stick, to the canal museum to dispose of the body. But she'd wondered about that, since as far as she knew, Michelle was just learning to drive stick. Like the mixed-up date in the journal, here was another one of those little problems, a chink in the prosecution's case that defense attorneys could exploit.

"In the statement that you gave, again, to Inspector Golazeski, you indicated that Michelle was learning to drive a standard vehicle, right?" Monahan asked.

"Yes."

"From your information, from your understanding, she couldn't drive a stick shift, right?"

"From what I was told," Cara agreed.

Monahan wrapped up his cross-examination by reemphasizing that Cara had done nothing after the chilling conversations with Michelle. "You hung out with Michelle and Brandon several times after that, after she related the story to you, right?"

"Yes."

"You were in her presence, right?"

"Yes."

"Cross," Panella called, summoning Keith Szachacz to question the witness for Brandon's side. He kept it brief, pointing out that Cara had written her journals three months before the preliminary hearing, and that she'd voluntarily come to the police station at Golazeski's request and then turned over her journals to police. "You are not friends with Natalie anymore, are you?" Szachacz asked.

"No," Cara replied.

It mattered, because if she was still dating Natalie, some might view her as having reason to be partial toward her girlfriend's brother. Szachacz, who had every reason to want the jury to believe her testimony, wanted to establish her as an impartial witness.

The attorney strolled to the witness-box and handed Cara an item.

"Do you recognize that?"

"Yes, I do."

"And what is it?"

"It's a 'number-one godmother' bookmark that we got at Unclaimed Freight after we were asked to be godparents . . . of Michelle's babies."

"Michelle told you that she was pregnant?"

"Yes."

"As a matter of fact, she said that she was having twins?"

"Yes."

Szachacz had her step down and parade the bookmark

in front of the jury for all to see. When she'd completed the loop, he said, "Judge, that's all the questions that I would have at this point."

When the cross-exams concluded, Cara Judd was excused, at least for the time being. Brandon's attorneys noted that they had her under a subpoena from which they didn't want to release her just yet. They might need her if Michelle took the stand and testified to a version of events that differed from what was recorded in Cara's diaries. Judge Panella told her to make sure the attorneys had a number where she could be reached. After that, he announced the conclusion of the day's session, and told the jurors that tomorrow the commonwealth would rest its case and the defense would take over.

"You're at the homestretch now," he told them. He reminded them not to talk to anyone about the case, read or listen to news accounts, or conduct any personal investigations or research into the matters at hand. Court adjourned at 3:50 P.M.

When the jurors and spectators left, Judge Panella said he'd hear any motions the defense teams wanted to make, now that the commonwealth had presented all of its evidence. This was an opportunity for the defense teams, if they did not believe the commonwealth had met its burden of proof, to move for acquittal. It was something of a formality, in a case such as this, but still an opportunity neither defense team was about to pass up.

"We'll start with Defendant Hetzel first," Panella invited.

"I would make a motion for judgment of acquittal to all counts, particularly the conspiracy count," Scomillio said. He maintained that the commonwealth's last witness contradicted the idea that a conspiracy existed. "Same thing with the act, Your Honor," he continued. "There's been no evidence of my client committing this act, other than this last statement from this last witness, which is contradictory to the other evidence offered by the commonwealth."

Panella turned to Morganelli. "Does the commonwealth wish to be heard?"

"I think there is circumstantial evidence that there was an understanding to lure this girl in a situation where harm might be caused to her, and that's up to the jury to decide. We only have to go forward with enough evidence to show that there was some overt act. I think the overt act is they ask her to come and then they sent her away when she shows up and ask her to come back this time alone." As for the murder itself, Morganelli said Cara Judd's testimony was evidence enough against Michelle.

Panella turned to Brandon's lawyers. "Let's hear on behalf of Defendant Bloss."

Sletvold, the Easton attorney consulting on the team, argued for dismissal of the conspiracy and murder charges. "It's not as Mr. Morganelli would suggest, that they both had a—their own independent motive and somehow that can be bootstrapped into a conspiracy. There has to be some evidence that there was a meeting of the minds for the conspiracy to go to the jury, and it has not been evidenced." He also argued that evidence that Brandon committed the murder was insufficient.

It was again Morganelli's turn to counter.

"Your Honor, the court knows that circumstantial evidence is sufficient to prove all these elements. There's very rarely situations where we have direct evidence of conspiracy. It is often proved through circumstantial evidence, through the actions of parties, what they do, what their motives are, what they do before the killing and after the killing, and I think—this certainly has been proven sufficiently to get to the jury as to these people acting in concert in luring Devon Guzman to their home, in turning her away when she shows up with another person, and then asking her to come back."

He argued that Cara Judd's testimony didn't take Brandon off the hook for murder. "If Devon Guzman bit him, you know, that doesn't mean that he was not involved in the planning to kill her prior to the bite taking place, and then Michelle Hetzel gets the job done on her own because there's an injury to Bloss that he has to attend to, intervening. You know, these are all issues that have to be resolved by the jury, and they have to hear all of the case and make up their minds."

Panella commended all of the attorneys. "Arguments were well done," he said. But he rejected the motions for acquittal. "I believe Mr. Morganelli correctly summarizes the evidence that's been presented, as well as the law. The law in Pennsylvania only requires that said agreement can be developed over seconds, even without words at times. Both motions for judgment of acquittal are denied."

40

The court proceedings on Tuesday, October 2, 2001, began with a debate in chambers over Michelle's defense team's first witness, Audra Maynard, the Mineral Springs patron who'd told police she'd overheard a fight in Keary and Devon's apartment the night of the murder. John Morganelli wanted to know what the defense hoped her testimony would prove or disprove. Scomillio answered that it would show that "the nature of this altercation was more than just slap fighting as Ms. Renner would like to allude."

This wasn't good enough for Morganelli, who put Michelle's attorneys on the spot. Were they trying to show that Keary and Devon were breaking up, or did they mean to imply that Keary was the one who killed Devon?

Brian Monahan dodged the question by saying that the testimony would establish that Keary might have caused bruising to Devon (bruising was noted at autopsy, so it was a relevant issue). Morganelli accepted this answer, and the conference in chambers concluded.

Since the turn-taking order in cross-examining commonwealth witnesses had been Hetzel's attorneys, then Bloss's, Judge Panella decided to keep the order for presenting defense cases. Michelle would present her defense first. When she was done calling witnesses and presenting evidence, Brandon would get his turn.

As expected, Audra Maynard was the first witness called. Scomillio began the questioning. Maynard revealed that she lived in the first house up from the Mineral Springs Hotel, on the opposite side of the road.

She told the jury that on the night of June 14, 2000, she crossed the road to the Mineral Springs at about eleven-thirty for a couple of drinks in the first-floor bar.

"While you were in the bar, did you hear anything?" Scomillio asked.

"Yes."

"What did you hear?"

"Very loud thumps and abruptlike slamming, if you would call it."

"OK. How long did you hear that for?"

"About, I would say, twenty to twenty-five minutes, almost a half hour."

"Was there any music playing?"

"Yes, there was. The jukebox was on."

"Were there people in the bar?"

"Yes, there was about five people in the bar, six people."

"You were able to hear this over them?"

"Yes. The ceiling tiles were shaking, that's how loud this was, how much percussion there was to this."

Later, after the noise had stopped, Maynard went upstairs to visit a friend. It gave her an opportunity to talk to Keary Renner and look inside the apartment.

"And what did you see?" Scomillio asked.

"I saw something on the couch with a blanket covering it, a green comforter."

"To the best of your ability and what you observed, what did the apartment look like?"

"It was a mess."

"When you say a mess, can you describe that for the jury?"

"There was glass broken on the floor. There was like over-turned furniture, a table that was broken, just everything was a mess."

Scomillio concluded his questioning, having mentioned nothing about bruising. Morganelli had no questions for the commonwealth, silently conveying the impression that her testimony held no relevance, so Kepler Funk rose to cross-examine the witness. Funk established that it had been about 1:00 A.M. when Maynard left the bar and went upstairs, and that she was able to see into the apartment through a screen door. With that, Maynard was dismissed, and Richard Deemer was called to the stand.

Deemer identified himself as the highway supervisor for the city of Easton. He had been an equipment operator for the city the year before, and had been working at the canal museum when Devon Guzman's body was discovered.

He described how he had been locking up the steel gate between the parking lot and the falls area on June 15, 2000, when a Red Honda Accord pulled in and the two occupants got out. One came over and asked him how long the silver Pontiac had been parked in the lot. The other went over to take a look at the car.

Deemer pointed out Michelle Hetzel in the courtroom, wearing a blue shirt and sitting with her attorneys, identifying her as the one who'd come over to talk to him.

He said the person who'd gone to look at the car called out frantically. Michelle went to take a look, and when Deemer finished locking the gate, he went over to the silver car, too.

"What were they saying when you went over to the car?" Scomillio asked.

Deemer said one of the girls was on each side of the car. "Miss Hetzel at that time was on the passenger side of the car. The other individual was on the driver's side. Again, they were just frantically crying, screaming, 'Is she alive, is she breathing?' I just told them to both back away from the car [and] calm down.

"At that point I proceeded to look into the car. Now, when I went in between the door and the car itself, I had both hands in the air, because I didn't want to touch nothing. And once I looked down in and took a glance and pulled back out, I called it in right away."

Scomillio asked Deemer to describe Michelle's reactions. He said that both girls were crying and "worked up." The crying persisted while they waited for police. An officer arrived less than five minutes after Deemer placed his call. If the jurors were keeping score, they might have remembered that Officer David Beitler, a prosecution witness, had testified that Michelle "appeared nervous" at canal park that day. Deemer didn't report the same impression.

Next to testify in Michelle's defense was Palmer Township police officer Jill Siegfried. Brian Monahan handled the direct examination. The thrust of the testimony was that Siegfried had conducted a strip search of Michelle while she was in police custody and that she had observed no visible injuries on her body at that time. On cross-examination Kepler Funk established that the date of the search and examination was June 29, 2000, two weeks after Devon's murder. The testimony was something jurors might or might not consider important, given the fact that Devon's body had been badly bruised, and Brandon had come away with a serious bite wound.

* * *

Elbert Hetzel, Michelle's father, a retired heavy equipment operator with a penetrating gaze, took the stand next. Victor Scomillio did the questioning. He wanted to establish that Michelle and Brandon were on the verge of divorce, and could not have conspired in a murder together. He asked Elbert Hetzel to think back to Memorial Day, 2000, when Michelle had run off with Devon to the islands, prompting him to describe a conversation he had with Brandon at that time.

"Well, it was at a family picnic," Elbert began, "and he just wanted to talk to us, and we just talked about Michelle being with Devon. And I guess we told him that, you know, he probably should see a lawyer and get a divorce."

"Did you extend an offer to help pay for the divorce?" Scomillio wanted to know.

"I said that I would help him, whatever he had to do."

Scomillio asked if Elbert had ever spoken to his son-in-law about kicking Michelle out of the house.

In the spring of 2000, he said, "I told him to tell her to leave."

That was when Michelle went to live with Keary Renner at the Mineral Springs.

Michelle's father went on to testify that while cleaning out the contents of the couple's house at Brandon's request, he'd come across a piece of paper in a black briefcase in an upstairs storage room, with Brandon's handwritten notes regarding getting a divorce.

Scomillio entered the letter as a defense exhibit and handed it to Elbert Hetzel to read. The handwritten notes referred to divorce, closing accounts and taking Michelle off a car insurance policy.

In the drawer of a desk in the living room, he'd found a letter from attorney Joseph Corpora to Brandon stating his retainer fee and billing procedures for divorce cases. The letter was dated May 31, 2000.

The last item Scomillio asked him about was Brandon's résumé, which Elbert Hetzel had found in the briefcase with the divorce notes. The attorney had him read off Brandon's educational background.

The last point Scomillio made before turning the witness over for cross-examination was that neither Elbert Hetzel nor his wife had ever been asked to sit down for a formal police interview. This point would become an important factor soon, when Michelle's mother took the stand.

Morganelli started his cross-examination by winning Elbert Hetzel's admission that he'd gotten along well with Brandon.

"In fact, you thought that he was a pretty nice fellow, didn't you?"

"Yes, I did."

"And you realized, didn't you, sir, that your daughter was not a very good wife for him, was she?"

"Yes."

"She wasn't, was she?"

"No. She was out partying every night."

"And she was out running around with Devon Guzman, correct?"

"Yes. They were out partying every night."

Morganelli confirmed with the witness that while Michelle and Devon were on their vacation, he'd offered to help pay for a divorce.

"That relationship between Devon Guzman and your daughter, and her going out, was interfering and was causing Brandon's marriage and your daughter's marriage to be pretty much a bad situation, is that right?" the DA asked.

"Yes."

Keith Szachacz objected on Brandon's behalf, on the grounds that the question had called for an opinion, but the point was made. The prosecution maintained that a key motive for murder for both defendants had been Devon's interference in Brandon and Michelle's marriage.

The DA had a few more questions. "You were aware, weren't you, Mr. Hetzel, that your daughter wasn't even working around this time frame, was she, in June of 2000?"

"It's hard to say. She worked and she didn't work. I mean, I believe her activities at night, partying, that she couldn't get up the next day."

"But Brandon Bloss was paying all the bills for her, wasn't he?"

"Yes."

"And she used credit cards, she went to Puerto Rico and ran up bills, correct?"

"Yes."

"And that was all being paid by Brandon Bloss?"

"I don't know who it was paid by."

That concluded the DA's questions.

Scomillio rose for the redirect, again working to establish that Brandon was the one who had a motive to murder Devon. "From what you observed of Brandon Bloss, from what he said to you, was Brandon Bloss happy about Michelle spending time with Devon?"

"No."

"Were you happy about Michelle spending time with Devon?"

"No."

Scomillio concluded his questions with inquiries as to Michelle's athletic prowess, which was a relevant consideration given that Devon had been described as feisty and athletic, once sending a grown man, George Vine, toppling on his rear. The implication was that it would have taken a strong, fit person to overcome her.

"Now, your daughter, was she ever an athlete?" Scomillio asked.

"No."

"Was she ever one that kept physically fit, you know, by working out?"

"No."

"Was she ever a violent person?"

"No."

Morganelli objected to the last question, but Panella overruled him.

Before calling a morning recess, Judge Panella summoned counsel for a sidebar to discuss the remaining witnesses. Monahan said he was going to call Michelle's mother. He didn't know if Michelle herself was going to elect to testify, but if so, she would take the stand after her mother.

After the recess Brian Monahan summoned Mary Hetzel to the stand. Throughout the trial so far, she had been a quiet presence in the courtroom, sitting with her husband toward the back. When she was seated, Monahan moved right to the night of the murder, asking her to recall the substance of the half-hour-long telephone conversation she'd had with Brandon while his wife was out that night.

"Well, when Brandon called, he told me that Michelle was out with Devon again, and he said he wondered what her excuse was going to be this time. He said that he can't just take it no more. He said, as long as Devon was around, him and Michelle will never be happy. And he said—and he said this, not only that night, but other nights on telephone conversations, that he could just kill her."

"Now, this conversation was a lengthy conversation, or was it a short conversation?"

"It was a lengthy conversation."

"OK. Let's—did he . . . he seemed agitated and aggravated?"

"Yes, he was upset."

He next asked about the phone call Michelle made from the canal museum the following day.

"It was around one or one-thirty in the afternoon, and she told me they found Devon's body. And she asked me if I could come down," Mary Hetzel told him.

She described her daughter's demeanor when she got there. "Michelle was upset. She was talking with the detective. And then the detective said that he was going to take her down to police headquarters for questioning. I asked if I could go along, and the detective said no, so I went on home."

"Was she crying at the time?"

"Yes, she was."

"OK. Sobbing?"

"Yes."

Mary Hetzel testified that Michelle had been dropped off at her parents' house on West Nesquehoning Street in South Side after being interviewed by police. Brandon showed up at the house after his shift at Ashland Chemical. She said she'd called him at work to tell him Michelle had gone in for a police interview.

"How did he appear to you at that point when he came to your house?"

"When he first came in, he just asked about—first thing he said is, 'Where's your car?' to Michelle."

"OK."

"And Michelle said that it was at the crime scene. And he said, 'Oh, shit, we have to get that car.'"

"OK. And then what did you do?"

"So he—Michelle was upset, so he asked me if I would drive him down to get the car, and I did."

"So he got into your car and you went where?"

"We went down to the canal museum at six-eleven."

"And what happened?"

"And there were people around, so he told me to turn around and go home, and I did."

"And did he say anything to you at all during the conversation—during the drive?"

"Just that he had to get the car and that's it."

"OK."

"I just felt he needed the car."

"OK. You went back to your house. Did anything else happen? Did Brandon ask you to do anything else after you arrived back at the house?"

"Yes. He asked me to call the police and see when we could get the car. So I called and I talked to a Lieutenant Riley, and he said the car was on a rollback."

"OK."

"And I wasn't sure what that meant, but then he said, well, let's go down again and see if anybody is around. So I took him down the second time, and there were people around, so we drove and we came back home."

Back at the house, she said, "He was asking Michelle what the—what the police questioned her about."

The next morning, Friday, June 16, she went to her daughter's house, two blocks from her home, for coffee.

"I called down there and I told them I was coming down for a cup of coffee, it was early in the morning. I can remember almost the time, because we were leaving for Missouri that Saturday morning, and I had a nail appointment at eight o'clock. So it had to be like seven o'clock in the morning, around there."

"Could you describe how the house looked that morning?" Monahan asked.

"It looked normal to me."

"OK. You didn't see anything, any tables broken or anything unusual?"

It was a pointed question, most certainly crafted to contrast deliberately the South Side home of the newlyweds to the trashed Mineral Springs apartment of Keary Renner.

Mary Hetzel answered that she'd seen nothing out of order.

Michelle was in the kitchen, while Mary was in the living room with Brandon that day, she recalled.

"During the course of having coffee with Brandon in the living room, did Brandon reveal anything to you or say anything to you that relates to this case?" Monahan prompted. This was the bombshell he had been leading up to.

"Yes, he did."

"And what did he tell you?"

"That—he told me that he—he—he murdered Devon."

Monahan asked if she could be more specific.

"He just said that he did it in the backyard. He said that he lost it when Devon said to him that she wouldn't bother with Michelle anymore, because Devon had said that so many times before. And he said that he did it, he slit her throat and he said he hosed everything off in the backyard and hosed everything down."

Monahan asked if she'd noticed anything unusual about Brandon's physical appearance that day, and Mary Hetzel replied that she'd seen something on his arm. "It was a nasty mark," she said.

"And did you ask Brandon about it?"

"Brandon said that he burned it at work."

"Could you describe it for us, what you saw?"

"I just saw an area on his arm. It looked like something very—you know, it looked sore, it looked bad."

Monahan next wanted to know if Mary asked Brandon where Michelle was when he committed the murder.

"Yes, I did," the witness said.

"And what did Brandon tell you?"

"She was asleep on the couch."

"OK. Did Brandon, at that point, ever say Michelle had anything to do with this?"

"No, he did not."

The attorney asked if she'd had any further such conversation with her son-in-law after that Friday, June 16. Hetzel claimed she had, a couple of weeks later, and that this time Brandon told a different tale.

"This time he told me that he asked Devon to go for a ride. He wanted to talk to her and they went down to the canal museum and they parked and they were arguing and then they started physically fighting and he killed her in self-defense."

Monahan's last effort was to emphasize, as he'd done with Michelle's father, that Michelle was nonathletic and petite. Mary Hetzel guessed Michelle weighed 105 pounds at the most and wore a size three or five at the time of the murder. This had to be pointed out for the benefit of the jury because by the time of the trial, her appearance had changed drastically, and now she wore a size nine/ten.

Keith Szachacz handled the cross-examination on Brandon's behalf. He moved quickly to discredit the preceding testimony, homing in on the fact that Michelle's mother had never told her story to police. He specifically referred to Detective Golazeski, who'd been present throughout the trial.

"Did you ever tug him on the shoulder and say, 'I have something to tell you that might save my daughter?'"

"No."

"Did you ever tug him on the shoulder, saying 'My daughter didn't do this; let me tell you what I know'?"

"No."

He asked about a conversation between Mary Hetzel and Brandon's mother later in the day after Brandon's early-morning confession. "Do you remember Friday, June sixteenth, calling or having a conversation with Mr. Bloss' mother, Pauline?"

"I did have some conversations with her, yes."

"Exactly. And you told Pauline that Brandon is not a murderer, didn't you?"

"No, I did not."

"And you told Pauline that you're mad at [Michelle] for what she did, and Brandon would never do that?"

"No, I did—"

"And you told Brandon that Brandon was going to pin it on Keary and come out of it smelling like a bed of roses, didn't you?"

"No, I did not."

After the heated attack, Szachacz withdrew, then reapproached with an envelope and a greeting card. Hetzel confirmed that the return address on the envelope was her own. The postmark read December 2000, four months after Michelle and Brandon had been charged with the murder. Szachacz asked her to identify the handwriting on the envelope, but the effort was like pulling teeth.

"Do you recognize the handwriting as being Mr. Hetzel's handwriting?"

"It may, I'm not sure."

"You don't recognize your own husband's handwriting, ma'am?"

"This is printed."

"Do you recognize your husband's printing?"

"It may be his, yes."

The attorney asked her to read the card. She retrieved her glasses and complied: "It says, 'For a special son-in-law. Brandon, at Christmas I just want to thank you for being part of many special family memories and to remind you how nice it is to have a son-in-law like you. Dad.'"

"Dad, meaning Mr. Hetzel?" Szachacz asked.

"Yes."

"Mr. Hetzel sent that card to Mr. Bloss, didn't he?"

"I was not aware of it. My name was not on there. I mean, if he sent it, he didn't tell me."

The greeting card made a strong point. Brandon had allegedly confessed to his mother-in-law to a crime for which her youngest child was sitting in jail, possibly facing the death penalty, and yet his father-in-law sent him a Christmas card?

Szachacz wasn't finished. He again hammered the fact that Mary Hetzel never went to police with her story. He pointed to Golazeski.

"Did you ever go tell this officer that your daughter is innocent?"

"No."

"And that somebody else did this. Did you ever tell him that?"

"I never had the opportunity to talk with him."

"Excuse me?"

"My husband did, I did not."

"You never had the opportunity. You just testified on direct exam that you picked up the phone and you called the police department and you spoke to a Lieutenant Riley?"

"Yes, I did."

The attorney kept turning up the heat.

"You testified on direct that Mr. Bloss called you the night of the fourteenth, right?"

"Yes, he did."

"And you had a lengthy conversation with him, right?"

"Yes, we did."

"And during that conversation, he said to you, 'Michelle

is out with Devon again. I'm tired of this and I could kill Devon,' right?"

"Yes."

"And after that, on the fifteenth or the sixteenth of June, after that alleged conversation, you called Lieutenant Riley, a police officer, didn't you?"

"Yes, I did."

"You never told Lieutenant Riley about that conversation, did you, ma'am?"

"No, I did not."

"Because it never happened?" Szachacz charged.

"Yes, it did."

Before concluding the scathing interrogation, Szachacz drove the point home one final time. He pointed out that police had been to her house several times during the course of their investigation. "Your daughter's life was at stake, ma'am. You didn't go tell the police officer that somebody else did it?"

"No, I did not."

Szachacz turned to Panella. "I don't have any other questions, Judge."

Judge Panella requested a glass of water for Mary Hetzel while John Morganelli readied himself for his cross-examination. Morganelli began by going back to the phone call the night of the murder and emphasizing Brandon's antagonism toward Devon. This supported the prosecution's assertion regarding his motive for murder, so he used the witness for his advantage.

"And is it my understanding then that in that conversation with Mr. Bloss, you indicated that he was expressing to you frustration about the relationship between Devon Guzman and his wife?"

"Yes."

"And he was saying to you that she was out again with Devon, right?"

"Yes."

"Was he upset about that?"

"Yes."

"And he was mad about that?"

"Yes."

"And he indicated—I think you said that he said something about, 'I could just kill her,' or something like that?"

"Yes."

"Was he referring to his wife or Devon Guzman?"

"He was referring to Devon. He said that him and Michelle would never be happy as long as Devon was around."

The DA next moved to establish that Michelle, too, frustrated over the situation with Devon, also had a motive for murder: the interference the relationship with Devon was causing in her marriage.

"Now, you observed the marriage and the relationship between your daughter and Mr. Bloss from February, when they got married, until they separated. And you would agree, wouldn't you, that Mr. Bloss wanted to try to make the marriage work?"

"Yes."

"But the problem was that this Devon Guzman was constantly out with your daughter, running around with her, and your daughter would go out with her and that was a problem, an interference in his marriage, wasn't it?"

"Yes."

"Now, were you aware of the fact that Ms. Guzman, in addition to having a relationship with your daughter, was also living with another woman, did you know that?"

"Yes, I did."

"Did you ever meet Keary Renner?"

"Yes, I did."

"And you were aware, weren't you, that your daughter was bisexual?"

"Yes."

"And that your daughter was having an affair with Devon Guzman at the same time she was married to Mr. Bloss?"

"Yes."

"And you were aware also—weren't you—that Keary Renner was also living with Devon Guzman?"

"Yes."

"And you would agree—wouldn't you, Mrs. Hetzel?—that the relationship between Guzman and Miss Renner often was a bone of contention for Michelle, she did not like that, did she?"

"No."

"And she actually wanted Devon to end her relationship with Keary Renner, didn't she?"

"I'm not sure. I—"

"You're not positive?"

"Right, yes."

"But you do know that your daughter was not happy with the fact that Devon was living with Keary Renner, correct?"

"Correct."

The DA wanted to know if Michelle ever told her mother she was pregnant.

"Yes, she did."

When was it, the DA asked.

The witness waffled. "I'm not sure. She thought she was pregnant." She said her daughter's irregular period caused confusion.

Morganelli started over. "Did she ever tell you that she was pregnant?"

Mary Hetzel's answer this time was "Never."

Letting her reversal speak for itself, the DA moved on, bringing her to the conversation with Brandon the day after the body was found, taking issue with the reason Brandon allegedly gave her as his impetus for the murder.

"And this is when he tells you he murdered Devon, he said that he did it in the backyard, he lost it, is that right?"

"Yes."

"But he—but according to you—he said that Devon had said she was no longer going to see Michelle, isn't that right?"

"That's when he said that he lost it."

"OK. But—and it was because Brandon had heard that before from Devon?"

"Yes."

"But, in fact, on this occasion, at least from what you allegedly are saying he told you, he was saying that Devon was agreeing not to see Michelle anymore, right?"

"Yes."

"But that caused him to lose control?"

"Because he said that she said that so many times before."

"I see," the DA said.

She was excused from the stand.

In support of his case that Brandon rather than Michelle was the culprit, Monahan called Michelle and Brandon's neighbor Joseph Welsh back to the stand very briefly to reiterate that it was Brandon he'd seen working in the backyard of 120 West St. Joseph Street for several hours the weekend after the murder. As Welsh left the stand, one last witness for Michelle's defense remained.

41

When Victor Scomillio summoned his final witness, the astonishment rippled in whispers through the courtroom. Her recorded voice had been heard already, but few expected to hear her speak live in court. When she was sworn and seated, Scomillio requested, "Please state your name for the ladies and gentlemen of the jury."

"Michelle Mae Hetzel," came the reply from the young woman in the black pants suit. Despite her young age, and circumstances that intimidated people twice her age, she appeared remarkably comfortable and composed. She would need that composure during the heated exchanges to come. The beginning was the easy part, fielding questions from her own attorney. Scomillio reminded her to keep her voice up and to reposition the microphone if necessary.

Michelle informed the jury that she'd gone to Easton Area High School through eleventh grade, and had since earned her GED.

"Describe a little bit about your relationship with Mr. Bloss," Scomillio prompted.

"We argued a lot," Michelle said. "We didn't get along at all."

He asked about her relationship with Devon Guzman.

"She was my best friend. We were very close. And around the age of sixteen, we started dating."

Now it was time to begin poking holes in the evidence against her. Scomillio started with Cara Judd's recollection that Michelle said she'd driven Devon's car to the canal museum after the murder. "Did you ever know how to drive a standard car, a manual transmission?" he asked.

"No, I did not."

"Was Devon's car manual or automatic?"

"It was manual."

The next topic was the testimony of George Vine. Scomillio asked her to explain the context of the conversation and what she'd said that night.

"It was about two months before Devon was killed, and I was at his house drinking with Devon, and Keary showed up and she found Devon and I there together. And Devon and her began arguing, and she threw a remote control at Devon. And they began fighting, and Devon got a bloody lip."

"OK. Describe what you said to George Vine and what you meant by it."

"I said I could just kill her."

"Why?"

"Because she was leaving with Keary; I don't know if she was afraid of her or not."

"OK. But why would you say that?"

"I was upset with her," Michelle explained. "Her and Devon had a history of physical fights. It always usually ended up in a physical fight."

He asked the reason for the Memorial Day trip to the islands.

"Devon and I needed to get away."

"How did you go?"

"I paid for the plane tickets on my credit card, and we flew from Newark to Puerto Rico."

"OK. While you guys were down there, did you purchase rings for the two of you?"

"Yes, we did."

"Describe those rings."

"Two of them are almost identical, and there was one for me and one for Devon. And then I bought Devon another ring with diamonds on it."

"OK. Did you guys exchange rings when you were down there?"

"Yes, we did."

"Why didn't you get legally married?" Scomillio wanted to know.

"I was already married to Brandon Bloss," Michelle said. She explained that she'd wanted to get out of her marriage before the trip and had intended to pursue a divorce, but claimed Brandon wouldn't let her leave. "Every time I was going to leave, Brandon always asked me to stay. And he said that we would work it out. And I would stay and it would go back to being the same thing."

Upon returning from the islands with Devon, "we were a couple," Michelle said. "We were going to be exclusive." But first they had to deal with the relationships they were in, and it was hard for Devon to leave Keary and for her to leave Brandon, she said.

Scomillio asked her to explain the argument between herself and Devon the night of the murder.

"She wanted me to spend the night at her father's house with her," Michelle said.

The answer disagreed with the reason given by Rick Guzman, Holly Ronco and Keary Renner, not to mention that given by her own attorney in his opening remarks. They all said it was because Devon was still living with Keary.

"Why didn't you?"

"Because I did not know what to tell my husband."

Prosecution witnesses had said that Devon had rejected Michelle, not the other way around, and that she'd thrown the wedding rings back at Michelle. Michelle now disputed this, saying that the reason the rings had wound up back in her possession was for safekeeping from Keary. "I gave Devon a class ring and Keary ended up taking that from her and I never got it back," she said.

Michelle moved ahead to when she arrived home that night after leaving Devon's father's. "Brandon was there. He was talking on the phone to my mother, and I laid down on the couch." She continued: "Brandon was telling my mother that I was out drinking again with Devon, and Brandon was asking me what was wrong with me, and I would not talk to him."

"OK. Did you go back outside of the house again?"

"Yes, to get cigarettes out of my car."

"Describe what happened when you went outside again."

"Brandon followed me out. I guess he thought that I was leaving, and we got in an argument. He pushed me on the ground and I dropped my keys and I asked him, 'What the fuck do you want from me?'"

"OK. What happened after that?"

"I went back in the house and I laid back down on the couch. And I believe Brandon called Keary's apartment."

"OK. What did Brandon say when he was on the phone?"

"He wanted to know what was wrong with me and why I was not talking to him, and if Devon was there."

"Did he say anything else?"

"He asked her to come over."

About twenty minutes later, Michelle said there was a

knock on the door and she heard Devon's voice. Brandon met Devon at the door and told her to take Keary home.

"OK. After that, did you hear Devon again?"

"No."

"Did you see Devon again?"

"No."

Michelle said she had an unexpected encounter with Brandon later that night. "He came in the back door where our laundry room is, and I heard him rustling around back there. Garbage was the next day, so I thought that he was cleaning the litter box. And he finally came into the living room and he was naked. He might have had boxers on. He was behind me."

When she asked him why he was naked, "he said that he was out with the dog and that he put his clothes in the laundry basket, which we have on top of our dryer."

Scomillio asked what she had done between the time Devon left to take Keary home and when she encountered Brandon at 2:00 A.M. She said she'd paged Devon and called her apartment, speaking with Keary. He asked about going to the Mineral Springs with Brandon.

"I went upstairs and I told him that I was going to go to Keary's house. And he said he wanted to go with me, because I was drinking. I went to the bathroom and Brandon was waiting for me in my car and he let me drive. He was in the passenger seat and my car was turned on. And he said that he was too tired to drive."

"Describe how the apartment looked when you walked inside."

"It was a mess. There was papers all over the floor. The coffee table was overturned, pots and pans were all over the place."

Michelle admitted it was her idea to call 911 several times from the apartment.

"OK. Where was Brandon when this was going on?"

"He was in the car. He wouldn't get out of the car for some reason. He didn't want to go into Keary's apartment."

Michelle described taking Brandon home. "I had to take Brandon home because Brandon had to be at work, and Keary went with me to take him home. And when I dropped him off at the house, he asked if I would be home when he got home from work; he wanted me home. And I said that I would be. And we went to Wawa and we got coffee and we went back to Keary's apartment."

Describing her reaction upon finding Devon's car at the canal museum, something for which she had been attacked by the prosecution, she explained, "We were both very angry when we saw her car. We thought that she was probably passed out."

"OK. Why would you think that she was passed out?"

"Because she had an argument with Keary that night, and we thought that she just drove there and hung out and fell asleep."

"What did you say when you pulled into the falls?"

"I said 'I could just kill her.'"

Scomillio asked what she saw when she approached the car.

"Keary opened up the door with her keys."

"Do you know which door?"

"The driver's-side door. And she opened it up and it smelled. And I saw blood on the back of Devon and dirt."

"Did you see Keary doing anything when you were over there?"

"Yes. Keary shook her and was cradling her head."

"So was Keary in the car?"

"Yes."

"And how was she cradling her head?"

"She had her arms around Devon's head."

From there, Michelle said she was taken to the police station to give a statement.

Her attorney asked, "Why didn't you tell the police that you saw Brandon Bloss at two o'clock in the morning half-naked?"

"That was the last thing from my mind, I mean, what my husband was wearing," she replied. She added that at the time, "it didn't seem awkward to me."

"At that time, did you talk with Brandon or have any idea that he might have been involved?"

"No."

"Did you talk to Brandon before going to the police station?"

"No."

"OK. What happened at the conclusion of your statement to the police officers, after the tape was shut off?"

"They asked me if I wanted to go back and get my car, and I told them no, I'd like to be taken to my mother's house."

The point of this was that she hadn't known about the bloody clothes and gloves in the trunk. She also denied knowing how her Tommy Hilfiger jeans got in the washer or a syringe cap found its way into the back pocket.

"OK. Describe Friday morning, June sixteenth, to the ladies and gentlemen of the jury."

"I woke up and I heard Brandon yelling. And I went down the steps and I saw Brandon burning his arm, burning his arm with a cigarette lighter."

"Did he say why he was doing that?"

"No. A couple minutes later, he said he needed to talk to me about something."

"OK. What did he talk to you about?"

"He told me last night he got in a fight with Devon and he killed her and it was self-defense. He said that she came after him."

Throughout the trial the defendants, through their attorneys, had blamed each other for the killing, but that made it no less jarring to hear the accusation for the first time directly from Michelle's lips.

"OK. Did he ever talk to you again about what happened?" her attorney asked.

"Several times."

"What did he say?"

"Different things every time. Devon took him down to the falls, and he said that they got in a physical fight in the car and she came after him with a knife. And then he went and he said something about [in]side of the car at the falls. And then later on in the month, he told me that it happened in our backyard."

Scomillio addressed very briefly the preceding day's testimony of Cara Judd. "You heard what she said yesterday?" he asked.

"Yes."

"Did you ever make any type of statement like that to her?"

"No, I did not."

"Did you talk to her about anything personal?"

"No, I did not."

"Why not?"

"I did not know her very well."

He moved on to the trip after the murder, asking her to explain how it came about and why she went.

Michelle said the idea of the trip originated outside of her presence during a visit with Brandon's mother, sister and Cara Judd. "Pauline and her ex-husband went to the bank to get money," she said. She and Brandon flew from Philadelphia to Houston, and then on to Cancun.

"Did you and Brandon get into a discussion in Houston, Texas?" Scomillio queried.

"Yes, I didn't want to go any further."

"Why?"

"Because I didn't want to go to Mexico. I had no reason to go to Mexico."

"Where did you want to go?"

"Back home."

"Where did he want to go?"

"To Mexico."

Scomillio's next questions pertained to whether Michelle had told anyone about her husband's confession, and why she stayed with him after the murder. Michelle said she'd told two friends, one of them being George Vine.

"Why did you stay with Brandon after he told you this stuff?" her attorney asked.

"I was scared. I moved in with my mom and my dad and I just—I didn't do anything to make him mad."

He talked about the blood Michelle said she saw on Devon's back. "You—when talking with the Easton police, you said that on direct that you saw blood around Devon when you approached the car. Do you remember exactly when you saw that blood?"

"When I went over to the car."

"OK. There's been talk about a green jacket being placed over Devon, do you remember seeing a green jacket being placed over her?"

"Not when I first approached the car with Keary, no."

"When Keary was holding Devon, was there a green jacket on her?"

"No, there was not."

"So, at that time, were you able to see her back?"

"Yes."

Scomillio's direct examination was almost complete.

"OK. Ms. Hetzel, was Devon Guzman your best friend?"

"Yes, she was."

"Did you have any other friends?"

"No, not after I got married."

"OK. Did you—did you consider her to be anything more than your friend?"

"Yes."

"Describe that."

"She was my lover."

"OK. Did you have any intention to stay with her—"

"Yes, I did."

"—in your relationship. Did she ever tell you her intentions with you?"

"Yes."

"Did you ever want to do any harm to her?"

"Never."

"On the night of June fourteenth, into the early-morning hours of June fifteenth, did you kill Devon Guzman?"

"No, I did not."

"On the night of June fourteenth, to the early morning hours of June fifteenth, did you plan with anybody, including Brandon Bloss, to kill her?"

"No, I did not."

"On the night of June fourteenth, into the early hours of June fifteenth, did you do anything to cover up Brandon's actions?"

"No, I did not."

"Did you move the body?"

"No, I did not."

"Did you hose down the backyard?"

"No, I did not."

"Did you, at that time, on June fourteenth into June fifteenth, did you know what happened to Devon Guzman?"

"No, I do not."

"Thank you," Scomillio concluded. His direct examination was brief and gentle, compared to the arduous going ahead.

* * *

Kepler Funk took the floor for Brandon's defense, getting off to a commanding start. "Miss Hetzel, step down, please. Look at photograph number six," he said, bringing her to the display of crime scene photos. "Look at it. Do you see the green jacket?"

"Yes, I do."

"And it's your testimony now that when you looked in the car, that jacket wasn't there?"

"Right."

"OK. Tell this jury who the person was that moved that jacket, tell the jury that."

"Keary was shaking Devon. That jacket was not on Devon when we got there."

"The question was, who removed the green jacket when Officer Beitler got there?"

"I'm not sure."

"You're not sure?"

"Keary might have put it on," Michelle proposed.

Funk moved on. "The pregnancy issue. I'm not going to ask you whether or not you were pregnant or not. What's important is that you told Brandon that you were, right?"

"I told him that I thought I was, not that I was."

"OK. You told him that after, after you got back from the islands?"

"Yes."

"That's the first time that he thought that you were pregnant, right?"

"Right."

"After he found out that you went to the islands?"

"Right."

"That's when you decided to tell him?"

"Right."

"After he thinks about and goes to see an attorney to get a divorce from you, right?"

"Right."

"Your response to that is 'I'm pregnant, Brandon'?"

"No. I said that I thought I was pregnant."

The attorney moved on again. "The wedding rings. Ms. Guzman threw them at you, didn't she?"

"No, she did not."

"On the fourteenth of June?"

"No, she did not."

"She didn't throw them at you?"

"No, she did not."

"You heard Ms. Renner testify?"

"No, that's what supposedly Devon told Keary."

"So they ended up with you, all three rings?"

"Yes."

"So the rings were for this quasi marriage for Ms. Guzman?"

"No, they were not [wedding] rings, they were promise rings."

"One of the rings for Guzman?"

"Yes."

"You had all three of them?"

"Right."

"She rejected you on the fourteenth, didn't she?"

"No, she did not."

"Did she have you hold those rings, or what's the purpose of you having her ring?"

"I had them so Keary wouldn't take them."

"Is anything Ms. Renner said here accurate, or did she make up everything?"

"Yes, what she said is accurate. It's what she heard."

He picked a new target. "Did you ever tell your husband that the falls was a special place between you and Ms. Guzman?"

"Yes, he knew."

"This was a place where you and Ms. Guzman, if you had an argument, would go and make up, fair to say?"

"Yes."

"It's not a coincidence that Ms. Guzman—her final resting place is at the falls. It's not a coincidence, is it?"

"I'm not sure why she was there."

"It just so happens to be that her body is found at the place that's special to you and her?"

"A lot of people know about that place; a lot of people go there."

"So then it's a coincidence in your mind?"

"I'm not sure. Brandon Bloss knew that."

"You're just a victim of that coincidence, is that it?" he charged.

He questioned her about how she had deceived Brandon during their brief marriage, probing her psychology and manipulative capacity. "You told Brandon that you had a lump on your breast and you and Dr. Oza were going to San Diego, right?"

"No, I did not."

"That was the line that you told Brandon so that you could go to the islands with Devon?"

"No, I told Brandon that I was going to San Francisco."

Funk continued to grill her about whether she'd claimed to have a lump on her breast or to be attending a conference in California with her boss. Michelle steadfastly denied both.

"So the lie you told Brandon was 'I'm going to San Francisco by myself,' is that it?" Funk asked.

"Right."

"To do what?" he fired back.

"I didn't tell him where I was going."

"I'm sorry?"

"I didn't tell him why I was going."

"'I'm getting on a plane and I'm going to San Francisco, see you later'?"

"I told him that I was going there, yes."

"For what?"

"I just told him that's where I was going."

"And he said, 'OK, honey, see you later, bye-bye'?"

"No, he didn't."

"What did you tell him, Michelle?" Funk demanded. It was a confrontational exchange. In the interests of professionalism, Judge Panella had asked the attorneys not to address or refer to the defendants by first name, except sparingly for tactical purposes. Funk took the liberty now, overtly challenging the young woman.

"I hung up on him," Michelle shot back.

"You called him on the phone and said that you were getting on a plane?"

"Yes. I said, 'I'm going to San Francisco.'"

"That day?"

"Yes."

"Did you—would you at least admit that you lied to him, you would admit that?"

"Yes, I did."

He raised another example of deception, asking if she'd ever faked illness to bring Devon to her side.

"No."

"You were here when Ms. Renner testified?"

"Right."

"Remember she used the phrase 'cry wolf,' do you remember that?"

"I never had to do that."

"It's your testimony that you've never done that, you never feigned being ill?"

Michelle said she'd never done that with Devon.

"To get Devon away from Keary?"

"No."

"You've never done that?"

"No."

"What Ms. Renner said in here was made up?"

"I'm not sure what Devon had told her."

"So you're blaming Devon for that?"

"No, I'm not blaming Devon. I don't know what was said to Ms. Renner and what wasn't."

He proceeded to ask about her marriage to Brandon. "In part, why you married Brandon was because he had some money and a steady job?"

"No, I don't know what Brandon's financial situation was."

"You're his wife, you don't know what his finances are?"

"No, I do not."

"You know that he worked two jobs?"

"Yes."

"That didn't come into the equation at all?"

"No."

"That he had a steady job and was a good guy?"

"No."

Funk won admissions from Michelle that she'd put in only about three weeks of work during the four months of her marriage, while Brandon worked steadily and paid all the bills. "That wasn't appealing to you?" he asked.

"I wasn't thinking about that."

"You married him just because you loved him?"

"At the time I did, yes."

"I'm sorry?"

"At the time I loved him, yes."

"You loved Devon when you married him, didn't you? Didn't you?"

"Yes."

Funk retrieved a piece of evidence, a black-handled Cook's Club kitchen knife, which police had collected from the kitchen sink in the Bloss/Hetzel home. He approached her with it, the blade glistening before him. "Miss Hetzel, you have knives in your kitchen, right?"

Not liking where this was headed, Victor Scomillio interrupted. "Your Honor, may we approach?" At sidebar Scomillio asked, "Can I have an offer as to where he's going with this line of questioning? It's my understanding that he's going to eventually put that knife in her hand."

Funk denied this. "I'm not going to give it to her, don't worry about that."

"I only do stuff like that," John Morganelli joked.

"I'm not going to do that," Funk insisted.

"It's clearly permissible," Panella said.

Resuming his questioning, Funk held up the knife. "Do you recognize this one?"

Michelle said she did.

"Now, you've been here through this whole trial; you're not suggesting that you don't have the ability to, with any of these knives, to cut someone's skin, you're not suggesting that, are you?" Funk was astute to pose the question, and it dangled like bait. Michelle had so far denied anything that could be construed as even remotely incriminating. Would she go so far as to deny even the physical ability to cut flesh with a knife?

"I'm saying that I wouldn't," Michelle answered.

"OK. I'm asking you if you have the ability to; you're not claiming that, are you?"

"No, I don't have the ability to," she answered this time, taking the bait.

"You don't have the ability to cut someone's skin with any one of these knives?" Funk reiterated.

"No, I wouldn't."

"I'm not asking if you would or not. I'm asking you if you have the physical ability to."

"No."

"So you don't?"

"No."

Now that he had her on the hook, he wasn't about to let her go. "Is it because of an injury you have or you're too weak to cut, or what? Why are you claiming that?"

"I'm saying that I wouldn't."

"I know you wouldn't."

"I can't physically do that to somebody, no."

"I'm asking you if you have the physical ability to do that."

Scomillio objected. "Your Honor, it's been asked and answered."

Funk complained that she hadn't answered his question.

"Ask it one more time," Panella told him.

"It's an easy question," Funk resumed. "Are you claiming that you do not have the physical strength or ability to use one of those knives from your kitchen to cut skin?"

"Yes."

"You're claiming that?"

"Yes."

Satisfied, Funk moved on. "You heard Miss Renner say, because you got to sit here, that sometimes you would take Ms. Guzman to the Ramada Inn, do you remember her saying that?"

"We went there once."

"OK. And that was in an effort to lure Devon from Keary?"

"No."

"It wasn't?"

"No."

"OK. That was so you and Devon could—"

"We went there for the night."

"I'm sorry?"

"We went there for the night."

"There's more to it than that, though. You and Brandon had your reception at that Ramada Inn, didn't you?"

"Yes."

"And there's more to it than that. The room you guys had was room two fifty-two, you and Brandon, right?"

"I don't remember what room Brandon and I had."

"When you took Devon to the Ramada Inn, you took her to room two fifty-two, didn't you?"

"We were in the suite, yes."

"The same suite that you and Brandon had?"

"I don't remember if it was the same one, but yes."

"So that's a coincidence then that happened, you had a suite with Devon, it's just a coincidence?"

"We went to the Ramada Inn and we asked for a suite and we were given that room, yes."

"So you admit that it was the same room?"

"Yes, I don't remember if it was the same room or not, but we went to the Ramada, we asked for a suite, and that's the room that they gave us."

"And you and Brandon had a suite, right?"

"Yes."

"It's a coincidence?"

"That we got the same room, yeah."

In answer to subsequent questions, Michelle denied having taken a syringe from the doctor's office, and said she didn't know what time Devon died.

"Let's talk about some facts for a change," Funk said. "Step down here, please." He brought her over to an exhibit of the log of pages made to Devon that night, pointing specifically to a thirty-one-minute gap between 12:15 to 12:46 A.M.

Keary Renner had testified that Devon left the Mineral Springs around 12:15 A.M. If she were "driving like a bat out of hell," as Devon was known to do, Funk calculated that she would have arrived at Michelle's house seven minutes later, at 12:22 A.M.

"Devon came to your house, you had your wrestling match?" he asked.

"Devon and I never got in a physical fight, ever," Michelle said flatly.

Funk persisted. "Brandon gets bit. Brandon got bit, didn't he? He got bit?"

"He got bit by Devon. I don't know when or where, but he did that night when hc was killing her."

"OK. He tends to his wound, and shortly thereafter, around twelve-thirty, you're in the garage with Devon?"

"I was not in the garage with Devon."

"This is where the murder happened on or about twelve-thirty?"

Scomillio interjected. "Objection, Your Honor, she doesn't know when this occurred. She testified about that."

"Hold on," Panella said. "Ask it in the form of a question."

Funk continued, coming back to the thirty-one-minute gap between calls to Devon's pager. "You paged at twelve-fifteen, that's your last page until the phone call at twelve-forty-six?" he asked.

"I was talking to Keary in between there."

"You're on the phone?"

"Yes."

"So when she died, you were on the phone?"

"I'm not sure when Devon Guzman died. You should ask Brandon Bloss."

"Twelve-thirty," Funk declared.

"Your Honor," Scomillio protested.

Panella told Funk, "I'm sorry, you'll have to form a question."

Funk obliged. "The murder happened at twelve-thirty, didn't it?"

"You should ask your client," Michelle retorted.

Funk next questioned her about the disposal of the

body, drawing upon never-before-revealed information that could only have come from Brandon Bloss. The form of questioning he was forced to take to introduce this new information would have been comical, if not for the ghoulish undertaking being detailed.

"I want to focus in on after you helped Brandon put Devon in her car," Funk began.

"That never happened," Michelle replied.

"OK," Funk said, continuing undeterred. "You asked Brandon to drive Devon's car because you couldn't drive a stick?"

"That's not correct."

"OK. Brandon pulled her car out of the garage onto the alley—you agree with me that's Holt Street, yes?"

"That's Holt Street."

"And he went the wrong way down the alley?"

"I wouldn't know that."

"You were in your red Honda Accord on St. Joseph Street, so you were parallel with each other, right?"

"That's where I park my car."

"I'm talking about driving."

Scomillio interrupted with an objection. "Your Honor, the question is assuming facts that are not in evidence here and have not been admitted to or stated by anybody in this case."

Funk replied, "I'll just ask her."

He turned to Michelle and continued. "Did you get in the red Honda Accord and come out of your driveway and go to be parallel with him while you were on St. Joseph Street? Did you do that?"

"No."

"OK. So then I take it, you did not take a left onto Folk Street?"

"No."

"And Brandon did not then, I guess, take a left to get behind you? That didn't happen, either, did it, I guess?"

"No."

"Then you didn't turn left into the alley behind Mr. Welsh's house, that would be—well, let me ask this, that's Orchard Street, isn't it?"

"Yes."

"You did not take a left there then?"

"No."

"And Brandon did not take a left to follow you?"

"I don't know what Brandon Bloss did or didn't do."

"So then did you not turn right onto St. John's?"

"No."

"Go down the hill?"

"No."

"You didn't do that?"

"No."

"You didn't go straight through the light?"

"No."

"And you didn't turn right to go on six-eleven under the train trestle? You didn't, right?"

"No."

"OK. And this whole time you're not doing that; and Brandon is not behind you, right, because you don't know?"

"No, because I didn't do it."

"So you drive down six-eleven, right, or you didn't do that?"

"No."

"And you didn't drive and then come to a spot across from the water treatment plant there on the right, where there's like a little cut-out? Let me ask you that, are you familiar with that little cut-out, little grass kind of dirt area with some trees?"

"No."

"Where the guardrail is there's a gap in the guardrail there—you're not familiar with that?"

"No."

"So then I guess you didn't turn left into that, right?"

"No."

"And Brandon didn't stay in that right lane in Devon's car, he didn't do that?"

"No."

"OK. And then when you found that that wasn't big enough, you didn't back out onto six-one-one, you didn't do that?"

"No."

"And you didn't keep driving up there southbound on six-one-one?"

"No."

"You didn't do that?"

"No."

"And then the Black Horse Inn on your left, you didn't turn your car into the Black Horse Inn?"

"No."

"You didn't do that?"

"No."

"And turn around in a stone parking lot, you didn't do that?"

"No."

"And then Brandon drove her car and pulled up at the Black Horse Inn, pulled up on your, what would be your passenger side, he didn't pull her car in next to you on her passenger side, he doesn't do that?"

"No."

"That didn't happen?"

"No."

"And you didn't put down your power window on your passenger side?"

"No."

"Didn't do that?"

"No."

"And Brandon asked you, 'What are we doing?' He didn't ask you that?"

"No."

"You didn't tell him, 'Follow me'?"

"No."

Scomillio interrupted again, renewing his earlier objection, that Funk was stating facts not in evidence, rather than asking questions.

Funk protested, "I'm asking it."

Panella gave him some leeway, warning, "It's almost time for you to move on."

Funk continued the absurd interrogation. "You didn't pull out and go back on north six-one-one?"

"No."

"Did you drive on six-one-one that early morning heading north with your lights off?"

"No."

"Cars weren't flashing you to remind you to put your lights on?"

"No."

"That didn't happen?"

"No."

"And you pulled into the first driveway of the canal museum, you didn't do that?"

"No."

"And then Brandon pulled Ms. Guzman's car?"

Scomillio objected a third time. This time Panella sustained it.

Funk backed up, bringing up the blood found on Brandon's clothes. "He got that because he helped carry Devon, he was on what would be the heavier side, and you had the foot side, and he was carrying her and got blood on his pants, isn't that true?" he asked.

"No."

"You don't know how he got blood on his pants?"

"Probably when he was killing her."

"You were on the phone when that was happening, is that it?"

"I was in my living room, yes."

Funk asked Michelle if Brandon had changed into sweatpants, sneakers and a Reebok windbreaker in her car that night. Michelle denied that he changed in her car and said she didn't remember what he wore that night.

"Brandon's clothes with blood on them ended up in your trunk, though?" Funk queried.

"Right."

At the conclusion of his cross-examination, Funk pointed out that Michelle hadn't attended Devon's funeral.

"This is your friend and your lover, your best friend and your only friend?"

"Yes."

"She had a funeral a few days after she died?"

"Yes."

"You didn't go, did you, though?"

"No."

"You didn't go?"

"Right. Keary said that her mom did not want us there."

"You didn't attend?"

"Right."

"Judge, nothing further," Funk said.

After a short recess, Morganelli took the floor, pouncing on some of the same issues Funk had. Again, Michelle denied that the fight at Devon's father's had been about Devon still living with Keary or that Devon had thrown rings back at her.

"So Ms. Renner must be wrong about that?" the DA asked.

"Right."

"Or she's lying about this?"

"Right."

Morganelli switched to the subject of George Vine. "Is George Vine wrong, too?" he asked.

She said Vine was uncertain of the conversation that night and had misconstrued its meaning.

Skipping ahead to Michelle's claim that she saw blood when she found Devon, the DA asked, "What I want to know, isn't it a fact that the only person that said that the green jacket was not there was you, isn't that right?"

"Yes."

"So that means then that Zachary Lysek and Officer Beitler and Keary Renner must all be mistaken when they say they saw the body covered with a green jacket, they must be wrong, is that right?"

"Right. The green jacket was not there when we got there."

"So they must be incorrect then?"

"Somebody put the jacket on top of her."

Returning to June 14, Morganelli asked, "Did you want Devon to come visit you that night when she showed up?"

"Brandon called her—no."

"You weren't asking to see her at all?"

"No."

"You had no reason to call her at that time?"

"No."

After Devon left, Michelle said she slept for maybe a half hour. She assumed Brandon had gone up to bed, but realized he hadn't when he came in the back door around 2:00 A.M.

"Now you're claiming to this jury that Devon Guzman

never came back to your house, isn't that right?" the DA queried.

"Right."

Morganelli pointed out that Michelle said she had been in the front room of the house all evening, while her husband somehow managed to meet up with Devon without Michelle's knowledge. "So the mystery, Ms. Hetzel, is how did Devon and Mr. Bloss get together when Ms. Guzman is coming back to your house? How does she know where to meet Mr. Bloss, if he's not home?"

"I don't know."

"You don't know?"

"I don't know."

"You think that Mr. Bloss got on the phone and contacted Devon and said, 'Don't come back here to our house; I want to meet you someplace'?"

"I don't know what happened."

The DA pressed her on how Devon could've returned to the house and met up with Brandon without her knowing. "If in fact the murder occurred at your house in the backyard, Ms. Guzman would have had to get entry into your front door and would have passed by you in this front room, correct?"

"No, she could have went around the back," Michelle replied, though admitting that Devon customarily entered through the front door.

The DA switched subjects. "And you realize and you know now that the cap of the syringe that was found in those jeans fit over the syringe—over the syringe that was found on Devon Guzman, you know that, don't you?"

"Yes."

"What I want to know, are you claiming then that someone planted that syringe cap in those jeans?"

"Yes."

"You didn't put them in there, did you?"

"No."

"Do you think that's just a coincidence that the cap that fits over the syringe that's on the body of Devon Guzman are in your jeans in soapy water that have blood in them, is that just a coincidence?"

"I didn't put them there."

"So who put them there then?"

"I don't know."

"Do you think Mr. Bloss might have?"

"He might have."

This was the first time Michelle suggested that it wasn't all just a collection of misunderstandings or coincidences that had led to her being on trial for murder. She was suggesting she'd been set up. Morganelli pounced on this, and made much of it throughout the rest of his questioning.

"You think that Mr. Bloss knew that the police were coming with a search warrant and he said to himself, 'I'm really going to throw the police off. I'm going to get some jeans of my wife's, and I'm going to put this cap in the pocket, and I'm going to put it in the washing machine with soapy water and make sure there is the presence of blood there, because I want to throw the police off.' Do you think he did that?"

"Yes, I do."

The DA brought up Brandon's alleged confession. "Now it's my understanding that you said that Brandon confessed to you and said that he killed Devon Guzman, correct?"

"He's made several statements to me, yes."

"And so then what you're telling this jury is that Mr. Bloss, on the evening of June fourteenth, left your residence, not telling you where he was going, correct?"

"Correct."

"Somehow met up with Devon Guzman, even though

Ms. Guzman was intending to come back to your house, correct?"

"Correct."

"That somehow Ms. Guzman would take him, or he would take her, to a special place that you two had, the falls—is that what you're saying, correct?"

"Yes."

"And that he then killed her, either at your yard and then took her body down there, or at the falls itself, correct?"

"Correct."

"And if we believe that Mr. Bloss did this on that night without your help, then Mr. Bloss acted by himself, correct?"

"Yes."

"Nobody else has a reason to hurt Devon Guzman, correct?"

"Not that I'm aware of."

"Why do you think Mr. Bloss needed two pairs of latex gloves instead of one pair when he put them in the trunk of the car? Why do you think that, Ms. Hetzel?"

Panella sustained an objection by Scomillio that the question called for speculation.

Morganelli resumed: "Isn't it a fact, Ms. Hetzel, that when the police opened up your trunk, they didn't find just one pair of latex gloves, they found two pairs of latex gloves? Isn't that true?"

"Yes, they did."

"Doesn't that seem to suggest that more than one person may have been helping with this murder?"

"Not necessarily, no."

Regrouping, Morganelli launched another attack. "Now, do you have any psychic abilities, Ms. Hetzel, at all?"

"No."

"You can't predict the future, can you?"

"No."

"At around, let's see—after you left—after you left Rick

Guzman's house on June fourteenth and you went home, you called up Holly Ronco, didn't you?"

"Yes."

"And you told Holly Ronco that you were concerned that Keary might hurt Devon this night, isn't that right?"

"I was afraid of Devon and Keary, yes, Devon and—"

"You called Holly Ronco on June fourteenth after you got home, and you said to Ms. Ronco, 'I'm concerned and worried that Keary might do something to Devon tonight,' correct?"

"Yes, because that night Devon broke up with Keary."

Pointing out that Keary had said otherwise, the DA asked, "Do you think that it's just a coincidence that [you said] someone might hurt Devon tonight, and she shows up dead a few hours later? That's just a coincidence?"

"Yes, I didn't mean for Keary—it wasn't meant like that."

He brought up the 911 calls. "She wasn't a missing person, yet you were trying to create a situation that made her look like she was missing, isn't that true?"

"No, that's not true."

"You wanted to create an impression that something had happened to her because you knew that sooner or later the police were going to find this car and her dead body in it, isn't this true?"

"That's not true."

"And you wanted to distance yourself and make it look like you were a concerned friend and that you were looking for her and she might be hurt someplace and you were hoping that the police would then find the body and you would look like you were concerned about her. That's what you were doing, isn't it?"

"No."

The DA continued to hammer the issue. "And you—all of a sudden because she's gone for an hour and a half—

are creating that she's a missing person? That's what you're doing?"

"It was longer than that."

"You called Holly Ronco up and you said, 'I think something is going to happen to Devon tonight; Keary might hurt her.' And in an hour-and-a-half time, you have a missing person, she might be in the hospital someplace, having the police look for her, because you wanted to create an impression that something was happening to her, correct?"

"That's not true."

"And you wanted someone else to find her, didn't you?"

"No."

"Except time was going on and it was the morning and they still hadn't found her yet, so you found her, didn't you?"

"Yes."

He brought up Cara Judd. "Cara Judd claims that on July the twenty-first—I'm sorry, July the twenty-second—she's with you and you tell her that you killed Devon Guzman?"

"That never happened."

"So Cara Judd must have lied about that?"

"For Brandon, yes."

"I see. So you think that Cara Judd, on July twenty-second, 2000, wrote this up in her journal and had the details of the murder just out of the clear blue sky?"

"From Brandon."

"Oh, OK," Morganelli said. "So Cara Judd is a co-conspirator with your husband to frame you, is that what you think?"

"Yes."

"You think George Vine is trying to frame you, too?"

"No."

"You think Holly Ronco is trying to frame you when she comes in court and says, 'Ms. Hetzel called me and said something might happen to Devon tonight'?"

"No."

"But Cara Judd is trying to frame you?"

"Yes."

"Didn't you ask Cara Judd to be a godparent of your baby?"

"No, I did not."

"So she just went out and bought that little item for no reason at all that said godmother or godparent?"

"I'm not sure."

"So then, as I understand it, then the detailed information that Ms. Judd got, and you would agree that Ms. Judd's version of how the murder occurred could very well be accurate, except that you didn't do it, correct?"

"I'm not sure."

"Well, you heard this read into evidence, right? And you know—don't you—that it's a detailed account of how the murder could have happened, correct?"

"Right."

"So you're saying then that Brandon said to Cara Judd, 'Listen, I killed somebody and I want to frame my wife. I need you to write this out in a journal for me so we could then frame Michelle Hetzel.' Is that what happened?"

"Yes."

"OK. And yet, Cara Judd never brings this to the police—does she—voluntarily? It's not until the police get to her, correct?"

"Right. She had a lot of time to put it together."

"Well, did you see this diary goes back until 1996 and goes beyond the date of the murder, doesn't it?"

"Yes."

"Ms. Judd was someone who kept a diary on a regular basis, wasn't she?"

"I'm not sure."

"So Mr. Bloss got together with Cara Judd, and Cara Judd said, 'Yeah, you know, I want to frame Michelle Hetzel for murder, so I'll write this all out for you and then I'm not going to tell the police about it, but I'll wait until they come see me.' Is that what you think happened?"

"I'm not sure."

"Don't you think, Ms. Hetzel, that if Miss Judd wanted to frame you by creating a false journal, that she would have done that and then called the police and said, 'Hey, I have some information for you.' She never did that, did she?"

"No, she did not."

"She wasn't trying to frame you, was she?"

"Yes, she was."

"Is she trying to frame you when she wrote in her journal that you said, 'I'm going to come out of this smelling like a bed of roses'?"

"I never said that."

"So she's lying about that?"

"Yes, she's lying."

Morganelli called her out on the carpet regarding attempts to pin the crime on Keary. "You thought, in the beginning—didn't you, Ms. Hetzel?—that you could make it look like Keary Renner did this, didn't you?"

"No."

"In the beginning, that's what you thought?"

"No."

"In the beginning you thought that you could show that Keary Renner and Devon were in this big fight in the apartment and somehow the murder occurred there?"

"No, that's not right."

"Isn't that what you were thinking when you called up Holly Ronco that night and said, you know, 'I think something is going to happen to Devon, and Keary might hurt [her]', isn't that when you were trying to put that into place?"

"No."

He switched topics to the argument at Rick's. "Now you indicate, Ms. Hetzel, that the subject matter of your disagreement with Miss Guzman June fourteenth, the night that you were at Rick's house, was that Ms. Guzman wanted you to sleep with her that night, is that right?"

"She wanted me to stay overnight at her father's house that night, yes."

"She wanted you to stay with her over at her father's house, and you said the reason that you couldn't is because 'What am I going to tell Brandon,' is that right?"

"That's right."

"This is a woman that you just got back from a week trip in Puerto Rico with and you didn't bother telling Brandon about that, did you?"

"No."

"So you were concerned that 'what am I going to tell Brandon about sleeping over one night at Rick's house,' but you weren't concerned about what you were going to tell Brandon about a week trip to Puerto Rico that costs seven thousand dollars, were you?"

"No."

"That doesn't make much sense, does it, Ms. Hetzel?"

"No," Michelle admitted.

He talked about her troubled marriage to Brandon prior to the murder, contrasting it with the decision afterward to go to Mexico with him. "Now, you have a—not a very good marriage, you claim, with Mr. Bloss, right?"

"No."

"He confesses to you that he killed his best friend—your best friend, right? You, of course, had nothing to do with this, and then you go to Cancun, Mexico, with him for a vacation?"

"It was not a vacation."

"Well, how long were you there?"

"A weekend."

Morganelli asked if she'd ever filed for a divorce from Brandon.

"No, I went to see a lawyer," Michelle said.

"Well, you went to see a lawyer, but you never engaged a lawyer, did you?"

"No."

"Mr. Bloss is the one that was making plans for a divorce, wasn't he?"

"Yes."

"He actually went to see a lawyer and the lawyer sent him a communication?"

"Right."

"And then he began to make a list, I think it's into evidence, about splitting up the assets between you and him, correct?"

"Right."

"Your money would come to an end if you and he got a divorce, wouldn't it?"

"No."

"All the money that you were spending, he made, I'm talking about?"

"Right."

Switching subjects, the DA attacked her on the basis of the phone records and pages made to Devon. He pointed out that although Michelle had returned home the morning after the murder, she never paged Devon from her home after 1:32 A.M. "You never paged her again, Ms. Hetzel, because you knew that she was dead, and you also knew that you didn't want to have any more records of any pages coming from that phone number onto her pager, didn't you?" he charged.

"No, that's not true."

Morganelli asked the judge for a momentary break while he prepared for his final attack. When he was ready, he began, "Devon Guzman was smaller than you, wasn't she, Ms. Hetzel?"

"Yes."

"How tall are you, about?"

"Five-seven."

"And Devon was about five-foot-four, wasn't she?"

"Yes."

"Now, the falls, which was where Devon Guzman's body was located, that was a special place for you and her, correct?"

"Right, and her and Keary."

"And what?"

"And her and Keary."

She was bringing Keary into it again. Morganelli let the remark stand without comment, moving on. "Now let me ask you this question, Miss Hetzel. You said that it wasn't until June sixteenth when you got up in the morning and you saw Mr. Bloss allegedly burning his arm with a cigarette lighter, that's the first time that he told you he killed Devon Guzman, is that right?"

"That's right."

"And, according to you, he tells you that he got in a fight and it was self-defense, isn't that right?"

"That's right."

"And he says—and then you claim that he said that Devon took him to the falls?"

"Right."

"And that she came after him with a knife?"

"Right."

"Did he explain to you how it was that if Devon was attacking him with a knife, that he was able to get behind her and cut her throat from behind, if she was in front of him?"

"No, he didn't give me the details."

"Now, you didn't tell anybody that you were pregnant?"

"I thought I was."

"Did you ever tell any of Mr. Bloss's relatives, like Natalie

Bloss or Pauline Bloss, that you were pregnant and expecting twins?"

"No, I did not."

"So, if they said that, they would be mistaken—"

"They would be lying."

"Was Cara Judd lying, too, then when she wrote in her journal that you told her that you couldn't drink alcohol or you could only drink a little alcohol because the doctor told you because of the pregnancies, is that a lie?"

"Yes."

"She made that up?"

"Yes."

"Was that part of the plan to frame you, you think?"

"Yes."

"Did you ever tell either Natalie Bloss or any member of his family that you were having papers drawn up to give total custody of the babies to them after they were born?"

"No."

"You never said that?"

"No."

"If Miss Judd heard that and wrote that, that would be a lie?"

"Yeah, they're lying."

"Miss Judd indicates that there was another occasion when you and her were together when you were crying and had the rings of Devon in your hand—Devon's ring and your ring and you told Cara how much you missed and loved Devon. Was that a lie?"

"No, that was true."

"That was the truth. So Miss Judd did get some of it correct then, is that right?"

"Yes."

"She only gets the things correct that are helpful to you, but she gets the things wrong that aren't helpful to you, isn't that correct?"

"That's correct."

"Did Miss Judd get it right when she said that you said, 'These people think that they are so smart and just keep checking my house. Well, go ahead, what do I care.' And then she said that you said, 'Anyway, my jeans were soaking for so long, they'll never find any blood from them.' Did she get that wrong?"

"I never said that."

"Did you ever tell Miss Judd about Brandon hosing down the garage to clean up the blood?"

"No."

"So, if she wrote that in her journal, she was wrong about that, is that correct?"

"I never discussed anything personal with Cara Judd ever."

"I have no further questions, Your Honor."

By now, it was late afternoon. Michelle had survived the major questioning, but her time on the stand was not over yet. Her attorney had the opportunity to redirect, to undo some of the damage done on cross-examination. After that, Brandon's defense and the prosecution could apply the heat again, recross-examining based on the redirect.

Scomillio asked his client to explain why she'd lied to police about her intimate relationship with Devon. Michelle said the reason was her family. "They never approved of my relationship with Devon. As a friend they did, but when it went to more, they wouldn't—they never accepted it."

Swinging the focus away from Michelle and toward Brandon for a moment, he asked: "When you were in Puerto Rico with Devon, were you two intimate?"

"Yes, we were."

"Did you tell anybody about that when you got back?"

"Brandon."

"You told Brandon that. What was his reaction?"

"He was angry."

Addressing Morganelli's argument that Michelle had to have seen Devon when she returned the night of the murder, Scomillio outlined a scenario in which Brandon could have slipped out of the house through the back door and waited for Devon, intercepted her when she arrived and brought her back to the garage on his own.

When Funk's turn came again, he hammered away on some of the same areas that had been touched upon before, noting that the time of the murder coincided with a crisis point in Michelle's two major relationships. "Devon rejects you, says, 'I'm with Keary, I've got plans to go to Arizona, have a baby'?"

"Devon never rejected me."

"Then you got caught in your lie from your husband and he says to you, 'That's it, I'm divorcing you.' Devon effectively divorced you, your husband effectively divorced you, was going to?"

"Devon did not."

"OK. And you were concerned that you were going to be left alone?"

"No."

"OK. That's when you told him that you were pregnant?"

"I never told him I was pregnant."

"You thought you were pregnant?"

"Right."

"And he didn't divorce you, did he?"

"No."

"Her death was two weeks—less than two weeks after you told him that?"

"Right."

Abruptly he switched subjects. "Brandon surprised you when he walked out into the garage, isn't that true?"

"That's not true."

"After he surprised you, he checked for a pulse on her?"

Scomillio objected, because the question assumed something Michelle had just denied. Funk withdrew it, posing a new one. "Brandon wanted to call nine-one-one, true?"

"No, no."

"You asked him to help you?"

"No," Michelle denied.

"No?"

"No."

"That didn't happen?"

"Right," she averred.

On his recross, Morganelli had a final trick up his sleeve. "Miss Hetzel, you would agree, wouldn't you, that it's important for all the witnesses who testified in this case to be truthful, wouldn't you agree with that?"

She agreed it was.

"Did you ever ask Cara Judd or Natalie Bloss to be godparents for your babies, and I mean babies plural?" the DA queried.

"No, I did not."

Scomillio broke in. "I'm going to object. This is beyond the scope of my redirect." The objection threatened to rob the DA of the opportunity to spring his trap. Fortunately for him, Panella granted some leeway. "Let's hear Mr. Morganelli's next question," the judge said.

The DA produced a sheet of legal-size-paper. "I would like to have this marked, if I may," he said, submitting it to be entered as evidence. The document was marked with the next sequential exhibit number.

"Now, Miss Hetzel," Morganelli said. "I would like to

show you what has been marked for purposes of identification as Commonwealth Exhibit Number fifty-two, and I would like you to take a look at that and tell me whether or not that is not, in fact, a letter in your handwriting that you wrote?"

"It is."

Much of the letter would not make much sense to the jury members, who had not been privy to Cara Judd's story about the night she believed Michelle drugged her and subsequently struck Brandon's mother. The letter read:

Pauline, Natalie, & Cara,

I'm writing to say I'm sorry! I do not know what was wrong with Cara other than she was drunk and I hope she is OK. I know your [sic] angry but I did not force her to do anything!! I was a little drunk myself so I am sorry for what I said and did to you Pauline! But I did not do anything to Cara. Yes there were people carding at Diamondz and my lawyer went there to verify that on Saturday! In any case I'm sorry and I'm half to blame. I'm just very stressed out. My husband is going to jail and I'm pregnant so my stress and hormones are at an all time high. I still would like you both to be godparents, but I guess that's up to you! But I know Brandon would be very hurt if his family weren't there when our babies are born. I know its [sic] easy to be angry and bitter but I'm asking you please forgive me! I'm not the same person or I would have turned Brandon in but instead I realized what's done is done and forgave him because I knew he was sorry! We need to be family and realize people sometimes make stupid mistakes, but now more than ever we need to stick together for Brandon. The most I have is a glass of wine usually only half now because I realized what I could do to my children. So again I'm

sorry and I hope you forgive me that is what familys are for right!
Love
Michelle

After showing the witness the letter, the DA asked, "This is a letter that you wrote to Cara Judd and Natalie in which you wrote in your own handwriting asking them to be godparents and saying that you were having babies, correct?"

"I wrote that for Brandon," Michelle replied. It was a letter that had never actually been sent.

"So this is another thing that is just misunderstood, I assume?" Morganelli asked.

"Yes."

At long last, after four hours on the stand, Michelle was allowed to step down. It was after 5:30 P.M., and it had been a long day.

"We're in the homestretch now," Judge Panella said before adjourning. In view of the conflicting testimony that had been offered, he reminded the jurors that they were the "sole finders of fact in this case," and that the responsibility was theirs to determine what the truth was. "It's up to you to decide which, if any, of the testimony to believe."

42

After Tuesday's dramatic turn with an embattled Michelle Hetzel holding forth on the witness stand, Wednesday, October 3, 2001, began in anticlimactic fashion. In chambers Judge Panella discussed the subject of whether the defendants would put on character evidence. It was an important issue, particularly in the eyes of the appellate courts, and Panella would be remiss if he overlooked it. He told the attorneys that he planned to talk to the defendants first thing, outside of the presence of the jury, about their right to call character witnesses— people who might testify regarding their reputation for truthfulness and nonviolence. In past cases this type of testimony alone had proven sufficient to create reasonable doubt.

DA Morganelli supported Panella's decision to give special instructions regarding character evidence, noting that the state supreme court had overturned at least one first-degree murder conviction solely because defense counsel had not considered the use of such evidence. He conceded that if character witnesses were to testify that both Brandon and Michelle had been peaceful, nonviolent people, he'd have no evidence to refute that. In essence, the defense had nothing to lose by calling such witnesses, he said.

But putting on witnesses who'd be open to cross-examination, not only by the prosecution but also by an antagonistic codefendant's counsel, could be a chancy proposition. For strategic reasons, neither defense team wanted to take the risk of calling such witnesses and having it backfire on them.

At the end of the conference in chambers, Michelle's attorney Brian Monahan asked Bloss's side if they would share how many witnesses they planned to put on the stand. Attorney Funk replied that it was going to be Brandon's call to make, when the time came, but that the only witness who might testify would be Brandon himself.

When the trial resumed in front of the jury, Monahan called Lieutenant Jose Garcia, a supervisor with the county corrections department. Garcia presented a visitor log showing that Brandon's mother and sister had gone to see him in jail. The inference Monahan was hoping jurors would draw was that it was possible that Brandon had conveyed information about the murder to his mother or sister, and that one of them in turn had relayed it to Cara Judd, who then incorporated it into her diaries as part of the aforementioned conspiracy to frame Michelle. It was probably a stretch to think they'd get the connection he was hinting at—a communication line between Brandon and Cara—but just in case they did, on cross-examination, Teresa Miranda clarified with Garcia that Cara Judd's own name appeared nowhere on the visitor log.

Detective Barry Golazeski was called next. He testified that police had toured Brandon's workspace at Ashland Chemical and received three types of rubber gloves used there. The implication was that Brandon, not

Michelle, had obtained and used the rubber gloves found in Michelle's car.

Panella called a recess at 10:17 A.M. While the jury was out, Monahan told the judge he was ready to rest his case. As a matter of course, he renewed a motion for Michelle's acquittal based on the arguments made when the commonwealth rested its case. Panella denied the motion.

With the jury gone, the judge spent considerable time explaining to Michelle her right to call character witnesses who could vouch for her reputation in the community.

"In cases such as this, in which it's word against word, credibility of the witnesses is of paramount importance, and character evidence is critical to the jury's determination of credibility," Panella said.

Panella sent her with her attorneys into a private conference room to review the decision of whether to call character witnesses. When they emerged, Monahan said they would stick by the decision not to. The reason was that if witnesses were put on testifying that Michelle was truthful, the DA would impeach that testimony with examples of untruthfulness. If they put on evidence that she was nonviolent, Brandon's attorneys planned to counter with evidence that she'd been violent with certain members of his family.

When the jury was brought back into the courtroom, Monahan rested his case on behalf of Michelle Hetzel. Now it was Brandon's turn. Judge Panella turned to his defense team. "Mr. Szachacz, we now turn to Defendant Bloss's side of the case. I'll hear from you."

Szachacz replied that he had no testimony to present.

Unlike Michelle, Brandon had decided not to testify on his own behalf. No witnesses would be called on his behalf, either, which meant that he was essentially presenting no defense. He was counting on the jury to find that the evidence put on by the commonwealth was insufficient to convict him.

Judge Panella excused the jury again, and proceeded to reiterate to Brandon the character evidence instructions that he'd given Michelle, granting him the same opportunity to review the decision in private with his attorneys. He reminded Brandon that both Michelle Hetzel and her mother had testified that he'd confessed to perpetrating a murder, and suggested that his reputation for being a law-abiding, nonviolent person could be a critical issue for the jury. But when Brandon and his defense team returned from the conference room, Szachacz said they would stick by their decision not to call any character witnesses.

The jury was brought back in, and Szachacz rested his case before them.

Panella reminded the jury that under the Constitution, every defendant has the right to remain silent. "You must not draw any inference of guilt from the fact that Defendant Bloss decided not to testify in this trial," he advised.

Before the evidentiary portion of the trial ended, Morganelli had the opportunity to present rebuttal evidence. He called Keary Renner to rebut Michelle's assertion that Keary might've placed the green coat on Devon's body at the canal museum.

Going to his crime scene photo exhibits, the DA asked, "When you looked in, did Miss Guzman have this green jacket on her as it's shown in these photographs here?"

"Yes, she did," Keary replied.

"OK. Did you at any time remove that jacket while you were trying to see whether she was OK or not?"

"No, I did not."

When Keary stepped down from the stand, the evidentiary portion of the trial ended. All that remained now were closing arguments and jury deliberations. It was just before noon, but Panella didn't want to squeeze in closing arguments today, because it would mean sending the jury into the deliberation room later in the day than he would like.

Before dismissing the jurors, he reminded them to heed the cautionary instructions they'd been given, such as to resist the urge to conduct investigations or visit the crime scene or other related locations on their own. It would be a shame if someone did something to jeopardize the trial at this late date. Thankfully, the run of bad luck that had depleted the pool of alternates at the start of the trial had ended. One more day and the case would be in the hands of the jury at last, provided luck held.

43

The trial ended the way it began, with three attorneys telling the same story, about a four-sided love triangle that came to a tragic end on a June night that felt like so very long ago. Once again they told the same story three times over, with minor variations that made all the difference in the world. This time the defense attorneys went first, delivering their impassioned closing arguments while Morganelli, hunched over laced fingers on the polished tabletop in front of him, watched pensively, waiting for his chance to have the last word.

Monahan maintained that Bloss committed the murder alone and confessed as much to Michelle and her mother. He referred to the 911 calls Michelle made, asking the jury to consider why, if she was guilty, she would call to report her friend missing. Finally he suggested that the high-school dropout was not smart enough to have planned the elaborate crime.

Funk, speaking for Brandon, described the crime as an act of passion on Michelle's part. "Hell hath no fury like a woman scorned," he said, pointing out Michelle's alleged confession to Cara Judd. Brandon's role had just been to help dispose of the body, he argued yet again.

"Did he make the right choice in helping dispose of the body? No. But you can't convict him of murder or conspiracy to commit murder for that."

When Brandon began to cry during Funk's closing argument, it was the first time either of the defendants had shown any such emotion during the nine-day trial. Minutes later, Michelle began to weep also.

When his turn came, Morganelli, who was after first-degree murder convictions, was obliged to counter the suggestion that the murder had been a crime of passion. If the jurors viewed it as such, they could reach a verdict of voluntary manslaughter, a lesser crime with lesser punishments. The DA stressed evidence of premeditation on Michelle's part—the warning call to Holly Ronco saying she was worried about Devon. "Is it just a coincidence that she was worried something might happen to Devon, and that it did?"

More evidence of premeditation, he stressed, was the fact that the couple contrived to bring Devon to their house alone, turning her away when she first arrived with Keary. "If all they wanted to do was talk to Devon, then why not let her in?" he pondered. "Keary Renner wasn't at the door. She stayed in the car to avoid a confrontation. Why? Because they wanted Devon alone. The murder plan was already in motion."

To persuade the jury that two people colluded in the crime, he pointed to the fact that two pairs of latex gloves were found in Michelle's car, and that both participated in cover-up. "Why would Brandon Bloss go over to Keary Renner's at two-thirty in the morning to look for a woman he hates, when he has to be at work at six-thirty A.M.?" Morganelli asked. "Because they needed to set up their cover story."

At 5:00 P.M., the jury of three men and nine women filed out of the courtroom, which had been their home for much of the past two weeks, and into the deliberation room, where they'd decide the fate of two young people.

At 9:45 P.M., an indication of the issues they were struggling with came to light when they requested a rereading of instructions regarding the degrees of murder or manslaughter they could consider. The reading of the in-depth instructions alone would take forty-five minutes, and given the late hour, Judge Panella asked if the jurors wanted to retire for the night and pick up deliberations in the morning. But they insisted they wanted to continue on, a strong indication that an end was in sight.

The time was 10:30 P.M. when the reading of the instructions concluded and the jury resumed deliberations. Two hours later, Judge Panella received word that they were ready to render verdicts.

It was the moment so many had been waiting for. Among them was John Morganelli. What conclusion had the jurors come to? How had they answered the questions that Morganelli himself had not been able to provide answers for?

"It was my judgment that it was better to let the jury decide the case rather than me, and let all the evidence go to the jury and let them figure it out," Morganelli said. He hadn't tried to pinpoint who wielded the knife for one simple reason: "I thought I might guess wrong." Now he was about to find out if he'd played it the right way.

Judge Panella addressed those present in the court room, which included the attorneys, family members of the victim and the accused, and reporters from various newspapers. Many of them had been in the courtroom since eight-thirty in the morning, and tensions were running high. Acknowledging that it had been an emotionally charged case, he cautioned those assembled to remain composed whatever the outcome. "We don't know what the jury's verdict will be, but there will be no acting u

in the courtroom and there will be no acting up immediately outside of the courthouse," Panella warned. Extra
deputy sheriffs stood by to keep the peace.

Once the verdict was received, Panella said, everyone
except members of the news media (who would be running out to phone in the verdict to their newsrooms for
the next morning's edition) would have to remain in the
courtroom for ten or fifteen minutes to allow the jurors
to exit the building first safely.

"With that, we'll bring the jury in," Panella announced.

In John Morganelli's ten years as district attorney, it was
the latest a jury had kept at it to deliver a verdict.

After the first couple days in court, hunched all day in
a rock-hard seat that felt like a church pew, and listening
to the agonizing testimony, Rick Guzman had endured
enough. "I couldn't take it anymore," he said. "I just stayed
home and got the heads up from my mom and family. I was
too broke up. You know, really to sit there and just—it's
tough. I wouldn't wish that on my worst enemy."

He was home sleeping when the jury was ready to deliver the verdicts. "I wasn't quite so sure if I could handle
the outcome," he explained. "So I kinda left and hid. I
knew my family was there." When the verdict came in,
he'd learn about it from his mother, who'd promised to
come over and wake him up.

The time was creeping toward 1:00 A.M. when the clerk
addressed the jury, asking the foreperson to rise to deliver
the verdicts on each of the two charges against the defendants. "Criminal homicide," the clerk called out. "On the
charge of criminal homicide, how do you find the defendant Michelle Hetzel?"

Anticipation created a deafening silence in the courtroom.

The foreperson replied, "Guilty of murder in the first degree."

"Criminal conspiracy. On the charge of criminal conspiracy to commit homicide, how do you find the defendant Michelle Hetzel?"

"Not guilty."

Michelle's fate had been declared. Now it was Brandon's turn.

"Criminal homicide," the clerk called. "On the charge of criminal homicide, how do you find the defendant Brandon Bloss?"

"Guilty of murder in the first degree."

"Criminal conspiracy. On the charge of criminal conspiracy to commit homicide, how do you find the defendant Brandon Bloss?"

"Not guilty."

Both defendants remained composed as the verdicts were read.

Brian Monahan asked for an individual polling of the jurors regarding his client. One by one they affirmed that they'd found Michelle Hetzel guilty of murder.

Immediately following the verdicts, sheriffs' deputies slipped handcuffs around the defendants' wrists and clicked them shut. Michelle marched first to the front of the courtroom to be sentenced by Judge Panella.

"Miss Hetzel, you have been found guilty of a crime for which the legislature has adopted a mandatory penalty. I have no discretion in this regard. The penalties for first-degree murder under the facts of this case are life imprisonment, as well as a fifty-thousand dollar fine. Based upon what I have heard at trial, I do not believe that you have any ability to pay a fine. You are, therefore, sentenced to life in prison and the payment of costs."

Ever thorough, making certain all bases were covered on the record, Morganelli said, "Your Honor, just one point—that the sentence is life without parole in Pennsylvania."

"That is the law in Pennsylvania," Panella agreed.

Monahan asked if Michelle could have a few minutes in private to say good-bye to her mother and father. In the interests of keeping order in the court, Panella denied the request, then summoned Brandon to approach the bench.

Just as he had done with Michelle, Panella cited Pennsylvania's mandatory penalty for first-degree murder and sentenced Brandon to life in prison, without the chance of parole.

At 12:58 A.M., court adjourned. Michelle Hetzel forced back tears as she was led past her mother and father, who held tight to each other and watched her go with red-rimmed eyes. As the courtroom emptied, Brandon's sister clutched attorney Szachacz and wept.

Outside the courtroom Morganelli and Miranda celebrated their victory. "This is the verdict I was looking for," the DA said. The acquittal on the conspiracy charge was of little consequence, as it had just been an avenue to get to the Murder One conviction, he said.

The defense attorneys, for their part, tried to make the best of the disappointment. Monahan said that Michelle would appeal. Funk declared, "I don't agree with this verdict." He, too, said an appeal would be forthcoming. "This is not over," he snapped.

But it was. Yes, there would be appeals, and as soon as morning, Michelle and Brandon undoubtedly would be discussing their options with their attorneys. But for now, it was over. At long last.

44

The jury settled the legal issue of innocence or guilt, but since many questions lingered, notably as to who wielded the knife against Devon, people inevitably asked: *did the jury reach the right verdict?*

John Morganelli remained emphatically certain it had. No one could say who used the knife, but under the law's accomplice liability provision, if Brandon and Michelle were both involved in the murder, that was enough to make them both guilty of murder.

Morganelli saw Michelle Hetzel as a girl of average intelligence but with a frighteningly above-average ability to make up stories. This ability occasioned him, in a news feature years later about dangerous female criminals, to single her out as a woman every bit as dangerous as any man he'd encountered.

"I thought Michelle Hetzel was a very dangerous person because she was a liar," Morganelli explained. "She was a very cunning woman. She would make up stories to suit her own needs. She told people she was pregnant, which wasn't true. She would say all kinds of nonsense, and she was deceptive, she was misleading. I think she was a manipulative woman, and I think that she was dangerous."

Having come face-to-face with her during the trial, he gained some insight into how she might have brought her strait-laced husband under her influence. "I always got the impression that she thought that she could manipulate men, particularly," Morganelli said, "that she thought she was sort of cute, and, you know, would, like, bat her eyes, sort of play an innocent little girl. I even got the impression at times that she was trying to manipulate me and the judge. You know, 'Oh, I'm just poor little Michelle Hetzel here, I'm so cute and sexy and whatever.' I just sort of ignored that, because she would sort of look at you, and just try to make eye contact with you; it was almost like she was trying to gain sympathy for her predicament, that you would feel sorry for her."

One of the people Michelle Hetzel thought might feel sorry for her after her conviction was none other than Devon's father, Rick Guzman.

"She had an investigator come to my house and appeal to me to help her get a new trial," Rick said. "Can you imagine that? Yes. The man came to my house. He was an ex–FBI agent. It was the summer of 2004. And I said, 'You gotta be kidding me.'"

Michelle had written Rick a letter from Muncy State Prison and sent it with the investigator, thinking Devon's father, someone she considered a father figure, might still harbor affection for her. "She actually thought that I would have a soft spot for her, and help the family get her a new trial," he marveled.

Through an appeal Michelle was seeking a new trial separate from Brandon. Even if she got it, Rick Guzman doubted it would do her any good, since he had concluded that Michelle had been the prime mover behind the murder.

"It was Michelle that was real pushy," he said. "She was obsessed with Devon, totally." Being spoiled and never having learned to take no for an answer, she was not about to take no from Devon, he believed. "No money could buy what Devon had," he said, and Michelle was too attracted to Devon's bright light to let her go.

Rick was sure Michelle contemplated the murder for months or longer, virtually sealing his daughter's fate first in her thoughts. "Given the human mind, you want something bad enough, you can get it. What the mind of man can conceive and believe, he will—*she* will—achieve. What the mind of man harbors, the body will bring forth."

Michelle would have had a hard time overpowering Devon on her own, Rick maintained. "Michelle couldn't stand on her own two feet. She wasn't athletic at all, where Devon was. Devon, as a little girl, took karate; she was athletic; she was nimble on her feet."

So Michelle needed the help of someone strong. "She needed the muscle," Rick said. "This was something that's been on the stove for months, if not years, you know, and she finally figured out a way to make it happen." The answer was Brandon. "He was a quiet individual. I always thought of him as 'still water runs deep.' He was college educated, and he had a decent job, comes from a good family—and she played the guy."

Rick believed Michelle used her feelings for Devon deliberately to incite her husband. "So she played the husband and his jealousies, and worked him to the boiling point of not giving a shit and just killing her."

As for why Michelle would do such a thing, Rick Guzman ventured that there was just something intrinsically wrong inside her. "You know it's just one of those things where you got a sick individual, a rotten apple in a healthy skin. What else can you say? You couldn't have picked her out of a basket."

Years later, he could speculate a little on his daughter's final, life-and-death struggle. "It must've been a hell of a time, you know, to literally bite a piece of flesh off a person," he reflected. "Well, she knew she was going down. What else is there?"

One thing he found remarkable was that despite Michelle and Brandon's combined intelligence, they committed such stupid blunders. For instance, leaving Brandon's clothes in Michelle's car. "That would've been the first thing I'd've took a match to," he said.

The existence of those clothes in Michelle's trunk had been among the most puzzling aspects of the case, especially since the couple had gone to such lengths to stage the crime scene and orchestrate a cover-up. *Had* there been some kind of setup? Why hadn't Brandon taken advantage of the 2½-hour wait in the car at the Mineral Springs after the murder to dispose of them?

Any number of places would have served the purpose. The Delaware River flowed silent and black on the other side of the road from the Mineral Springs. The bag could have been tossed into the river, to be carried miles away by dawn. If the river seemed an untrustworthy repository for such problematic items, there was the woods. In the country darkness behind the Mineral Springs stood a disused railroad bridge, from the base of which rose a set of tiered wooden steps leading to a hiking trail that skirted wooded ridge high above the river. Something well-hidden along that little-used trail would probably have gone undiscovered for ages.

It is dark and still out along the Delaware in the dead of night, and it would've been simple to slip out of the car and get rid of the incriminating clothes and gloves without being seen. Why had Brandon left them in the vehicle? It was one of many mysteries, little and big, that remained after the trial. This one, however, received an answer when Brandon filed an appeal in 2003 under the

Post-Conviction Relief Act (PCRA). His explanation was simple: Michelle was supposed to get rid of the bag.

The PCRA documents provided Brandon's story of the crime. It was a familiar tale—that he only had helped dispose of the body—but the new documents filled in some missing details. According to the appeal:

Fearing for his unborn child and concerned for his wife, Brandon broke up a fight between Michelle and Devon in his living room, which had started because Michelle was enraged that Devon had brought Keary to the house. Bitten by Devon, he went upstairs to tend to his bleeding wound. Meanwhile, Michelle followed Devon outside, through the kitchen and past a butcher block full of knives. In the garage Michelle launched a "vicious, and ultimately fatal, attack." Brandon came down, and at first could not find the girls. Then he discovered them in the garage, where Michelle was "sitting on the garage floor crying with the head of the victim in her lap, and exclaiming words to the effect of 'breathe, Devon, breathe!'"

Brandon checked for a pulse and found none. Michelle began giving "definitive directives," including telling Brandon to get a change of clothing, bring Devon's car to the back of the yard, hose away blood and help her move the body. Later, Michelle took off her jeans and left them to soak in the washer. At some point she got rid of the murder weapon.

While Brandon followed Michelle toward the canal museum with Devon's body in the seat behind him, he began to panic that she was leading him right into downtown Easton, so he reached behind, found Devon's green jacket and tossed it over her body. Here now was an explanation for the green jacket that caused Michelle such grief on the witness stand.

At the canal museum, Michelle told Brandon to leave the keys in Devon's car and roll up the windows. She pro duced a small steak knife and slipped it into Devon's left hand. She also produced a syringe and left it in the waistband. She told Brandon not to worry about the bag of bloody clothes—she'd get rid of them.

But there was one crucial thing Brandon's latest story still left unexplained. Why would Brandon have done Michelle's bidding and gone to such lengths to cover up the crime, if he had not helped commit it? This was one of the most compelling logical arguments for his guilt, and perhaps part of the reason why his appeals to date have been denied.

Michelle's appeals have been no more successful than Brandon's. Five years postconviction, the only things left for her appeals lawyer to challenge were the DNA lab work and the authenticity of Cara Judd's journals. But unlike Brandon and his family, who'd kept a public silence about the case and confined their appeals to legal channels, Michelle and her family went public shortly after the trial.

The year 2002 began with a concerted campaign to establish Michelle's innocence. A letter to the editor appeared in the *Express-Times*, submitted by a woman who said she'd attended the trial and concluded that the evidence had been sufficient to convict Brandon, but not Michelle. She believed conflicting evidence and testimony forced the jury to convict both defendants in a haste to get the decision over with.

A week later, that letter was followed by a similar one submitted by Michelle's parents, who vented about the gossip in South Side that still surrounded the murder. People wondered aloud to shopkeepers if the new owners of Brandon and Michelle's home knew a murder had been committed here. Michelle's parents asserted that their daughter had given truthful statements to police, passed a polygraph and voluntarily testified to prove her innocence. "The only thing Michelle was guilty of was having a relationship with her best friend," they wrote. The assertion that Michelle had passed a lie detector test came as a surprise to many.

A friend of Devon's didn't let the Hetzels' claims go unanswered, wagering in a letter of her own that Michelle may have passed a polygraph because she'd come to believe her own lies, "therefore having no detectable reaction."

Michelle's father didn't stop at letters to the editor to clear his baby girl. Elbert Hetzel, who'd cooperated with authorities during the murder investigation, believed that police had not returned the favor and done enough investigating to exonerate her. With the two-year anniversary of the crime approaching, he contacted the *Express-Times* to urge that a reporter look at the case anew.

45

When the *Express-Times* received Elbert Hetzel's request, Rudy Miller, a young general-assignment reporter, eagerly volunteered. "It was a big story around the newsroom at the time, and I wanted to be a part of it," he recalled. "Michelle's father approached us and said that he wanted us to look into this case because he thought that the jury made a mistake, that Michelle Hetzel was not involved in the murder, that it was all Brandon's doing. So he encouraged us to send somebody to go to prison to interview her. I thought that was a great opportunity, and I took that as a launching point for doing the story that I did."

The story would turn out to be an in-depth analysis of the case, headlined ANATOMY OF A MURDER, and running on Sunday, June 16, 2002, almost two years to the day from the date of the crime.

After her sentencing, Michelle had been transferred to Muncy, a close-security prison where Pennsylvania's most serious female offenders are held. Miller got his name on her visitor list, wrote up a list of questions, packed up his notebook and pen, and hit the road. From Easton, Muncy lay some three hours northwest by car.

It was a story for which Miller would go beyond the call of duty, devoting more time to it than most stories he'd done. He had a very personal reason for wanting to do a good job. "I had a friend who got addicted to heroin and disappeared one day," he said. "No one knew what happened to him, and years later, his bones, his skeletal remains, were found, and it was really a big event for me because he was a close friend of mine. And I remember the way that the media covered his thing. I remember the police reporter who covered a lot of this stuff was a person who tended to want to put a Pollyannaish spin on everything, and I remember thinking that I owed it to my friend, Dan, to try to do as good a job as I could to try to present everything accurately, even if there were ugly sides to it."

Going to Muncy, Miller wasn't out to hurt anyone, but he wanted to present a fuller picture than the many shorter pieces previously published had. "It really ended up being a story about three girls—Devon, Keary and Michelle—and what got them together, and what could lead these three to have such a tragic, fatal ending."

Miller took a wrong turn getting off the highway, but then found his way to the prison. When he got there prison officials wouldn't let him bring in his list of interview questions, but he was at least allowed to bring a notebook and pen.

Muncy's layout reminded him of a liberal arts college with stone buildings surrounding a quadlike courtyard only the entire place was circumscribed by two-story chain-link fencing trimmed with razor wire. Inside, he found himself in a large, open space where women in brown jumpsuits mingled with their visitors. He met with Michelle in a small room with bulletproof glass around the sides, overseen by a guard in a perch. The place felt almost like an airplane terminal. Almost.

Having put on weight at the time of her trial, Michelle was now thin again. Her dyed-blond hair had grown out, revealing a natural brown. She made an immediate impression. "I remember she just seemed very disturbed," Miller said. "People had described her as manipulative, to me, and that's very obvious to me that she's the kind of person who wants to convince everybody, including herself, that her vision of reality is the truth, even if it isn't. She seems like someone who has a very hard time dealing with unpleasant thoughts."

In his story, Miller described her manner: "She recalls emotional events with the levelheadedness of someone used to talking about the past but detached from the present. Sometimes she looks through you as though you are invisible."

The ensuing conversation illuminated some of the remaining dark recesses of the fatal love triangle and provided insight into the sense of urgency of youthful passions that caused so much torment.

Michelle told Miller that when Devon returned from Arizona, she posed a fateful question. "Devon asked if I had ever kissed a girl before. I never had, so I kissed her."

The two became inseparable, skipping classes together and dropping out of school as juniors. "Their world did not include school," Miller wrote. "Their world was inhabited by just the two of them. Their relationship was their secret."

However, Keary claimed to have also had a secret relationship with Devon that started before Michelle's, not to mention that Keary and Michelle had once been an inseparable pair themselves, before Devon arrived on the scene. Devon was someone whose very being seemed constantly attended by excitement and adventure. She quickly became the prize for which Michelle and Keary competed. Even so, the trio associated with few friends outside themselves.

Michelle confirmed people's suspicions that she married Brandon to please her parents. She wanted to give her dad the opportunity to walk her down the aisle. She loved her husband in the manner of a naive eighteen-year-old and enjoyed his attention at first, but soon found him tight with money and too controlling. When Miller interviewed Michelle's parents, Elbert Hetzel told him that if Michelle put something in the laundry after one wearing, Brandon would take it out, fold it, and put it back in her closet. Michelle, in turn, would lie to her husband about where she was going, then secretly go see Devon.

Miller tracked down George Vine for his story, too, cold-calling him at his apartment and gaining some further insight into the tensions within the love triangle. He concluded that although Keary was volatile, she was able to vent her rage. Michelle, on the other hand, channeled her emotions differently. "All I know is she used to get pretty tight," Vine told Miller, "like schizophrenic tight."

Devon's sway over Michelle was profound, perhaps more profound than anyone realized. "Elbert Hetzel regrets that he did not understand the strength of the bond between his daughter and Devon," Miller wrote. Before he departed Muncy, Miller became convinced of the strength of that bond as well, though he heard nothing that persuaded him of Michelle's innocence.

Two years had passed, but Michelle talked about how much she still loved Devon. "It's almost as though she had a hard time admitting that Devon was dead, you know?" Miller reflected. And Devon's death wasn't the only thing he got the feeling she hadn't made her peace with. "He rejection, the feeling of rejection she had from Devon was just so profound, it's something I don't think she'll ever get over."

46

While Michelle Hetzel lived out the consequences of the past within the stone walls of Muncy, and Brandon Bloss did the same at Somerset State Prison, life went on in the Lehigh Valley.

Rick Guzman and Holly Ronco have been raising two children from a brief marriage that dissolved due to their age difference. Derick, Devon's brother, graduated high school and served as a source of strength and pride to his father and mother, who both remained in Easton. Keary Renner reunited with her husband, who served his country in Iraq.

John Morganelli challenged the status quo with a second run for state attorney general and hadn't ruled out a third try. Barry Golazeski received a merit award for his work on the Guzman case and retired from the Easton PD in 2006 to head up a new antigang strike force for Morganelli. Zachary Lysek continues as Northampton County coroner.

Brandon's Florida attorneys returned south, and the local defense lawyers resumed their respective practices. Brandon and Michelle divorced from behind bars. Michelle continued to hope exoneration would come one day, and enlisted the help of appeals attorney John Waldron to challenge the authenticity of Cara Judd's journals. Her parents have made the long trip to Muncy twice a week. Brandon continued to maintain his public silence, but his appeals attorney, Michael Gough, voiced this prediction: "I don't think you've heard the last of this very troubling case."

Meanwhile in Easton, the Delaware and Lehigh rivers still collide violently at the Forks, just as they did before any of this ever happened, just as they have for ages, before the first pioneer ever set foot here and the original settlers called the turbulent confluence of rivers "Lechawitauk," revering it as a center of spiritual power. Time has passed, but the finding of Devon Guzman's lifeless body at this place, around which the close-knit city of Easton was built, has created a deficit, a nagging void, as if the spirit of the Forks had suffered from the desecration of life within its embrace.

Like all of Devon's closest loved ones, Rick Guzman was among those who felt the void most acutely. He has thought about Michelle's parents, who can still go and see their daughter, touch and kiss her, get to see what she looks like as she grows older. And then he has considered his own future. "I'm just left with pictures in a frame," he said.

He has been haunted by a ghostly vision shortly before his daughter's death. "About three months before this happened, I had a dream that I was at Devon's grave site with my mom and my sister standing about ten feet behind me talking like there was nothing wrong, and I was bawling my eyes out. And then a couple months later, she . . . this happens. Makes you wonder about the Supreme Being, you know?"

The man who once leapt for Brandon's neck had come to accept that he must curb his "uncivilized" impulses. He was grateful to the police, the DA's office and the jur that brought about justice for his firstborn, but now he knew that justice fails to fill the deeper yearning.

"Once it was over, I was really surprised how much satisfaction I *didn't* get," he remarked. "You know, you think about a trial, nailing these bastards, getting justice. I got really no satisfaction. I mean, what for? What do you say? I could give advice to someone—what to expect or don't expect. Don't expect to have a party.

"The judge bangs a gavel, that's all it is. You're still left with nothing. It's strange. You know what I mean?

"It wasn't what I expected, looking back," he said. "I didn't know what to expect. But I thought there would be something. Like you sit down to eat supper, and you eat and you eat and you eat, and you get up from the table and you're still hungry. 'Wait a minute, I just ate. Why am I still feeling these pangs?' Kind of like that."

HORRIFYING TRUE CRIME
FROM PINNACLE BOOKS

MORE MUST-READ TRUE CRIME
FROM PINNACLE